Also by Jessica B. Harris

The Africa Cookbook

The Welcome Table

A Kwanzaa Keepsake

Tasting Brazil

Sky Juice & Flying Fish

Iron Pots & Wooden Spoons

Hot Stuff

The Black Family Reunion Cookbook
(with The National Council of Negro Women)

Creole Fusion Food from the Atlantic Rim

Beyond Gumbo

Jessica B. Harris

SIMON & SCHUSTER
New York   London   Toronto   Sydney   Singapore

SIMON & SCHUSTER
Rockefeller Center
1230 Avenue of the Americas
New York, NY 10020

For information regarding special discounts for bulk purchases,
please contact Simon & Schuster Special Sales:
1-800-456-6798 or business@simonandschuster.com

Designed by Katy Riegel

Manufactured in the United States of America

1 2 3 4 5 6 7 8 9 10

Library of Congress Cataloging-in-Publication Data is available

ISBN 0-684-87062-2

7/03

Acknowledgments

SHORTLY AFTER MIDNIGHT on May 20, 2000, my mother died, leaving me alone in the world with no parents, no siblings, no husband or children. I therefore owe thanks not only to those who aided me in the completion of this book, but most important, to those whose love, concern, comfort, and constant and continuing support kept and keep me on the planet.

Thanks must first be given to those who took planes and crossed continents and oceans, drove cars, sent food, called, and sat and dried tears and held hands and taught me to move always forward: Gray Boone, Patricia, Charles Anthony and Jan'ie Hopkins, Vanessa and Lisa Abuksumo, Lucille Rich, Henriette Ferguson, Daphne Derven, Cathy Royal, Maria Williams Jones, Martha Jones, Liv and Willy Blumer, Kerry Moody, Carey Pickard, Nathaniel and Harlan, Alexander Smalls, Keren Tonneson, Maryse Pochot, Chester Higgins and Betsey Kissam, Trish and Tony Garnier, Cheikh Oumar Thiam, John Martin Taylor and the Charleston crew, Dolly McPherson, Maya Angelou, Joan Sandler, Ayo Fenner, Fritz Blank, Ariane Daguin, Sara Moulton, Michèle Marcelin, Marcella Martinez, Lou, Mary Len and Lenora Costa, Lolis Eric Elie and the Elie family, Madelon Stent, Gail and Birch McDonough, Audreen Buffalo, Pat Lawrence and Noel, James Noel, Simon and Shelly Gunning, Jan Brady and John Batty, Patrick Dunne and the staff at Lucullus, Carol Cadogan, Ellen Rolfes, Carole Abel, Judy Kern, Mammadou Sy, Charlayne Hunter-Gault and family, Betty Fussell, Ralph Taylor, Monty Cumberbatch Nello Bynoe and all at Almond Resorts, Mae Tata and my sisters and brothers at Casa Branca, in Bahia, especially Sinha and her sons, Theophile and Théodora, Aimée and Albert, and the members of my African Komaclo/Houémavo/ Grimaud family.

Then there are the friends in the world of food who have fed me literally and spiritually, allowed me to ask stupid questions and sometimes even play in their kitchens, and treated me as an equal. Thanks to Patricia Wilson, Robert Oliver, Ken Smith, JoAnn Clevenger, Paul Hamilton, Zarela Martinez, William Woys Weaver, Augusto and Claudia Schreiner, Fatéma Hal, Leah Chase, Michelle Nugent, Poppy Tooker, Carmelita Jeanne, Gérard Virginius, Delia Maduro, Gina Lee Johnson, Julie Sahni, Greg Sonnier, Susan Spicer, Karen Hess, Te, John Currence, Owen from Hudson Cafeteria, Angie Johnson, Imre and the staff at Galatoire's, Jasper White and all the folks at Jasper's Summer Shack, Mark Miller, all the folks at the Southern Foodways Alliance, Ann Abadie, Charles Regan Wilson, Mary Hartwell, Mary Beth at the Center for Southern Culture at Ole Miss, and the staff and members of the Caribbean Culinary Federation.

Thanks are also due Susan Tucker at Tulane as well as librarians at the Benjamin Rosenthal Library at Queens College, the Oak Bluffs Public Library, the Institute of Jamaica, the Barbados National Museum, and the wonderfully helpful staff at the Williams Research Center of the Historic New Orleans Collection, as well as booksellers and antiquarian book dealers too numerous to note who have filled my head with thoughts and my shelves with books.

Then there are folks met along the journey who have become friends and who also give me strength and keep me moving forward. Those met along the way include Jan de Costa, Andrew Hopkins, Jinx and Jeff Morgan, Leona Watson, Hetty from Curaçao, Don Richmond, Dennis Greene, Matt Rowley, Suzie Segal, Myrna Colley Lee, Nancy Civetta, Ron Bechet, Rita and John Scott, Kate Dyson and family in London, Michèle and Ulrick Jean Pierre, Olive Tomlinson, Gretchen Tucker-Underwood, Kim Dummons, John T. Edge, Blair and Baby Jesse, Matt and Ann Konigsmark, Dorothy and Tom Howorth, Jean Daniels Lear, Audrey Peterson, Jan Arnow and family, Vickie Fuller, David Eltis, and the numerous members of my very personal international rainbow tribe. Daily the QC lunch bunch makes me laugh; Ron Cottman keeps the rain off and the furnace chugging; Mr. Wright, Mr. Leslie, Leadfoot Louie, Kenny, M. Pierre, and the succession of taxi drivers get me where I'm going, and my neighbors—Monica Payne-Hall, Lance Hall, Amat, Julia, and Aubrey—put up with me, feed my cats, and water my plants when I'm out of town.

Finally, these efforts would not be a book without the ongoing ministrations and attentions of my agent, Susan Ginsburg, and her consecutive assistants named Ann; my long-suffering editor, Sydny Miner, with whom I have worked for over a decade; her new assistant, Laura Holmes; and the entire publication staff at Simon & Schuster who treat me as though I wore a crown.

To all of you and to the one whom I inadvertently forgot, my gratitude is as deeply heartfelt as it is endless.

The ultimate thanks go to God, the Orisha, and the creative spirits who gave me the parents I had, the brain I try to use, and the joy of being me in the world. I am grateful.

Contents

Beyond Gumbo

Banana seller in the French Caribbean.

Introduction: Beyond Gumbo

Creole Fusion Food
From the Atlantic Rim

MOST AMERICANS who see the word *Creole* immediately take a mental journey to the city on the Gulf Coast known as New Orleans. They think only of jambalaya and redfish court bouillon, of grillades and filé gumbo. Although the deep rich flavors of a Louisiana gumbo are definitely a part of the Creole world, the Creole experience extends beyond the Crescent City to encompass the food of the southern Atlantic rim. It's *gumbo z'herbes,* but it's also a dish of flaky grilled snapper topped with a *sauce chien* prepared with onion, shallots, garlic, scallions, parsley, vinegar, and biting hot chile in Martinique. Creole food is Puerto Rico's *lechon asado,* complete with crisp skin and a saucer of tangy, sour orange *mojo* for dipping. Creole is a peanut patty in Mexico called *prasle de cacahuatl* and okra soup in Savannah. It's crawfish and crab backs and, yes, it's even the taste of red beans and rice on a Monday morning in New Orleans.

Crioula, Kreol, Créole, Krio, and *Creole* all come together in the Creole world, as do the foods of Barbados and Bahia, Belize, Mexico's East Coast, and South Carolina's Gullah peoples. Creole food is the food of the descendants of Nigeria's Yoruba peoples in Brazil, the Sephardic Jews of Curaçao, and the Bahamians of Key West. In short, Creole food is the food of the Atlantic rim. It's the world's original fusion food, one that was created centuries ago when Africa and Europe met in the New World.

No word is more loaded with meaning than *Creole.* In the Crescent City alone, its meaning changes virtually block by block, from the Garden District to the Ninth Ward. In French, it can even include some of the food of the inhabitants of islands in the Indian Ocean. Perhaps it would be best, therefore, to begin our journey into the world of Creole food with a look at the word itself.

The debate is not new; even in 1914 in New Orleans, the word was much contested. According to *Louisiana: Comprising Sketches of Parishes, Towns, Events, Institutions, and Persons Arranged in Cyclopedic Form,* edited by Alcée Fortier of Tulane's Department of Romance Languages:

> **Creoles**—Webster defines the word creole as meaning "One born in America or the West Indies of European ancestors." Charles Gayarré, in a lecture on "Creoles of History and Creoles of Romance," at Tulane university on April 25, 1885, stated that the word creole originated from the Spanish word "criollo" from the verb *criar* (to create); that this word was invented by the Spaniards to distinguish their children, natives of their conquered colonial possessions, from the original inhabitants, and that to be a "criollo" was considered a sort of honor. The transition from the Spanish "criollo" to the French "créole" was easy, and in time the term was extended to cover animals and plants, hence such expressions as creole horses, creole chickens, creole figs, etc. Negroes born in tropical countries are also sometimes called creoles, but according to the definition above, this is an erroneous use of the term, as the negro's ancestors were not European.
>
> Among the white people of Louisiana during the French and Spanish dominations, *this use of the word was never tolerated.* [The italics are my own.]

That's precise enough for 1914 and, indeed, if one looks up *criollo* in the current edition of *Nuevo Pequeno Larousse Illustrado,* it reads, "*dices del blanco nacido en las Colonias; y de los españoles nacidos en America*" ("said of whites born in the colonies, and of Spaniards born in America"). Even the contemporary Spanish definition confines itself to discussing race. The *Random House Dictionary of the English Language* seems to clear up some of the confusion by including the following:

1) a person born in the West Indies or Latin America, but of European, especially Spanish ancestry. 2) a person of French ancestry born in Louisiana.

However, as 5th and 6th meanings under the same listing, the dictionary compounds the confusion by adding,

> 5) a person of mixed Spanish and Negro or French and Negro ancestry. 6) (l.c) Archaic, a native-born Negro, as distinguished from a Negro brought from Africa.

The traditional uptown New Orleans definition, cited by Lyla Hay Owen and Owen Murphy in *Creoles of New Orleans,* states, "Most old-guard New Orleanians declare that the only true definition of a Creole is one that states, 'a Creole is a person born in the colonies of pure Spanish and pure French parentage, a Caucasian,'" thereby asserting that the term *Creole of Color* is a contradiction in terms.

This is further confused by the first meaning in the recent *Webster's Unabridged Dictionary,* that a Creole is, "a slave born in his master's house, Negro born in the colonies, white person born in the colonies." The etymology of this definition is given as the Spanish *criar*—to be brought up—which, in turn, comes from the Latin *creare,* (to create or to beget.) The rest of the definition of the word covers the usual territory, but adds that, when the creole referred to is white or mixed, the word will take a capital letter. *Webster's* adds a note that Creole food is prepared in a style characterized by the use of rice, okra, tomatoes, peppers, and high seasonings (as in creole sauce or lobster creole). It further adds that, in Alaska, the term refers to a person of mixed Russian and Eskimo blood!

Finally, there is the Richard Allsopp's definition in the 1996 *Dictionary of Caribbean English,* published by Oxford University Press. A member of the editorial board for *The New Oxford English Dictionary* and a native of Guyana, he's well positioned to help us straighten out the confusion surrounding the origin of the word:

> [T]he term in all its senses, connotes New World, especially Caribbean, family stock, breed, and thence quality. Originally (17th C) it was evidently used with pride by European colonists (esp. the French) to refer to themselves as born and bred in the "New World" and spelt with a capital C. (ex. Napoleon's wife Josephine de Beauharnais was a Creole)

It was then extended to distinguish "local" from imported breeds, especially of horses and livestock, then slaves locally born as different from original African importees. With this sense the status of the word dropped (18–19C) among whites but rose among blacks and coloureds locally born, and freed men. In many post-emancipation Caribbean societies the term became (19–20C) generally a label either of a class embracing non-white persons of 'breeding' or an excluded class of ill-bred blacks.

This exhaustive definition further adds that the Spanish word considered to be its origin by *Webster* is, in fact, adapted from the Portuguese *crioulo,* and that Spanish etymologists Corominas and Pasual confirmed as recently as 1989 that the Portuguese origin is undisputed and goes back to the word *criar,* to create. More important for us, they suggest that the word may ultimately have been of African origin and cite Garcilaso el Inca who wrote in Peru in 1602:

> [I]t's a name that the negroes invented . . . it means among the negroes "born in the Indies," they invented it to distinguish those . . . born in Guinea from those born in America, because they consider themselves more honorable and of better status than their children because they are from the fatherland while their children are born abroad, and parents are often offended to be called *criollos.* The Spanish, in like manner, have introduced this name into their language to mean those born in America.

Where do these conflicting definitions leave us? To seek yet another definition of *Creole,* one that will keep all of its historic and social contradictions and yet will allow for the diversity of Creole life throughout the hemisphere and, indeed, in places in which several cultures come together. This definition is closer to the usage of the word by specialists in linguistics, who state that, although a creolized language is the result of the melding of two other languages, it becomes the mother tongue of its speakers. This is the closest parallel to creolized foods, as they have indeed become greater than the multiple dishes that spawned them. This definition of Creole, one of blending, allows for the coming together of diverse elements to create a vital, vi-

Cooking pots for sale in Cartagena, Colombia.

brant new entity; this is the case with the mixing of Native-American, European, and, African culinary arts, creating what is commonly called Creole cooking not only in New Orleans, but in Port-au-Prince, Haiti; Port of Spain, Trinidad; Pointe-à-Pitre, Guadeloupe; and Pointe Coupée, Louisiana. This is what we taste in the pots in Salvador da Bahia de Todos os Santos, Brazil; and in San Salvador in the Bahamas; in Brooklyn; Barbados; and Belize; Jamaica, New York and Jamaica, West Indies—the food that resulted when Africa and Europe came together in the Americas.

Resulting from the confluence of the Columbian exchange, the Atlantic slave trade, and the European age of exploration, and extending over subsequent migrations of Indians, Chinese, Levantines, and more Europeans, true Creole food has long been the hallmark of the Southern Atlantic rim. Ironically, although centuries older than Pacific-fusion cuisine, this cooking, with its international range, has not yet been presented to the eating public in all of its delicious complexity. Creole cuisine is at the matrix of *nueva cocina latina.* It is found in the Mexican food of Veracruz, the stews of Panama, and the *comidas criollas* of Colombia's coast. The food of the Creole world is the culinary soul of New-World Cuisine.

In this fusion cooking, the basic foods and cooking techniques of western and central Africa come together with the foodstuffs of the Americas, the culinary traditions of various colonizing European countries, and the influences of later immigrants from Asia and the Levant. The results are a multiplicity of dishes that reveal their Creole kinship in the use of marinades, the use of nuts as thickeners, the thought of seasoning well, spicy condiments, and leafy greens. It traditionally places the emphasis on vegetable-filled stews, and an abundant use of fish and seafood—what the world is now learning is an optimum diet. Most recipes are based on grains and vegetables, and flavorful fish and fowl are the main sources of animal protein. Other meats are used in festive foods or as flavoring. Tastes that are as bright as tropical sunshine are hallmarks of Creole cooking.

The people of this Creole world have a common history and many similarities in taste, but each has brought something different to Creole cuisine. Influences from France, Spain, Holland, Denmark, Portugal, and England mingled with those of the Yoruba in Brazil; the Ashanti, Fanti, and Denkiera in Jamaica; the Wolof in New Orleans; the Toucouleur, Igbo, Ewe, Fon, Kru, Hausa, Kalabari, Songye, and more. The native ingredients of the Americas crosspollinated, literally and figuratively, with those brought to the Americas from Europe, Asia, and Africa and went into the dutchies, iron pots, coui, and canaris of the New World.

The Americas have long been a culinary crucible. From the first inhabitants of Mexico, who began to domesticate grains, legumes, and tubers, to the native peoples who brought South American ingredients with them as they migrated northward to populate the Caribbean, to the early peoples of the American southeast, and beyond, food has been evolving in this hemisphere for millennia. Following the arrival of the Europeans, successive waves of settlers: explorers and conquistadors, pirates and peasants, missionaries and monarchs, the indentured and the enslaved—all brought the flavors of Spain, Portugal, England, France, the Netherlands, Africa, Asia, the Middle and Far East to American shores, making the hemisphere one of the world's original melting pots.

The Creole world is a major part of this melting pot, which extends from pole to pole and from sea to sea. The coastal cities of the Creole world were the first place that worlds collided in this hemisphere. It was in Veracruz, Mexico, that Hernan

Cortes stepped ashore and unleashed a wave of destruction that, even today, makes *conquistador* a synonym for destroyer or cultural terrorist. It was in a James River port town in Virginia, in 1619 that the first enslaved Africans came ashore in what would become the United States—one year before the arrival of the Mayflower and the establishment of the Plymouth colonies. It was in cities like New Orleans; Charleston; Savannah; Philadelphia; New York; Kingston, Jamaica; Pointe-à-Pitre, Guadeloupe; Georgetown, Guyana; and Cartagena de los Indios, Colombia, that the Creole world would define itself and begin to develop a cuisine that is recognizable even when its origin is not.

This is a cuisine that is defined by the simplicity and the freshness of ingredients, and by the intricate kitchen techniques required by festive preparations that call on culinary know-how from three continents, and an overarching insistence on taste. The original fusion food, the food of the Creole world, is truly multicultural. Here, vanilla borrowed from the Mexican Aztecs may meet up with rice grown by African agricultural methods, and European techniques of pudding making to produce a rice pudding—that is uniquely Creole.

Columbus's first taste of cassava, served to him by a *cacique* or Caribbean chieftain, was only the New World genesis of this mixing of cultures. Europe and Africa had come together several decades earlier as, first, Vasco da Gama, then others circumnavigated the African continent, leaving behind European outposts that would mark the beginning of the creolizing of the coastal food of that continent.

The African culinary matrix began with a diet of grains and tubers. These were used to produce porridgelike mashes similar to the *attiéké* and *ablo,* the *acaça* and *ugali,* the *fufu* and *couscous* of today's continent. They were topped with soupy stews prepared from meats ranging from guinea hen to bush rat and supplemented with onions, garlic, gourds, and a wide variety of leafy greens to form a culinary paradigm that is one of the prevalent ones of Creole food: a soupy stew served over, or with, a starch. The late anthropologist William Bascom in a landmark article on Yoruba cooking, cites five traditional cooking techniques that were used among the West African Yoruba, but that can be assumed to have existed continentwide, generally:

- boiling in water
- steaming in leaves
- toasting beside the fire
- baking in hot ashes
- frying in deep oil

These techniques are all abundantly evident in the creolized cooking of this hemisphere. In addition to these methods, I want to suggest several other culinary threads that seem to signal a transhemispheric web of culture that link the food of the creolized world:

- composed rice dishes
- abundant hot sauces
- dumplings and fritters
- seasoning and coloring foods
- seasoning pastes like *sofrito* and Bajan seasoning
- abundant use of okra
- use of pig and pig parts
- dried, smoked, and pickled ingredients as flavorings
- confections using nuts (including peanuts, pecans, and coconuts), fruit pastes, and cane sugar
- preponderance of professional women cooks and their importance

There are regional specificities, such as the use of codfish in the Caribbean and in South America, and techniques vary from place to place, but in general, the creolized food of the African Atlantic world has a flavor all its own.

Composed Rice Dishes

The Grain Coast of West Africa produces its own variation of rice—a wet rice that is worked agriculturally, according to a task system that is replicated virtually unchanged in South Carolina's Low Country, where the grain was the wealth of planters. The region of West Africa, which includes countries from Southern Senegal to Sierra Leone and Liberia, is noted for its rice cooking. The national dish of Senegal, *thiébou dienn,* a red rice and fish dish, is similar to the red rice that graces many of Charleston's and Savannah's tables. *Thiébou niébé* is a close Old World cousin of Hoppin' John, a traditional New Year's Day dish for much of the Low Country and the American South. It's also similar to the composed rice dishes served for luck throughout the Caribbean.

Creolized New World variants of these African dishes also include all of the rice and legumes dishes of the Caribbean basin, like Barbados's peas and rice and Jamaica's rice and peas, a dish so popular in Jamaica that it is known as its coat of arms. Puerto Rico's *arroz con gandules* and Cuba's *moros y cristianos,* as well as *congris,* made with red beans and served in both Cuba and New Orleans are other examples of creolized food. There's the *riz aux gombos* and the *matété crabes* of Guadeloupe, as well as myriad dishes that reflect a preference for rice over other starches. In New Orleans, this is seen not only in the red beans and rice that is the traditional Monday dish (which, by the way, is much loved in Haiti, where it is known as *riz national*), but also in the scoop of rice in the gumbo plate, and the many different varieties of *jambalaya*—one of the classic dishes of New Orleans cuisine.

Abundant Hot Sauces

The Creole cooking of the African Atlantic world is also known for salsas, *mojos,* marinades, sauces, *molhos,* rubs, seasonings, and pepper sauces—some of the most flavorful and the most piquant condiments in the world. They are evidenced in Trinidad's *kuchela*—a spicy shaved mango dish, perfect with everything from shrimp to grilled chicken; in the multiple sauces of Brazilian cooking; in the chutneys of the English-speaking regions; and in the *recaitos* and *adobos* of the Hispanic world. We like it hot, and it is not surprising that this area of the world, in which the chile originated, has its own particular way with hot stuff. Jamaica's Scotch bonnet is one of the world's most potent chiles and turns up in everything from the jerk of the Maroons to the Pickapeppa and planter's sauces of the big houses. Trinidad's turmeric-hued hot sauce is legendary among chile heads, and the sheer abundance of chiles available in a Mexican market would give pause to even the most savvy chile aficionados. Africa's pre-Columbian taste for the spicy adapted to the arrival of chiles from the Americas with alacrity on both sides of the Atlantic. Native peoples and enslaved Africans alike somewhat creolized the tastebuds of the transplanted Europeans, who found that using hot sauces aided their digestion, and also helped them to perspire and, thus, cool off in their new tropical environment.

Dumplings and Fritters

The fritter factor is nowhere more evident than in the cooking of the Creole world. New Orleans' *beignet* owes its name and its taste to the French, but the Crescent City's other famous fritter, the *cala,* that used to be hawked through the streets by women of color, crying *"bels calas, bels calas tout chauds,"* comes straight from Africa. It probably takes its name from a similar fritter sold in like manner by the women of Bong country, Liberia, an African rice-growing region.

Savory fritters abound as well. The bean fritter that is prepared by Yoruba women in Nigeria and sold throughout the streets as *accra* or *akara* has become so popular up and down the African coast that one apocryphal story suggests that the capital of Ghana is named for the fritter. It, too, has found a place in the New World. *Akara* turns up as Bahia's *acarajé,* the primary street food of that city, gives its name, albeit spelled *acrats* to the codfish fritter of Martinique and Guadeloupe. In Curaçao, in the cookbook of the sisterhood of the Sephardic temple of Mikve Israel, the hemisphere's oldest continuous Jewish congregation, it appears surprisingly under the name Kala, a rice fritter from Liberia. Recipes for fritters both sweet and savory make abundant use of ingredients, ranging from pineapple bits to pumpkin to leftover pieces of meat.

Dumplings also play a major role in the food of the Creole world, placing the starch *in* the soupy stew instead of under it. They are yet another example of how stretching a meal to serve many mouths became a regional taste. Philadelphia's pepperpot was traditionally served with *foufou* dumplings made from the plantains, which were available in that city as early as the eighteenth century. Jamaica's red-pea soup would be incomplete without a few of the flour dumplings known as *spinners.*

In Barbados, wise cooks always put a tiny pinch of sugar in their dumplings; in Guadeloupe and Martinique *dombrés* are so loved that they are served with everything from crabs to red beans.

Seasoning and Coloring Foods

Seasoning pastes abound in the Creole world, from the *sofritos* of the Hispanic world, green or the more traditional red, to the light cilantro paste used to season green rice in Curaçao. In Barbados, mixtures of verdant herbs and spices called *Bajan seasoning* are tucked into scores in fish or fowl prior to cooking. Elsewhere, lightly sautéed pastes of herbs and seasonings become the flavor base for soups and stews, and act as one of the building blocks of the intensity that defines Creole flavor.

Today's superstar chefs create flavors in food as artists prepare a canvas, layering flavors on top of one another. Creole cooks have done this for centuries. The unspoken, and virtually always unwritten, part of any Creole recipe from the Caribbean is to begin with a lime wash, in which the meat, fish, or fowl to be cooked is bathed in a mix of fresh lime juice, salt, and water. Although this is undoubtedly a holdover from the days when tainted meat or fish had to be doubly cleaned, the result is an underlying zest that is the foundation of many Creole dishes. In New Orleans, most cooking directions begin, "first, make a *roux*," as that flour and oil mixture is the flavor base into which the onions, celery, bell pepper, and the rest go. In Brazil, garlic is browned in oil at the start of many a recipe, giving the dish a unique flavor base: then and only then can the actual cooking begin.

Color is important, too. There is a tendency to tint food like rice with an orange hue, reminiscent of the foods colored by palm oil, which is used heavily in West Africa. Turmeric and saffron impart a yellowish hue, but palm oil, known in Brazil as *dende,* gives a brilliant orange, also produced by *achiote* or *annatto* in recipes from the Hispanic Caribbean and from parts of Brazil that don't use palm oil. Deep, rich, brown stews are another hallmark of Creole cooking in the Caribbean and New Orleans, and many old-style cooks caramelize cane sugar in oil to give a color and flavor base to their dishes. Others use a commercial product known as browning to achieve the same effect.

Abundant Use of Okra

When the African-American songwriter Olu Dara sings "Okra," he's singing of more than just a vegetable that has become emblematic of the food of the American South. He is singing of a food that is virtually totemic for all Africans in the diaspora; for everywhere that okra points its green tip, Africa has been. From the caruru of Brazil, to the fried okra of Mississippi to the sopa da guingambo of Puerto Rico, the scattering of Africans in this hemisphere has flung the seeds of this mucilaginous vegetable north, south, east, and west.

Some have written that the slaves brought okra over on the Middle Passage. I suspect, though, that anyone who has thought of the horrors of that journey would realize that this is likely to have been nigh unto impossible. It is far more likely that okra, like breadfruit and other items, was brought to this hemisphere to provide inexpensive fodder for the enslaved Africans who had to be nourished to work.

A taste for the "slimy" has long been an accepted and, indeed, a cherished mouth feel on the African continent, where it is given by indigenous ingredients such as okra and meloukhia. In the New World, this taste translates into many dishes. In Curaçao, the slipperiness comes from cactus tuna in dishes like *ka dushi*. But, in the rest of the Atlantic Rim we slide on okra, the one vegetable absolutely emblematic of the African presence in the New World.

Use of Pig and Pig Parts

Pig is so much a part of the diet of the Creole world that it seems difficult to believe that the little four-footed porkers didn't exist in this hemisphere until the arrival of the Spaniards. The omnivorous pig has walked this earth for centuries and is a relative of the wild boar. Easy to raise because they're docile and will eat almost anything, they have become the totemic meat for many in the Creole world. Brought by the Spaniards to the Caribbean in 1493, pigs rapidly acclimatized and became readily available. In 1514, Diego Velasquez de Cuellar reported to the Spanish king that the two dozen pigs that he had brought to Cuba in 1498 had increased to thirty thousand. In the 1600s, pirates, freebooters, and other brethren of the coast captured wild pigs and made an alternate business of selling their skins and meat. They preserved the meat by smoking it over a wood chip fire in *boucan,* or smokehouses and, therefore, were given the French name *boucaniers,* or in English, buccaneers. By the time Père Labat, a Dominican friar, arrived in the Caribbean region in the late seventeenth century, a *boucan de cochon* had become an acceptable way to party in the Caribbean. Settlers imitated the cooking methods of the buccaneers, albeit with domestic swine instead of wild hogs. Labat indulged in the feast and gave readers one of the first descriptions of New World barbecue.

During the period of enslavement, Africans benefited from the fact that almost every part of the pig is edible, and that its skin can be tanned into leather. It's said, laughingly, that Blacks in the southern United States eat everything on the swine from the "rooter to the tooter." Throughout the entire hemisphere ears, feet, snouts, maws, and chitterlings all go into the pots to emerge as *andouille, souse,* head cheese, *boudin, chicharron,* and more. And where would we be without the lard that is used in baking in much of the American South and in the cooking of Mexico and the Hispanic world? Indeed, from the *boucheries* of southern Louisiana, to the lechon of the Hispanic world, the *souse* of the English-speaking Caribbean, to the sausages that go into Brazil's *feijoada,* pork is one of the hemisphere's prime meats.

Dried, Smoked, and Pickled Ingredients as Flavorings

It is undeniable that there is a cultural curve that extends from Africa to the New World, then upward from coastal South America into the Caribbean and beyond. This curve is fascinating, as Africa's hold on culture mutates as the curve moves northward. Tribal influences change and vary, the intensity of Africanisms heightens or decreases all along the arc, but the African culture is always present. This also applies to the use of seasoning ingredients.

On the African continent, there is a tradition of using dried or smoked ingredients to season soupy stews. Senegal's *guedge* and *yète* and the superfunky dried, smoked shrimp of the République du Benin are examples. In the New World, dried ingredients are used as well, and dried, smoked shrimp are still a major seasoning ingredient in the Afro-Brazilian cooking of the state of Bahia. As the arc moves northward, the

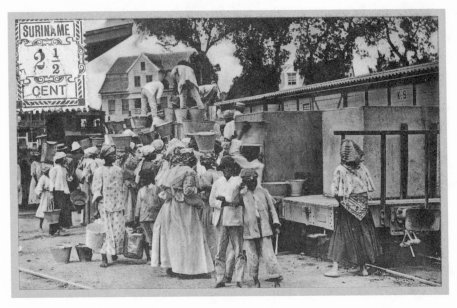

Water distribution during a drought in Surinam.

dried ingredients give way to the pickled pork and smoked and salted fish that are used to season the pots of the Caribbean. Salt cod, a legacy of the slave trade, pickled and smoked herring from the seafarers, and the pickled pork that was also aboard ship take over seasoning duty from smoked shrimp, and the result is a change in flavor. Further north, in the southern United States, smoked ingredients return with seasoning pieces of fatback or even leftover ham or ham hocks, when available. Codfish turns up rarely, if ever, unless the cook comes from the Cape Verde Islands or is a transplanted Caribbean native. The constant throughout is the cardinal importance of the flavoring piece of meat, and the need for getting as much flavor as possible from as little animal protein as possible.

Confections using Nuts, Coconuts, Fruit Pastes, and Cane Sugar

Less studied than other influences on Creole cuisine, but no less delectable, is the world of Creole confections. From the praline of New Orleans to the sugar cakes and rum-scented fudge of Barbados, to the cocadas and coconut sweets of Colombia and Brazil, the love of sugar in the Creole world is evident everywhere. It is highly ironic, given that no area of the world was more transformed by sugarcane! The monoculture of one region—Brazil—and, later, the Caribbean and parts of the American South, resulted in the depopulation of another: Africa. The culinary conjunction of the two brought about an abundance of desserts and candies that will please and delight even the most discriminating sweet tooth. New Orleans's praline may take its name from the French *Duc du Praslin,* but its taste is pure Creole. It turns up in variants: In Brazil, it is called *pé de moleque;* in Curaçao, where it is made with peanuts and called a *pinda,* and even in Texas border towns where it goes by the Franco–Aztec–Spanish name, *prasle de cacahuatl.* Fudges abound, as do preserved and glaceéd tropical fruits.

In the northern regions cakes and pies make their mark, and, throughout the Creole world, bread puddings and rice puddings deftly transform leftovers into culinary *tours de force.* The love of sugar is an acceptable vice in the Creole world, and one that is frequently indulged.

Preponderance of Professional Women Cooks and Their Importance

L'art culinaire créole is very much a woman's art. In many parts of the Creole world, the culinary dictum, "mistress of the stewpot, master of the flame," holds vibrantly true. Men may man the fire pits, the jerk, the *boucan,* and the barbecue but, women, the true keepers of the flame of this culinary tradition, are in charge of such dishes as the *blaffs* and *callaloos* of the Caribbean, the *moquecas* of Bahia and myriad other dishes of the Creole world. Another unifying element in Creole cooking is the predominance of professional women cooks. While Europe has made *haute* culinary matters the realm of men, the Creole world still celebrates the deft hand and sure judgment of women chefs. From Brazil's smiling *baianas de tabuleiro* through all of the madras-clad chefs of the Caribbean to—yes—Aunt Jemima, a Creole woman at the stove is the hallmark of authenticity and of good food.

For centuries, women in all parts of the Creole world have found freedom and purpose in the kitchen. The enslaved Africans and their descendants were able to triumph over the rigors of a system that gave them no control by controlling the diets of their masters. Incidentally, in many cases, the women cooks saved the lives of those who enslaved them by providing them with a diet that was based on their knowledge of tropical foodstuffs and of proper nutrition for the climate in which they were enslaved.

In the conditions of urban slavery, some of the women were sent into the streets to sell dainties—sweets or savories that they'd made on their mistress's account. In some cases, they were allowed to keep a small portion of the monies raised and, indeed, some women in New Orleans, Bahia, and other places, were able to purchase their freedom and that of their loved ones through this work. Free women sold items, and often huckstering was their financial mainstay. Food for freedom was more than a thought; for women cooks in the Creole world it was a way of life.

Anyone who has ever attended Guadeloupe's celebrated *Fête des Cuisinières* has seen some of the survivors of an earlier generation of Creole chefs as they strut their stuff in the streets of Pointe-à-Pitre. Women of immense style, they parade the streets bedecked in a king's ransom of gold jewelry, their ample shapes swathed in the flamboyant colors of their chosen fabric of the year. Their baskets, brimming with food, are draped with miniature kitchen implements and their aprons embroidered with the grill of Saint Lawrence, whom they have selected as their patron for his martyrdom on the grill. These women radiate contagious abandon and infectious joy, their deep-throated laughter echoing around the hall in which the luncheon banquet is traditionally held. Champagne flows, the sensuous coupling of the accordion and clarinet begins the *biguine,* and they sway contentedly, inviting all to join them in the dance. Seductive and coquettish, adept in the kitchen and perhaps in other rooms of the house as well, this image of the Creole cook has been mythologized and fantasized about by writers and artists for generations. She's the one in the *samba de roda* ring clapping and singing in Brazil; the one tempting the indecisive buyer in the praline shop in New Orleans; the woman behind the coal pot at Oistin's, inveigling the tourist to just try one more fish cake or another piece of fried chicken. She's been sung about in the lyrics of Dorival Caymmi in Brazil and pictured as Jorge Amado's Gabriela, praised in the works of Lafcadio Hearn, and painted by artists known and unknown. This jovial, gracious cook is only one side of the picture—the public view—whereby talented resourceful cook meets canny salesperson who knows she must hawk her wares to put food on the table for the folks back home.

The other side of the coin is less festive, but no less important to the equation. Here there is little music and even less jewelry; an inventive housewife with few resources and fewer pennies who must feed a large family and comes up with a stew or a dish that is so delicious that the family clamors for it even when money isn't tight. Creole food, the preeminent taste of the Atlantic Rim of the New World, is a triumphant food that comes from sorrow's kitchens. It was conceived in the kitchens of the hemisphere's big houses, *casas grandes, fazendas,* and plantations, and nurtured over coal pots and three-rock stoves in the slave cabins and in the shanties of the black shack alleys. Its African matrix was seasoned with the mixing and mingling of races and nations—Spanish, Dutch, French, Indian, Portuguese, Chinese, and more—that has produced words like *mulatto, mestiço, quadroon, marabout, mustafino octoroon,* among others. This Creole food is undeniably the true food of the Western Hemisphere, a food created from an international larder of ingredients and a world of techniques that make something rewarding from difficult circumstances.

Taking the goods to market, Jamaica.

Glossary

Achiote *(Bixa orellana)*

These small reddish berries are sometimes called *annatto, urucum,* or *roucou,* and were used by the early Native Americans in the Caribbean and the Amazon Basin to decorate their bodies. The berries still serve as a colorant today in the cooking of Brazil, and in the French and Spanish-speaking Caribbean. There, they are mixed with lard or other cooking oils to give the oil and the foods cooked in them an orange-yellow coloring. It is difficult to document, but it has been suggested that this method of cooking first developed as a means of replacing the reddish-hued palm oil prized in much West African cooking. In fact, in the Brazilian state of Vitoria, an *azeite de urucum* is used instead of *dende* or red palm oil in dishes that would call for palm oil in the neighboring state of Bahia. Achiote also appears in the *sofritos* of the Spanish-speaking Caribbean and in the *blaffs* and the *mignans* of the French-speaking islands.

Achiote seeds should be purchased when they have a bright brick-red color. They may also be called *annatto.* Once they have turned brown, they have lost much of their already faint flavor. The seeds may be kept indefinitely in a tightly covered jar in the refrigerator or in a cool, dark place.

Ackee (*Blighia sapida*)

A Jamaican riddle asks: "My father sent me out to pick out a wife; he told me to take only those that smile, for those that do not smile will kill me. What is my wife?" The answer, as every Jamaican child knows, is *ackee*. The fruit looks a bit like a large pink mango or guava, until it has ripened. Then it "smiles," bursting open, exposing yellow meat with black seeds. Until the ackee has ripened naturally and is smiling, it is poisonous. Ackee's yellow flesh has a scrambled-egg look. It is found most frequently in ackee and saltfish, the Jamaican national breakfast dish.

Jamaicans have to worry about ackee smiling, but those in northern climes do not, as ackee is most frequently found there in canned form. Banned until recently in the United States, ackee is now available in markets selling West Indian products.

Aji Amarillo (*Capsicum baccatum*)

This is the most commonly used chile in Peru. *Aji Amarillo* add heat, flavor, and color to a variety of dishes. They are usually used as a paste, which is prepared by boiling the chiles in water and then processing them in a blender or food processor.

The *aji mirasol* is simply a dried version of this chile. It is prepared by sautéing it in a dry skillet, then grinding it into a powder and adding a bit of water to make a paste. Occasionally, *mirasol* pastes can be found at purveyors selling Latin American ingredients.

Aji Limo (*Capsicum chinense Jacquin cv. "Limo"*)

This is a Peruvian chile that is a habanero relative with yellow or red versions. It can be obtained fresh from mail-order sources.

Allspice (*Pimenta dioica*, syn. *Pimenta officinalis*)

This berry, the size of a large peppercorn, has the taste of nutmeg, cinnamon, black pepper, and cloves. The berries are also known as *Jamaica pepper* and, to the eternal confusion of many, as *pimento.* In the French-speaking Caribbean, allspice is known as *bois d'Inde,* and is used extensively to season seafood dishes, like *blaffs* and *boudin,* or blood sausage of the French-speaking Caribbean. Other parts of the tree are also used. The leaves, which are similar to European bay leaves, appear in spice baskets in Grenada and on other islands. Even the wood is used: True Jamaican jerked foods are grilled over a fire of allspice branches, which gives jerked foods some of their characteristic flavor.

Allspice is available in supermarkets. Purchase whole berries, not the powdered form. Also note that the berries can vary widely in size—use your own judgment when a recipe calls for a particular number.

Amchar

This Indian addition to the cooking of Trinidad and Tobago is prepared from powdered, raw, green mangoes. It is used as a souring agent for chutneys, soups, and vegetable dishes.

Amchar (sometimes called *amchur* or *amchoor*) can be found in shops that sell Indian ingredients. Sometimes, slices of dried raw green mango may be found as well. These may be pulverized at home and used in the same manner.

Arrowroot *(Maranta arundinacea)*

This rhizome is dried and powered into one of the most easily digested of all starches. In the Caribbean, it is used rather than cornstarch to thicken sauces. Saint Vincent is the source of the majority of the world's supply of arrowroot.

Bananas *(Musa sp.)*

Any northerner who journeys to the Caribbean region is astonished at the number of varieties of bananas. In fact, it was only in 1948 that botanists agreed on the origins of this plant, which is really not a tree at all, but a large perennial herb.

Green bananas are frequently peeled before cooking. To peel them cut off both ends with a sharp knife. Slit the banana skin lengthwise down to the flesh in three or four spots. Be careful not to cut too deeply. Then, lift the skin with the dull edge of a knife until the banana is completely peeled. Finish off by scraping away any green fibers still on the flesh.

Banana leaves add an extra fillip to steamed, poached, and baked dishes and give a great subtle flavor.

Bananas should be purchased when their skins are unblemished and when they are firm to the touch. Anyone who remembers the old Chiquita jingle knows that they should never be refrigerated. Banana leaves are available at specialty stores or via mail order.

Baton Lélé *See* Lélé.

Beans

They call them beans; they call them peas; they call them just about everything. What would Caribbean food be without rice and peas (Jamaica), peas and rice (as it's called in the rest of the English-speaking Caribbean), *arroz con gandules* (Puerto Rico), *riz au pois* (Haiti), and *moros y cristianos* (Cuba)? Beans also appear in soups, stews, and as side dishes. Historians report that at least ten types of beans were cultivated in slave gardens in the Caribbean in the seventeenth and eighteenth centuries. Some of them, like Congo or gunga peas (pigeon peas)—also known as *gandules* or *gungoo peas*—are still used and appear regularly in variations on the peas-and-rice theme. Black-eyed peas (cowpeas) are less frequently used in the Caribbean but do show up on the plate in the United States and Brazil. Some of today's favorite beans in the Caribbean are kidney beans, black beans, turtle beans, red beans, and pink beans. Culinary anthropologist Maricel E. Presilla, a specialist in the history of Cuban cooking, notes that Cuba's population is divided according to its bean-eating habits. The western part of the island including Havana enjoys black beans. The eastern side agrees with its Haitian neighbors and prefers kidney beans (as do Jamaicans).

All beans are readily available dried or canned. Find a market at which they are sold frequently, so that they will not have weevils, and pick over them before cooking, no matter what the package directions say.

Black-Eyed Peas *(Vigna unguiculata or vigna sinensis)*

Legumes are among the world's oldest crops. They have been found in Egyptian tombs, and turn up in passages in the Bible. Some say they may have originated in North America; others suggest West Africa. As there are over 7,000 different varieties, the nomenclature often gets very confusing. The black-eyed pea, with its distinctive black "eye," is often called *cowpea,* which sometimes refers to a smaller variety. The important thing to know is that they are used in everything from soups to fritters and can be purchased fresh, canned, or dried.

Broad Beans *(Vicia faba)*

These beans are believed to have originated in North Africa or the eastern Mediterranean, and were the only beans in Europe until the Spaniards brought the string bean back from South America in the sixteenth century. Fresh young beans can be eaten raw without their thick skin, but the more mature beans are used in soups and stews. An excellent source of folic acid, broad beans are also called fava beans (from their Latin name), and are used in areas of the Creole world where there is Latin influence.

They are available dried or canned and are seasonally available fresh.

Black Sugar *See* Sugarcane.

Bois d'inde

Some suggest that these are bay-rum berries. French sources, though, seem to think that they are just cousins of allspice.

Breadfruit *(Artocarpus altilis)*

Captain Bligh of *Bounty* mutiny fame brought the first breadfruit to the Americas as food for the enslaved Africans of the Caribbean. The fact that the limited amount of water on board was given to the young seedlings and not to the crew produced the mutiny. Descendants of the original breadfruit tree can still be found in Kew Gardens in London and in the Botanical Gardens of Saint Vincent. The large, round-cannonball-sized relative of the mulberry provides starch in many Caribbean dishes. Breadfruit is cooked when green or ripe, and can be substituted for white potatoes in many recipes. It can also be thinly sliced and fried as chips, or roasted, either in an oven or over an open fire.

Fresh breadfruit can occasionally be obtained in large cities where there is a significant Caribbean population. Be sure to look for a globe with no blemishes or soft spots. Frequently, in Caribbean markets, you can buy part of a breadfruit. Purchase only what you need, as it will keep only a few days in the refrigerator.

Brown Sugar *See* Sugarcane.

Buttermilk

Traditionally, this is the milky, slightly sour liquid that separates from cream during the production of butter. Today, in the United States, adding bacteria to milk is the mass-market method to produce buttermilk. Buttermilk is available in the dairy cases of most supermarkets.

Calabash *(Lagenia leucantha)*

After maturity, the skin on these pumpkinlike gourds hardens and becomes impermeable to water; thus, they are frequently used as cooking utensils in the Caribbean. They are called *coui,* from the original Arawakan word. Dippers, soup bowls, and large service pieces made from calabash can be found in local markets, and make an innovative way of setting the table for a Caribbean meal.

Calabaza *(Cucurbita* species)

When you have pumpkin soup in the Caribbean, odds are that the calabaza is the vegetable used. Called *pumpkin* in the English-speaking Caribbean, *giraumon* or *calebasse* in the French-speaking Caribbean, and West Indian pumpkin in North America, this large yellow-skinned pumpkinlike squash is cut into chunks and added to stews, pureed by modern chefs, and fried. It was thought that this member of the squash family originated in Egypt, but recent studies indicate that it actually comes from Peru.

A winter squash, *calabaza,* like its cousins the butternut and the acorn squash, is increasingly available in supermarkets, where it is often called West Indian cooking pumpkin or, simply, pumpkin. Because of its size, it is usually sold in pieces in Caribbean and Latin American markets. Look for firm pieces with bright-orange flesh with no blemishes or dark marks. They can be kept whole for several months in a cool, dry place, but use calabaza pieces soon after purchase because they will only keep a few days in the refrigerator. If calabaza is unavailable, use Hubbard acorn or butternut squash.

Callaloo *(Xanthosoma* species)

This is the name of a classic Caribbean soup that appears in different guises in various islands—it's called *pepperpot* in Jamaica. Callaloo is also the name of the greens that go into the soup. The leaves will often be called *calalu* (or *callaloo*) while the roots have a different name entirely. At least two different leaves are called *callaloo* in the Caribbean. The first is the elephant-ear-shaped leaf of the plant, variously known as *dasheen, tannia, yautia, taro, malanga,* and *chou caribe.* The second is better known as Chinese spinach or Indian kale and is sometimes called *bhaji,* its Indian name, in Jamaica and Trinidad.

These leafy greens can occasionally be found fresh in Caribbean markets in large cities. It is also possible to find canned callaloo; Jamaican's Grace brand seems to have the widest distribution. Fresh spinach can be substituted.

Cane Syrup

This light-colored sugar syrup has a hint of the molasses taste found in sugarcane. It is used in preparing the 'Ti Punch and Punch Vieux (*see* "Beverages"), ubiquitous drinks of the French Antilles. A simple sugar syrup is a good substitute.

Another version of cane syrup is the Louisiana type, which goes under the name of *melao de cana* in the Spanish-speaking world, and *sirop de batterie* in the French one. This is a heavy, dark syrup made from pressed sugarcane. Lighter in taste than molasses, it is used when making syrup cake, *gateau sirop,* and other Louisiana confections. Steen's is the brand of choice in Louisiana and can be mail ordered. If you're fortunate enough to make it to the farmer's market in New Orleans, you may purchase cane syrup made by local farmers from heirloom canes.

Cane Vinegar

The molasses taste of sugarcane is again the attraction in this white vinegar widely used in Jamaica. It is virtually impossible to find in the United States, but you may substitute distilled white vinegar mixed with a tablespoon or two of brown sugar. Steen's in southern Louisiana makes a darker-hued, but similar-tasting, cane vinegar. It can be purchased by mail order (*See* Mail-Order Sources).

Carambola *(Chrysophyllum cainito)*

Called *star fruit* or *star apple* (or *five finger,* in Guyana), this multisided fruit becomes a translucent yellow when ripe. Its juice is consumed in the Caribbean, and the fruit is frequently used in salads and desserts as garnish or because of its unusual star shape. There are two versions, one more tart than the other.

Carambola is readily available at specialty grocery stores. The yellow version tends to be the sweeter.

Cascadura

Found in Trinidad and Guyana, the cascadura, or *hassah* is elsewhere known as *poisson coffre,* or *trunkfish,* a type of mudfish with a white, tender flesh that is similar in taste to shrimp. *Cascadura* is such a delicacy that only the rare visitor to Trinidad has a chance to sample it. Legend has it that visitors to the island who eat *cascadura* curry will return there.

The fish can occasionally be found frozen in fish markets in Caribbean neighborhoods. Shelled and cleaned shrimp are an acceptable substitute.

Cassareep

Made from the juice of the boiled-down grated *cassava,* flavored with brown sugar, cinnamon, cloves, and other ingredients, cassareep is one of the oldest condiments in the Caribbean. Its origins go back to the early Indian inhabitants of the region. It is even mentioned in chronicles of the area dating back to Columbus's time. Today, the condiment is mainly found in Guyana and some of the English-speaking islands of the southern Caribbean, where it is used to season pepperpot stew.

Cassava *(Manhiot esculentar* or *Manhiot dulcis)*

Bread made from the flour of this starchy tuber, known as *yuca* or *manioc,* was on the menu when Christopher Columbus dined with the king of the Caribe Indians on December 26, 1492. He would have perhaps declined to try it if he had realized that the bitter version of this tuber can be poisonous; its high percentage of prussic acid is dispelled by cooking.

Today, the sweet version of the tuber is found in most of the Caribbean, and is used to make everything from tapioca to *pain de kassav, pan de casabe,* and *bammie,* the Haitian, Dominican, and Jamaican versions of the same cassava bread that was served to Columbus. Travelers to Port-au-Prince, Haiti, can stock up on *pain de kassav* at a small town on the outskirts of Cap Haitien, where it's still baked in the old style, over open-air, cast-iron griddles. In Jamaica, inventive chefs have cut *bammie* into star- and baton-shaped pieces, which, when fried, are the perfect accompaniments to many modern dishes.

Ready-made *bammie* can occasionally be found in Caribbean markets in the United States, but you can also prepare it yourself. The flour (also known as *manioc* or *cassava meal*) used to prepare it is available at health-food stores.

The tuber itself is also widely available and is known as *manioc* or *yuca.* Its long, tuberous root and dull, green leaves turn up in the cooking of the Creole world as well. In Cuba, cassava is cooked and eaten in many forms and is mashed into *fufu.* The tuber is also used to prepare cassava meal, known as *farinha* in Brazil. Cassava meal can be found in stores selling Latin American and Brazilian products; fresh cassava tubers and cassava can be found in grocery stores in Latin America, and West Indian neighborhoods in the United States. If you wish to purchase the leaves, you may have to ask for *dasheen* or *malanga.* Cassava tubers should not show mold or have sticky spots and should smell fresh.

Chadec *(Citrus grandis)*

Chadec is the French name for this fruit, also called shaddock or pomelo. Thought to be the ancestor of the grapefruit, *chadec* is used in marmalades, for juice, or candied.

Channa

Channa are roasted chickpeas, an Indian snack food transplanted to the Caribbean. Channa can be simply salted, flavored with curry powder, or toasted with a biting hot chile covering. Often purchased from street vendors, in Trinidad and Guyana, channa are nibbled like peanuts.

Channa can be purchased in shops selling Caribbean spices, or easily prepared at home.

Chayote *(Sechium edule)*

Also known as *christophine, chocho, mirliton, xuxu,* and *vegetable pear,* this delicately flavored squash is used in everything from soups to main dishes. The vegetable looks like a light green or whitish pear with a puckered-up mouth at the bottom. It was introduced to the Caribbean from Mexico in the eighteenth century. Chayote is particularly prized in gratins and souffles in the French-speaking islands and in New Orleans, where it is usually served stuffed with savory seafood. There, it is known as *mirliton.*

The peel and the seeds of the young chayote are edible. Once the chayote is older, the peel and the seeds should be discarded. Look for firm ones with no blemishes. Chayotes are available in supermarkets, and will keep for up to three weeks in the refrigerator. Chayotes can be substituted for zucchini, but will produce a more lightly flavored dish.

Cherimoya *(Annona cherimola)*

Sometimes called *custard apple,* this fist-sized fruit has a custardlike flesh that tastes like a mixture of vanilla ice cream and banana. Cherimoyas range in color from green and grayish brown to black. They are frequently used as the basis for fabulous tropical ice creams and sorbets. Cherimoyas should be eaten exactly like Goldilocks' porridge . . . when it's just right. In the case of the cherimoya, that means when it gives slightly when pressed, and has a sweetish smell. They are found fresh only in specialty shops and in the subtropical areas of the United States. Canned pulp and juice can be found in most markets.

Chiles *(Capsicum frutescens)*

They crosspollinate with the speed of rabbits, and have different names wherever you find them: Chiles. Called Scotch bonnet, *bonda man'jacques, piment négresse, wiri wiri,* and bird peppers among other things, chiles turn up in every course except, usually, dessert.

Seemingly related to the Mexican *habanero* chile, the lantern-shaped Scotch bonnets of the Caribbean add flavor to the pot, as well as heat. If unavailable, substitute a habanero or Scotch bonnet pepper sauce. Tabasco sauce may be used as a substitute only as a last resort; it will add heat, but the subtle flavor of the chile will be lost.

In traditional Creole cooking, chiles are always used fresh. No self-respecting rural family is without a chile bush, and many a transplanted Caribbean native has a well-nurtured pot of their favorite chile growing in a sunny kitchen window.

Scotch bonnet chiles can be purchased fresh in most markets. Look for those with bright color and no blemishes. You can have the flavor of the chile and less of the heat if you remove the seeds and membranes from the chile before using it, but be careful! When working with chiles, use rubber gloves or coat your hands with oil to avoid the stinging capsaicin (the compound that gives chiles their heat). Wash your hands thoroughly after handling chiles, as the capsaicin will seriously irritate your eyes and mucous membranes.

Chocolate *(Threbroma cacao)*

Unless you are very familiar with tropical fruits and vegetables, you'll probably never recognize the cocoa trees growing by the roadside as you drive through the lush countryside. You might even miss it in the marketplace on islands like Martinique and Guadeloupe, where it appears in two-inch-thick dark brown logs, because log chocolate, as it is found in the Caribbean, is unavailable in the United States. Mexican chocolate comes already flavored with cinnamon and may be found in gourmet shops or those selling Latin-American products. Bittersweet chocolate may substituted in some recipes. However, if Mexican chocolate is called for, the addition of cinnamon and other spices may be necessary in order to get the same flavor.

Chou Palmiste *See* hearts of palm.

Cinnamon (*Cinnamomum verum* and *Zeylanicum cassia*)

The rolled-up quill of the dried, pale-brown inner bark of the cinnamon tree was one of the most precious spices of the ancient Romans. On Caribbean islands like Grenada, cinnamon literally grows on trees. Cinnamon is a commonly used spice in the Caribbean along with its coarser, close cousin, *cassia*. When you go into supermarkets in Barbados, the spice shelves do not contain cinnamon packages; they simply have packets and boxes labeled spice. The generic term is used only to refer to cinnamon spice and indicates the frequency of its use in Caribbean cooking.

When purchasing cinnamon, look for the quills and not the ground spice, which is usually a mixture of cinnamon, cassia, and Lord knows what else. You can grind your own in a spice grinder or a coffee grinder used only for spices. Look for quills that are highly aromatic; store in an airtight container so that they do not lose their potency.

Clove (*Eugenia caryophyllata* and *Syzygium aromaticum*)

Cloves, the pink, unopened buds of a tropical evergreen plant, were one of the spices for which Columbus was searching in 1492. Cloves are indigenous to the Spice Islands of Southeast Asia. They arrived in the Caribbean, and are now quite at home on a number of islands, notably Grenada, the Caribbean's very own spice island.

Cloves should be highly aromatic when purchased, and stored in an airtight container. If powdered cloves are needed, grind your own in a spice grinder.

Coconut (*Cocos nucifera*)

No one is sure exactly how the coconut arrived in the New World. The coconut is thought to have originated in Southeast Asia, but the nut can float, and may have arrived in this hemisphere before the Europeans. For centuries, the coconut palm was the stuff of life for the peoples of the Caribbean. From the fronds, which were used for roofs; to the logs, which were used for houses and rafts; to the rough husk, which made rope, the tree fulfilled many needs. Culinary needs were also well taken care of.

Green, jelly, or water coconuts provide liquid that is so pure that it was occasionally used in place of plasma in the South Pacific during World War II. Coconut oil is the traditional Caribbean cooking oil of choice, while the grated meat of the brown ripe coconut appears on the table in all courses, from appetizer to dessert.

In Caribbean neighborhoods, jelly coconuts (the green fruit whose meat is still a jellylike mass) are sometimes hawked on the streets by vendors who open them; then pour the coconut water into plastic containers. Most folks, though, remain ignorant about the differences between coconut water and coconut milk.

The liquid in a coconut is coconut water. Coconut milk is the liquid of the coconut mixed with the grated coconut meat. To prepare coconut milk, open a brown or dry coconut by heating it in a medium oven for ten minutes. (The coconut will develop fault lines.) Remove the coconut and with a hammer, break open the coconut along the fault lines. Remove the shell, scrape off the brown peel, and grate the white coconut meat. (Using a food processor for this step prevents skinned fingers.) Add 1 cup of heated coconut water or 1 cup boiling water to the grated coconut meat and allow the mixture to stand for one-half hour. Strain the mixture though cheesecloth, squeezing the pulp to release all the coconut milk. Unsweetened canned coconut milk can be used. If you're preparing a dessert and really desperate, you may dilute coconut cream.

Floating Market, Curaçao.

Coconut water can be purchased at Caribbean markets where enterprising folk set up stands, complete with machetes, and open the coconuts for you. (Avoid the canned sweetened Asian type of coconut milk and look for the water straight from the coconut, or settle for the unsweetened kind.) Coconut oil is readily available, as is canned coconut cream, which is frequently used in Caribbean drinks such as the piña colada. And, of course, there are always the hairy brown coconuts that peer out at us in the grocery store. They can be transformed into coconut milk, grated coconut, and just about any other coconut product you may need.

Colombo *See* Curry.

Conch *(Strombus gigas)*

This large gastropod mollusk is found in the Caribbean, where the shell is used as a horn. The large and singularly unattractive inhabitant of the shell is considered a delicacy in the Caribbean and eaten in many guises. The mucilaginous string that attaches the conch to its shell is considered an aphrodisiac in the Bahamas, and consumed with gusto by the men who frequent the conch stands under the bridge heading to Nassau's Paradise Island. Conch salad, which is made from chopped conch, raw onion, and bird peppers mixed together and served with a squirt of lime juice, is another popular conch dish.

Called *lambi* in the French-speaking Caribbean, after the Caribe word, it is often served in stews or grilled. An amazing sexist Creole proverb says of a wife-beating husband that *"I bat li con lambi"* (He beats her like a conch). It is an unpleasant reminder of the way that conch must be thoroughly beaten to tenderize it before cooking.

Today, because of overfishing, conch is increasingly endangered in parts of the Caribbean.

Coriander *(Coriandrum sativum)*

The leaves of this plant, which is a relative of the carrot, are also known as *Chinese parsley* and *cilantro*. Brought to the New World by the Spaniards, it is still emblematic of the foods of the Spanish-speaking world. What would Mexican salsas and guacamole be without it? The pods and seeds of the plant are used to make several West Indian curries. Coriander leaves are an important ingredient in the *sofritos* of the Hispanic Caribbean.

Corn *(Zea mays)*

This cereal grain is native to the Americas. Corn turns up in many guises throughout the Creole world. As cornmeal or corn flour it is used for everything from breading for frying to breakfast porridges. It's roasted and served for a favorite roadside snack, sometimes with a piece of coconut on the side. *Hominy,* which is prepared from flint or dent corn, is the base for soups in Mexico and is a dessert in Brazil, where it is also fermented. It also turns up as pastes that hark back to West Africa, where the adopted grain has become extremely popular.

Fresh corn is available year-round, although it's at its peak in summer. The best corn is picked, then cooked immediately. Hominy is available canned or dried; cornmeal is available in a number of degrees of coarseness, and in either white or yellow. Corn flour is finely ground cornmeal.

Cowpea *(Vigna unguiculata* or *vigna sinensis)*

These are relatives of the black-eyed peas. For some people, cowpeas mean the smaller variety; others simply use the terms interchangeably. *See also* Black-eyed peas.

Crapaud

This is a French word to describe the large frogs that can be found on the islands of Montserrat and Dominica. They are also known as *mountain chicken* and considered a local delicacy. They are not available in the United States.

Creole Cream Cheese *See* recipe p. 319.

Curaçao

The name of one of the islands of the Netherlands Antilles is also the name of a liqueur produced on the island. Excellent in cooking, for making mixed drinks and on its own as a perfect after-dinner drink, it has spawned many imitators, but true curaçao comes only from Curaçao.

Curry

Anyone knowledgeable about spices will tell you that there's no such thing as curry powder. Curry powders are prepared spice blends that were designed for particular dishes. Premixed blends are simply labor saving. Transported to the New World by the colonial British, who took a liking to it in the subcontinent, as well as by the indentured servants who migrated to the Caribbean from India in the late nineteenth century, this mixture of spices varies from dish to dish. Allspice, an unheard-of ingredient in many Indian curries, is frequently the prime ingredient in West Indian curries. Trinidadian curries tend to be fiery hot; Jamaican ones run the gamut from mild to hot. In the French Antilles, curry is called *colombo,* taking its name from the former capital of Sri Lanka. Dishes like *colombo de porc* mix India's spices with the New World's favorite meat—pork. Curry is the basis of Trinidad and Tobago's popular street food, *roti,* a chicken, beef, or vegetable curry wrapped in a plain, flat crepelike bread. In Guyana, curry is eaten with roti, as well. Pieces of the roti are torn off and dipped into the curry in a style closer to that of India.

The Madras curry powder mixtures that are usually used in Jamaica and the southern Caribbean contain saffron, ginger, turmeric, cumin, coriander, and several types of chiles. Madras curry powders are some of the hottest.

When purchasing curry powder, look for a blend that is aromatic. Purchase in small quantities so that you do not keep the spices for too long. Better yet, prepare your own blend using this recipe:

5 dried bird chiles
2 teaspoons coriander seeds
½ teaspoon mustard seeds
½ teaspoon black peppercorns
½ teaspoon green peppercorns
½ teaspoon fenugreek seeds
7 curry leaves
½ teaspoon ground ginger
1 tablespoon turmeric

Seed the chiles and place them with the whole spices in a heavy cast-iron skillet. Toast over medium heat until they darken and perfume the air. Allow the spices to cool, then grind in a spice mill. Toast the curry leaves separately; then grind. Mix all the ingredients together and place in a jar. Cover tightly. Personalize the recipe by adding varying amounts of the spices that you like. You may consider adding cumin, cardamom, cloves, and cinnamon, among others.

Dasheen *See* Callaloo.

Dewberry *(Rubus caesius)*

This fruit is closely related to the blackberry, but has smaller berries. They are not readily available unless grown locally, except for the Pacific variety, which are sometimes found dried. Blackberries may be substituted for them in any recipe.

Djon-djon

These tiny black mushrooms are only available in Haiti, and are used to add color and flavor to such local dishes as *riz djon-djon,* a Haitian rice and mushroom dish in which the mushrooms are used to flavor the rice.

Djon-djon can be found in markets in Haitian neighborhoods. If you cannot find them, substitute reconstituted dried dark European or Asian mushrooms for an approximate taste.

Dried Shrimp

Used in Afro-Brazilian dishes from the state of Bahia, dried smoked shrimp also appear in a few Caribbean dishes and some New Orleans gumbos, for which they are ground and used to flavor rich sauces. Dried shrimp and the more pungent dried smoked shrimp can be found in Asian markets.

Fanner Basket

This is a large flat basket that is used for winnowing rice in the coastal areas of South Carolina.

Garlic *(Allium sativum)*

This "stinking weed," as it is sometimes known, is one of the treasures of the food world. Thought to have originated in the Middle East, garlic was known to the ancient Egyptians who fed it to the builders of the pyramids in large quantities. Garlic can be very pungent, and its fragrance makes some shy away from fresh garlic cloves. Garlic powder, garlic granules, and garlic salt, however, are no substitute for fresh garlic, which is used sparingly in many dishes of the Creole world. Those who prefer the more robust side of Creole cuisine will enjoy dishes like Guyana's garlic pork, where garlic's pungency is exploited with culinary glee.

Garlic is simple to use. To crush a clove, simply whack it with the flat end of a chef's knife. For those who are garlic phobic, you can get a bit of the flavor by impaling a peeled clove on the tines of a fork and stirring it through the food that is being prepared.

When purchasing garlic, look for heads that are heavy and firm. (Light ones may contain cloves that have dried out.) Store garlic in a dry, cool place. It will keep for several months.

Geera *(Cuminum cyninum)*

This is an Indian term for cumin, a spice that frequently appears in the curry powders of the Caribbean.

Genip *(Allophylus paniculata)*

The fruit of the *genip* tree look like enormous grapes, and are relatives of the lychee. *Genips, guineps, quenette,* or *genipa,* however, have thick slip skin and a small pit surrounded by a translucent pinkish pulp that can be tart or slightly sweet. Sucking the meat off the pit is a Caribbean children's delight. Kids always seem to know where to find genips growing, but the rest of us can find this fruit in markets, sold in bunches or clusters. Note that what are called *genips* in Jamaica are called *ackee* in Trinidad.

For some reason, *genips* have become popular with street vendors in New York City, turning up not only in Caribbean neighborhoods but virtually all over town. If you don't live in Gotham, try a Caribbean neighborhood. Otherwise, this might just be one you'll have to sample *in situ.*

Ginger *(Zingiber officinale)*

This rhizome of a tropical plant is probably a native of Asia. It has done so well in the New World, though, that Jamaican ginger has become synonymous with the spice for many of us. Ginger is used fresh, dried, or powdered in many of the region's recipes, where it turns up in everything from curry powders to ginger beer to candies. One Jamaican lemonade recipe even calls for a few gratings of peeled fresh ginger to give it some zing.

Ginger can be found fresh in virtually all grocery stores. If purchasing powdered ginger, look for Jamaican ginger, which is more delicate in flavor. Purchase fresh ginger when it is firm. It can be stored in the refrigerator, wrapped in paper towels or in a plastic bag. Dried ginger, which is used in desserts and in some spice mixtures, is best kept in an airtight container in a cool, dry place.

Guava *(Psidium guajava)*

This fruit is native to the Americas; there are over 100 edible varieties. Père Labat, the French priest to whom we owe much of our knowledge of things gastronomic in the seventeenth-century Caribbean, transcribed several recipes for guava, including one for baked guava. A rich source of minerals and vitamins A and C, guavas are eaten at various stages of their development. When green, they are slightly tart; when ripe they are sweeter. In the Caribbean, guavas are eaten in all forms—cooked and raw—but, more often than not, they are used to make jams, jellies, and chutneys.

You may find fresh guavas in markets that sell Caribbean produce. If so, look for fruit that is firm with no blemishes. If fresh guavas are unavailable, you'll have to content yourself with guava paste, which is eaten with cheese as a dessert on some Spanish-speaking islands.

Hearts of Palm

Those swaying palm trees that make Caribbean beaches postcard paradises also leave their culinary offerings in various guises. One species produces the form of reddish-hued palm oil that is a hallmark of Brazilian cooking. Others offer a cluster of co-conuts, and still others give us hearts of palm. These are exactly what they are called: the heart of a palm tree. It is found fresh in the Caribbean, Brazil, and in parts of Florida, where it is known as *swamp cabbage.*

If you are fortunate enough to happen across fresh heart of palm, remove the coarse outside husk and boil the heart in water, adding a bit of lemon juice to keep it from discoloring. When the heart is tender, remove it, drain it, and serve it either with a vinaigrette as a salad, in fritters, or with a hollandaise sauce and asparagus.

Fresh hearts of palm are as rare as hen's teeth in northern climes, so we have to content ourselves with the canned variety, which is best used in salads.

Igname *(Members of the dioscorea family)*

Known as yam, *ñame, yautia,* and *tannia* in the Caribbean, this large hairy tuber has nothing to do with what people in the United States call yams. True yams have flesh that can range in hue from white to purplish, and the largest of them weigh in at several hundred pounds. For many African nations, yams were a symbol of life's continuation, because new yams grow from older cuttings. The religious significance continued in the New World, where new yams are consecrated in voodoo temples in Haiti during a ceremony known as *mangé yam* (yam eating), and in Brazilian Candomble *terreiros* in a ceremony honoring Oxala the Orixa, who loved white yams. An astonishing number of different types of yams are sold in the Caribbean, each with its own local name in English, French, Spanish, Dutch, and *patois,* which makes identifying them a Herculean task. If you want to sample some of the varieties, head for your local Caribbean market. Yams are served in a variety of ways in the Caribbean, ranging from boiled and puréed (like mashed potatoes) to French fried or added to soups and stews.

When purchasing yams, look for firm ones with no signs of mold or insects. Larger yams are usually sold in pieces; look for pieces that are not soft or spongy.

Jackfruit *(Artocarpus integra)*

This fruit is so often confused with its close cousin, the breadfruit, that it has become a bit of a joke to Caribbean folk, who are used to seeing one labeled with the other's name. Introduced to Jamaica at the end of the eighteenth century by Admiral Rodney, it made its way to Hispaniola and, from there, to the rest of the Caribbean. Less aromatic than its notoriously funky Asian relative, the *durian,* the fruit can grow up to ninety pounds; thirty- or forty-pound jackfruit are not uncommon. Unripe fruit is often cooked; the ripe fruit is much like a custardy pineapple in taste. Even the seeds can be roasted—they have a flavor similar to chestnuts. Jackfruit are not often available in American markets.

Jamaica *(Hibiscus sabdariffa)*

The deep red flower of the hibiscus family is sometimes known as *sorrel* or *roselle* *(rosella)* and, in Spanish, as *flor de Jamaica*. It is African in origin and is consumed in Egypt under the name of *carcade* or *karkadeeh*. The podlike flowers of the plant are dried, then steeped in water to make a brilliant red drink that has a slightly tart taste. The drink can be consumed as a nonalcoholic beverage, but becomes another thing altogether with the addition of rum. It is a traditional Christmas drink. Formerly found in Caribbean markets only at Christmas, dried sorrel is now available almost year-round.

Jamaica Pepper *See* allspice.

Kid

The meat of young goats is occasionally used in West Indian cookery, most notably in Jamaica's curry goat and *manish* water, a fortifying soup. The meat has a slightly gamey taste.

Kid is available from butchers in West Indian and Greek neighborhoods. If you cannot find it, it can easily be replaced by mutton.

Lambi *See* Conch.

Land Crabs

These small, hard-shelled members of the crab family are not sea dwellers but, rather, just what the name implies—land crabs. They are found strung together in bunches in markets in the Caribbean and coastal areas of northern South America. They are put in pens and fed a diet of bread and spices. Land crabs are the main ingredient in one of the French Antilles's favorite appetizers, *crabes farcies,* or stuffed crab backs. Called *jueyes,* their meat is served up in turnovers, *empanadillas* that are delicious when served with coconut water in Loiza Aldea. Brazilian writer Jorge Amado was known for his love of the *casquinha de siri*—Bahia's variation on the stuffed crab theme. The taste of land crab is sweeter, and without the sea-tang of its water loving cousin. However, if you must find a substitute for land crabs, find and use the smallest, most delicate sea crabs that you can. They are occasionally found in Caribbean markets.

Langosta

Known in the French islands as *langouste* (as opposed to *homard*) and in the English-speaking ones as *spiny lobster* or *lobster, langosta* is a surprise for many northerners traveling to the region. Unlike its cousins from New England, the tropical lobster has no pincer claws. It makes up for this by having some of the tastiest lobster meat available.

Langosta can occasionally be found in specialty fish markets; they are best served grilled so as not to destroy their delicate taste. In other recipes, you can replace langosta with regular lobster meat.

Lard

Rendered fatback is known as *lard*. Lard is frequently found in Hispanic recipes, in which it is known as *manteca de cerdo*. Purists will want to render their own lard but, for the rest of us it is available in the meat departments of most grocery stores and from butchers.

Lélé

A *lélé* or *baton lélé* is a small branch of a tree with several offshooting branches trimmed in such a way that it can be used as a whisk. This stirring stick is used in Caribbean cooking to whisk such dishes as *callaloo voodoo* or *mignan de fruit à pain*. A *baton lélé* can be purchased inexpensively in any market on Martinique or Guadeloupe, or it can be made from a small stick with three or four smaller branches growing from the end, with bark peeled off and dried. They are sometimes called *swizzle sticks* in the English-speaking Caribbean.

Limes *(Citrus aurantifolia)*

A member of the *Rutaceae* family, which also includes oranges and lemons, Caribbean limes have yellow skins and look like small green lemons; they only turn yellow when overripe. Limes are the basis for numerous dishes and are the prime ingredient in most of the region's drinks, such as rum punch and the *'Ti punch* of the French Antilles. In the French-speaking islands of the region, they are cut *en palettes,* that is, sliced around the outside so that each slice is seedless. They are served as condiments for everything from *callaloo* to grilled fish to salads.

Caribbean limes rarely make their way to northern markets. Instead, select the juiciest limes you can find, with no blemishes or soft spots, or purchase key limes.

Mace *See* Nutmeg.

Mango *(Mangifera indica)*

This tropical fruit *par excellence* is known by some as "the king of the fruits." Over 326 varieties have been recorded in India, although the fruit is thought to have originated in the Malaysian archipelago. Mangoes arrived in the New World (Brazil) in the fifteenth century, and in the Caribbean after 1872. It's difficult to be exact about the date for, in 1872, a French vessel carrying a cargo of mangoes from *Iles Bourbon* to Hispaniola was captured by the English off Jamaica, the cargo was jettisoned and then floated to various Caribbean islands where the mangoes reproduced. The most common mangoes in the Caribbean are Julie mangoes, which are flattened, light-green ovals.

Mangoes are used in many different ways in the Caribbean. Green mangoes are used in hot sauces and in condiments such as *kuchela.* Ripe mangoes appear in desserts and candies and even pureéd and used in drinks. Needless to say, to many a ripe mango simply sucked on or cut open and eaten is one of the delights of the tropics.

Once a hard-to-find specialty fruit, mangoes are readily available in North America and Europe. If you cannot find them at regular grocery stores, look for them in shops selling Caribbean and tropical produce. There are numerous varieties of mango—some claim over a thousand—so choosing them by color or size can be very risky business indeed. Select them instead by touch. Mangoes should be purchased when they are firm but yield slightly to the touch. Green mangoes are still difficult to find outside of Caribbean or Indian neighborhoods but, if you're lucky enough to locate some, think of making a condiment like *kuchela* or a *souskai*.

Manioc *See* Cassava.

Mauby *(Colubrina elliptica)*

This is a cooling beverage made from the bark of a small tree. In the Caribbean from the late nineteenth to the latter third of the twentieth century, vendors could be found on the streets of villages and cities selling mauby from containers that they carried on their heads.

Mauby bark can be found in Caribbean markets and a mauby syrup is available from shops selling Caribbean items.

Mirliton *See* Chayote.

Molasses

Called *melasse* in French and *melao de caña* in Spanish, this by-product of the refining of sugarcane is a spicy thread that runs through the history of blacks in the New World. Molasses, along with rum, was one of the products of the triangle trade that brought most of the slaves to the New World; it was one of the Americas' principal sweeteners until the middle of the nineteenth century. As a result, the dark, spicy taste of molasses can be found in the traditional sweets of the area such as Jamaica's Bustamante's jawbone and Bullas and Guyana's Christmas cake, although many now replace the traditional sweetener with brown sugar. In Brazil, molasses is the main ingredient in some of their confectionery as well as in *pé de moleque.*

Molasses can be found right where it's always been, waiting for you at the supermarket near the sugar products. Try using a spoonful instead of sugar in some of your dessert recipes.

Name *See* Igname.

Naseberry *(Lachras zapota)*

A native of the Caribbean, this fruit is known as *sapodilla, nispero* in Spanish, and *sapotille* in French. The French say that the color of the kiwi-sized fruit is the color of the skin of beautiful mulatto woman. Indeed, it is a lovely golden brown fruit that has a slightly grainy pulp of honey-brown hue. The Aztecs ate the fruit. The Mexican name for the tree is *chicozapote* and the sap from the tree is known as *chicle,* the substance from which chewing gum is made. Naseberry are usually eaten simply as fruit. Recently, though, they have begun to appear in tropical fruit salads and sorbets.

If selecting a naseberry for eating, look for one that is soft to the touch, but without blemishes. When they are too firm, they are underripe and have an unpleasantly sour taste.

Nutmeg and Mace *(Myristica fragrans)*

Two of the spices that Columbus was looking for when he stumbled upon the Caribbean—nutmeg and mace—are actually from the same tree. The nutmeg is the seed and the mace is the lacy aril that covers it. Grenada, the Caribbean's spice island, is one of the world's largest producers of nutmeg today, and the tall, tropical evergreen from which the nuts come scents the air. Nutmeg has been a popular spice in Caribbean cooking for centuries: A grating is indispensable to a true rum punch, and the grated spice subtly enhances curries, stews, soups, and desserts. Mace is an ingredient that frequently turns up in the Creole dishes of the Carolina and Georgia Low Country.

When purchasing nutmeg, forget about the powdered stuff in cans or jars. Get a nutmeg grater and whole nuts, which will release a small bit of oil when pressed if they are good quality. Mace can be found in its natural form, called *blades*. These are good for adding to soups and stews but, for baking and other uses, you will have to resort to ground mace. Buy it in small quantities and store it in an airtight container, as it rapidly loses its aroma.

Okra *(Hibiscus esculentus)*

Outside of the American South, this relative of cotton is perhaps one of the least-liked vegetables of the Western world. People just don't like its slimy texture. In the creolized areas of the hemisphere—from New Orleans to Bahia—cooks simply let okra be itself, and prize the pods for their ability to thicken sauces and soups. Okra is native to Africa, and its origins are trumpeted by its name in a number of languages throughout the world. The American okra comes from the *twi* of Ghana, while the French opt for *gombo,* which harks back to the Bantu languages of the southern segment of the continent. Okra is known as *gombo* in France, *guingambo* in Puerto Rico, *malondron* in the Dominican Republic, and sometimes, by its East Indian name, *bindi,* in Trinidad and Jamaica. It adds the sticks-to-your-ribs quality to *callaloo* and to Jamaica's pepperpot and turns up in Puerto Rico's *sopa de guingambo.* It also appears as a vegetable, and blanched as a salad.

When buying okra, look for small pods that have no blemishes. The smaller pods are more delicate in taste and not as fibrous as the larger ones. In cooking okra, remember: The more you cut it, the slimier it will be. The slime, though, can be minimized, if not eliminated, by selecting small pods and leaving them whole.

Select pods that are green in color; black stripes often indicate that the pods are fibrous. The okra should be tender, not soft, and without bruises or marks. If you're not using it right away, blanch and freeze for storage.

Frozen okra is readily available and can be substituted when fresh is unavailable. Okra is still one of those vegetables that has not become "mainstream," so you may have to look for it in African-American neighborhoods and in grocery stores catering to a Middle-Eastern clientele. Cooks should note that okra has a chemical reaction with cast iron and copper pots, which affects the color, not the taste, of the pod. I once said that wherever okra points its green tip, Africa has passed; I still believe it.

Otaheite Apple *(Syzygium malaccense)*

Also known as a *pomerac,* this fruit looks too good to be true. The pear-shaped fruit has a waxy, burgundy-red skin and pristine white flesh. Eaten mainly as a fruit, it can also be sliced thin to add color and a very subtle taste of apples—with a hint of roses—to salads.

Oursin

This is what islanders on Martinique and Guadeloupe call small spiny sea urchins, which are no fun to step on at the beach. At the dinner table, it's another story; *oursin* are delicious when they appear as appetizers, either baked or raw. Those sea creatures are occasionally found in fish markets, and are extremely perishable.

Papaya *(Carica papaya)*

Known as *fruta bomba* in Cuba, *lechosa* in the Dominican Republic and Puerto Rico, *papaye* in the French-speaking Caribbean, and erroneously as pawpaw or melon tree on many English-speaking islands, the papaya is native to the Caribbean. Papayas can vary in size and appearance, ranging from small, unripe melons to misshapen yellow squashes. The flesh varies in color from light pink to deep orange and even red. When cut open, papaya has a myriad of small black seeds, which are not usually eaten, but which have a taste between watercress and pepper. Sliced papaya often ap-

Monkey pots for cooling water, Barbados.

pears on tables at breakfast or at dessert, accompanied by a wedge of lime; it is also eaten green in salads and condiments.

A surprising characteristic of the papaya is its remarkable ability to tenderize meat, thanks to the large quantity of the enzyme *papain,* which also aids in digestion. Tough pieces of meat are made virtually fork tender by wrapping them in papaya leaves or rubbing them with papaya juice. For this reason, papaya is the basis of many commercial, natural, meat tenderizers.

Papayas are almost as common in markets as mangoes. Be sure that it is slightly firm to the touch and has no blemishes or soft spots. You can also get canned papaya nectar and other papaya products at specialty shops carrying Latin-American and Caribbean products.

Passion Fruit *(Passiflora incarnata)*

This fruit of the passionflower can resemble a thick-skinned yellow or purple plum. Inside, numerous small black seeds are encased in a yellow or orange-colored translucent flesh, which is wonderfully tart and almost citrusy. Called *maracudja* in some parts of the French-speaking Caribbean and *granadille* in others, it's known as *maracuja* in Brazil, and *granadilla* in the Spanish-speaking Caribbean; the fruit is a delight.

Better known for its juice than its seed-infused slurry of tart pulp, its acid taste can be found in sorbets and in desserts throughout the region. The juice's distinctive tart taste can be found in numerous liqueurs mixed with everything from rum to Cognac, and many commercial fruit juices.

Passion fruit is increasingly available in the northern United States; the juice, as well as passion-fruit–flavored liqueurs, are readily available.

Peanuts *(Arachis hypogae)*

This native of the New World was thought by many to have originated in Africa, because its popularity in North America harks to the era of the slave trade. The peanut is not a nut at all; it's actually a legume, and closer to the black-eyed pea than it is to the almond. Peanuts were first grown in pre-Inca times in ancient Peru. (Garcilaso de la Vega wrote in 1609 that it was being raised by Indians under the name of *ynchic.*) The Aztecs called it *thalcachuate,* the word from which the French take their word, *cacahuete.* Peanuts were brought to Africa by Portuguese slave traders and slowly became popular. The Mandinka of western Africa refer to the legume as *tiga,* a diminutive of the Portuguese word *manteiga,* meaning butter, as the oil of the peanut was used for cooking. Peanuts returned to many parts of the hemisphere from Africa with slave traders. In Veracruz, Mexico, one of the culinary links that can be seen with the African continent is the abundant use of the peanut sauces. In North America, the African connection led to many thinking that the *goober* (from the Kimbundu language of Central Africa, *nguba*) actually originated in Africa.

Roasted peanuts are ubiquitous in all grocery stores, and raw peanuts are becoming increasingly easy to find, particularly in the South, where they are much loved. If purchasing peanuts in the shell, be sure they are fresh, since peanuts are susceptible to *aflatoxin,* a mold.

Pepper *(Piper nigrum)*

This spice is the most widely used in the West. In fact, it is so popular that in ancient times a market in Rome was named the *Piper Horatorium* for the main spice that was traded there. In other times, pepper was so highly prized that it was literally worth its weight in gold. While English speakers get our word *pepper* from the Sanskrit *pippali,* the French get their word *poivre* from the name of one of the early traders in the commodity. Pepper is one of the spices that has had the greatest influence on the history of the world. Desire to control the pepper trade sent Portuguese explorers around the Cape of Good Hope to India, and a desire to break the Portuguese monopoly on the trade routes prompted Columbus to venture out toward the West.

The pepper plant is native to the Malabar Coast of southwestern India, but today's pepper comes from Malaysia, Indonesia, or even Brazil. Pepper loses its potency after it is ground and, for that reason, anyone who wants to use black or white pepper in cooking should have a pepper mill. It doesn't have to be fancy, just a serviceable, functioning grinder. Use it, and you'll be surprised at the difference it makes.

As with all spices and herbs, purchase pepper in small amounts to ensure freshness. The larger the grain, the more expensive the pepper. Look for even-sized berries. Many consider the finest black pepper in the world to be India's Tellicherry pepper. Black peppercorns are the fermented, sun-dried berries of the pepper plant. White peppercorns are the ripe berries with the outer skin removed, which are then dried until cream-colored. Green peppercorns are the fresh berries. They are usually available either freeze-dried or in brine. Tree-ripened red peppercorns are virtually unavailable outside pepper-growing countries.

The pink peppercorns that are sold in markets and that turn up in peppercorn mixtures are not pepper at all, but the berries of a South American tree, *Schimus terebinthifolius.* They should be used sparingly, as in large quantities they can be toxic.

Pepper Sauces

The Arawaks of the Caribbean made several pepper sauces like *taumalin,* prepared from limes, chiles, and crabmeat. The tradition goes on today with the Caribbean region producing a seemingly infinite variety of pepper sauces. Any hot-stuff–loving individual making a trip to the Caribbean should attempt to sample as many sauces as possible, because each has its own zing. Jamaica's Pickapeppa sauce has a rich brown coloring and a heartiness somewhat like a peppery Worcestershire sauce. Bellos, from one of the smaller islands, is like red liquid fire. Barbados's Bonney Pepper Sauce mixes Scotch bonnet chiles with a mustardy base. Matouks from Trinidad use a tamarind or papaya base in their hot sauces. Brazil weighs in with its own pepper sauces, usually prepared at home from chiles. Then, there's the incendiary *pimenta malagueta* that comes preserved in oil or in *cuchaça.* In other parts of the hemisphere, salsas or the simple mix of chiles and limes gives flavor to dishes and are used in place of hot sauces.

As northern taste buds are turning more toward things piquant, Caribbean pepper sauces are widely available. Head to your local market and sample what's there.

Pigeon Peas

Called *gungo* peas, *Congo* peas, or *gandules,* these are the peas that frequently go into rice and peas. Of African origin, this field pea is usually found dried in U.S. markets. Fresh ones are occasionally available; they can be prepared and eaten like regular garden peas.

Pisquette

This is one of the names in the French Caribbean (the other is *titiri*) for the whitebaitlike fish that is prepared in omelets, fritters, or fried, and eaten with gusto. In Brazil, they are known as *pititinga.* These small fish are found in the mouths of rivers and caught with fine nets. They can be replaced in recipes by whitebait or similar small fish.

Plantain (*Musa paradisiaca*)

This is the big brother of the banana family. Plantains are never eaten raw, and are starchier than bananas. Available in markets selling Caribbean and Latin American produce, the ripeness of the plantain determines its cooking use. Green plantains are suitable for chips, and adding to stews because of their high level of starch. Yellow medium-ripe plantains are good for dishes such as Puerto Rico's *mofongo,* as they are soft but still have not lost their starchy taste. Black-skinned ripe plantains are those where the starch has turned to sugar. They are perfect for dessert dishes. Green plantains should be peeled under cold water to avoid staining your hands.

Rice (*Oryza sativa*)

Although Asia is the continent that immediately comes to mind when rice is mentioned, some parts of Haiti grow rice in paddies very much like their Eastern and African counterparts. The world's second most popular grain is also a major part of many Creole meals. What would island cooking be without rice and peas? Rice turns up in Guadeloupe's *colombos,* Trinidad's curries, and Puerto Rico's *asopaos.*

In the northern part of the hemisphere, rice was the wealth of the creolized coastal areas of south Carolina and Georgia and everything from the agricultural methods for raising it to the dishes it was served in harken back to Africa.

Several varieties of rice are available throughout the Creole world. In Carolina, Carolina gold, a faintly golden variant on the original rice, is much prized, but those unwilling or unable to go to the expense will not compromise their taste with anything less than Carolina rice. Purists in Louisiana swear by Louisiana rice. In the Caribbean, "pickin' " rice (removing the stones and impurities from it) is still a necessity, and an occasion for talking among cooks as they sit and pick. For others, Uncle Ben's seems to be the rice of preference.

Rum

Visions of piña coladas and rum punches are immediately conjured up by the mention of the word *rum* in conjunction with the Caribbean. Few, though, will remember the tempestuous history of the beverage in the region. Rum is a distilled spirit made from sugarcane, molasses, or sugarcane by-products. Columbus is said to have brought the cane to the Caribbean from the Canary Islands on his second voyage. The plant thrived and, by the sixteenth century, rum was on its way to becoming a regional delight. Called *Kill Devil* and *Guilldivel,* the raw spirit was said to be responsible for Port Royal in Jamaica becoming the wickedest town in the world. Rum fueled the British Navy and brought comfort to European planters and African slaves alike.

Each Caribbean island produces its own rum. You can tell who lives in a particular Caribbean neighborhood by looking at the rum shelves of the local liquor shop. If you see Brugal, Bermudez, and Barcelo, you're guaranteed a Dominican population; XM or El Dorado and you've found your way to a Guyanese enclave; Barbancourt, and you're in a Haitian hangout. Puerto Rico favors Don Q, Palo Viejo, and Barcardi (which originated in Cuba, but is now produced in Puerto Rico); Barbados produces Cockspur, Mount Gay, and H.L. Seale; Jamaica has Appleton, Meyer's, and Wray and Nephew; Martinique features Rhum Negrita and Rhum Maulny; Trinidad makes Old Oak. Because these are products of larger distilleries, they are exported to Europe and the United States and, therefore, tend to be among the best known. However, other areas of the region also produce their own rums: the *Ile des Saintes* honors old Père Labat; Barrilito is made in small batches in Puerto Rico, and Pusser's, the rum of the Royal Navy, is still made on the British Virgin Islands.

Up until the early twentieth century, many large landowners in the region produced their own rums for their families and friends. These smaller distilleries are the origins of many of the specialty brands today, such as Cuba's Havana Club and some of Guadeloupe's *rhums agricoles.* Sought after by rum connoisseurs for their individual flavors, these brands, when aged, frequently have many of the characteristics of fine cognacs.

The lighter Puerto Rican rums are perfect mixers and can also substitute for other liquors. Try a rum bloody Mary, or a rum and tonic, or a rum and water using Añejo.

Jamaica's Appleton and Meyer's rums are the quintessential rum-punch rums. Barbados's Cockspur and Mount Gay are good with mixers like ginger ale, which allow the taste of cane to shine through; this is also true of the light rums of Martinique. For an afterdinner treat, try a snifter of twelve-year-old Barbancourt from Haiti or one of the aged or millennium bottles of Mount Gay or Appelton.

Saffron *See* Turmeric.

Saltfish

What is usually called saltfish in the Caribbean is salted codfish. Known as *morue* in the French-speaking islands, and *bacalao* in the Spanish-speaking ones, saltfish is another part of the history of the region. In the days of the Atlantic slave trade, the slave price was paid in Spanish coins, rum, or salted codfish. Because it was easily transported, saltfish was sometimes fed to slaves on the middle passage, but it was expensive and did not appear often.

Up until recent years, saltfish was an inexpensive item in Caribbean households. It is found in dishes throughout the area, such as Jamaica's stamp and go, and ackee and saltfish; in Guadeloupe's *calalou;* and Puerto Rico's *bacalaitos.* Times have changed, though, and now it is not uncommon to hear folks complain that saltfish has become so expensive that it is prohibitive for many of the poorer households. Imagine a northerner's amazement at being asked to bring pieces of saltfish down to the Caribbean.

Saltfish is readily available in Caribbean markets. Look for pieces with white flesh (yellow flesh indicates age).

To prepare, soak the fish overnight in cold water. Drain, then place in a saucepan and cover with fresh cold water. Bring the water to a boil and simmer for 15 minutes, or until the fish is tender. Skin and flake the fish.

If you are in a hurry, and unable to soak the fish overnight, wash it in several changes of water, bring it quickly to a boil, and drain immediately. Then skin, flake, and proceed with the recipe.

Sapodilla *See* Naseberry.

Seasoning

This is a Barbadian term for the mixture of chives, fresh thyme, and other herbs that is used to season chicken and fish. It is also sometimes called *Bajan seasoning.*

Sofrito

This mixture is a seasoning staple in most Puerto Rican kitchens. There are as many variations to the *sofrito* recipe as there are Puerto Rican grandmothers. Most mixtures contain pork, lard, green peppers, tomatoes, onions, and coriander. They are prepared in advance and stored in the refrigerator and then added to a variety of dishes.

If you do not wish to prepare your own *sofrito,* Goya produces a readymade variety.

Sorrel *See* Jamaica.

Soursop *(Annona muricata)*

The shape of this tropical fruit has earned it the nickname *bullock's heart* in some countries. Inside the spiny, leathery, dark-green skin, the pulp is white and creamy and slightly granular. Called *corossol* in the French-speaking Caribbean, and *guanabana* in Spanish-speaking countries, the soursop is native to the Caribbean and northern South America. It's spiny like an artichoke, but may also have a smooth green or greenish brown skin. The thick skin covers a creamy white fruit that has a sweet, slightly acid flavor. French missionary Père Labat, who left many testimonies to Caribbean gastronomy in the eighteenth century, recorded a recipe for baked soursop with orange-flower water and cinnamon that still sounds good today. However, the fruit is usually consumed raw or in juices like Cuba's champola or Puerto Rico's *carato,* and in sorbets, ice creams, and candies throughout the Caribbean.

The soursop rarely appears in northern markets, as they don't travel well. However, if you do find a store that carries them, select one without too many blemishes and that is slightly soft to the touch. The pulp is available canned and frozen.

Spice

This is a Barbadian term for cinnamon.

Sugarcane *(Sacharum officinarum)*

This "honey-bearing reed" was brought to the Caribbean from the Canary Islands by Columbus on his second voyage in 1493. The plant grew and thrived and, by the seventeenth century, the sugar revolution changed the face of the Caribbean socially, politically, agriculturally, and economically. Small land holdings became outmoded, as sugar could only be grown profitably on large estates. The arduous task of growing the cane and processing it into sugar, molasses, and rum was the labor of the hundreds of thousands of slaves imported from Africa. These were the glory days of the West Indies when the phrase "as rich as a West Indian planter," was heard in the fanciest salons of Great Britain.

Until recently, we haven't been exposed to true sugar, seeing instead refined, superfine, white crystals. A push to natural foods has shown that the unrefined sugar is better for us, and many people will opt for the cane taste of *muscovado sugar,* if available, which is the last sugar in the barrel after the molasses has been drained. Brown sugar and the darker black sugar are still available in the Caribbean and are a treat for those who get to cook with them. They appear in Jamaica's bun and in Guyana's Christmas cake, and in virtually all of the region's baking.

Unrefined sugars are available in shops selling Caribbean products, and are easy to find elsewhere. If not, you can substitute muscovado or dark-brown sugar.

Sweet Potato (*Ipomoea batatas*)

The confusion between what are yams and what are sweet potatoes reigns only in the northern hemisphere. Elsewhere, folks are very clear as to what's what. According to botanists, the yam is a thick, hairy, tuber that may have flesh in hues ranging from pristine white to slightly purple. They are all members of the Dioscorea family (*See* IGNAME). Sweet potatoes grow on a trailing perennial plant, are related to hibiscus, and usually have orangey skins and flesh that can range in color from pale white to deep reddish orange. Both yams and sweet potatoes are eaten extensively in the Creole world. Sweet potatoes are called *patates douces* in the French-speaking, and *papas dulces* or *papas boniato* in the Spanish-speaking ones.

Sweet potatoes are available at all grocery stores year-round. When selecting sweet potatoes, look for those that are firm, with no blemishes.

Tamarind (*Tamarindus indica*)

This tropical tree produces a brown pod, which is processed into an acidulated pulp, used in the Caribbean for flavoring everything from chutneys to guava jelly. Tamarind balls are a favorite of all Caribbean school children.

Tamarind can be purchased in shops selling Indian or Caribbean products. It usually comes in a prepared pulp, which can be kept for a week or longer in the refrigerator. Prepared tamarind can also be frozen. Tamarind juice is also available, but has prodigious laxative qualities.

Thyme (*Thymus vulgaris*)

A relative of the mint family, thyme is frequently used in Caribbean herb mixtures. It appears fresh in Barbadian seasoning, in numerous dishes from the French-speaking Caribbean, and dry in a salt-and-herb mixture from Saint Croix.

Fresh thyme is usually available in supermarkets, but dried thyme may be substituted.

Turmeric (*Curcuma domestica* or *Curcuma longa*)

In the Caribbean, outside of the Spanish-speaking areas, and in Brazil, more often than not what is sold as saffron is really turmeric. This rhizome, which is a relative of ginger, adds color and taste to many West Indian curries. It's called *safran-pays* in the French-speaking Caribbean. If you happen upon a spice basket from Grenada, the small dried root labeled *saffron* is turmeric, and can be grated as needed. Turmeric is usually found dried and powdered in the United States. If purchasing dried turmeric, do not depend on color as a guide to freshness, as different intensities of hue exist. Buy in small quantities, and keep in an airtight container in a cool, dark place. If purchasing fresh turmeric, look for thick rhizomes without soft spots or cracks. Turmeric can be found in shops selling Indian ingredients.

Ugli (*Citrus* species)

This grapefruit-sized fruit of Jamaican origin isn't ugly at all. It is a cross between a grapefruit, an orange, and a tangerine, and is often called *tangelo*. It appears on Caribbean tables as juice and as marmalade, and is also glazed and dipped in chocolate. *Ugli* fruit can often be found in grocery stores in the United States.

Vanilla (*Vanilla planifolia*)

Native to the Central American fringes of Mexico's forests, this is another of the New World's gifts to cooking. The pods of this relative of the orchid develop their deep coloring and taste after a lengthy period of processing. First used by the Aztecs, vanilla is one of the world's master spices and is used in much of the baking of the Creole world. Anyone who has seen the fat, oily beans in the market in Guadeloupe will never want to buy commercial vanilla extract again but will, instead, opt to prepare their own by adding a vanilla bean to a small vial of dark rum for a particularly Creole flavor. Others may wish to take a hint from Montezuma, who is recorded as having consumed a beverage known as *tlilxochitl,* prepared from chocolate flavored with vanilla.

Yam *See* Igname *and* sweet potato.

Z'habitant

This is the French-Antillean name for a large crayfish frequently used in Creole cooking.

Z'oiseaux

These are bird peppers used in the French Antilles.

Z'yeux noirs

This is the French-Antillean term for black-eyed peas (cowpeas).

Mail-Order Sources

Aji limo chiles

www.chileguy.com

www.dagiftbasket.com

Andouille Sausage

Poche's Meat Market and Restaurant

Route 2 Box 415

Breaux Bridge, LA 70517

318-332-2108

Pap's Louisiana Cuisine, Inc.

162322 Highway 929

Prarieville, LA 70769

225-622-3262

paps@intersurf.com

Banana Leaves

www.friedas.com

Bajan Condiments and Hot Sauces

www.native-treasures.com

Cane Syrup, Cane Vinegar

Golden Kentucky Products
PO Box 246
Lexington, KY
606-453-9800

Steen's Syrup Mill, Inc.
P.O. Box 339
Abbeville, LA 70510
800-725-1654
www.steensyrup.com

Carolina Gold Rice

www.hoppinjohns.com

Cassava Meal

Emporium
31-88 30th Street
Astoria, NY 11102
718-204-8181

Discover Brazil
844 Grand Avenue
Saint Paul, MN 55105
612-222-4504

Chiles and Tropical Fruits

Frieda's by Mail
PO Box 58488
Los Angeles, CA 90058
www.Frieda.com

Stone Ground Cornmeal

www.hoppinjohns.com

Coffee from Around the World

J Martinez and Company
3230A Peachtree Road NE
Atlanta, GA
888-642-JAVA

Crawfish

Handy Soft-shell Crawfish
10557 Cherry Hill Avenue
Baton Rouge, LA 70816
504-292-4552

Battistella's Sea Foods Inc.
910 Touro Street
New Orleans, LA 70116
800-375-2728
504-949-2724
batpak@bellsouth.net

Creole Cream Cheese

www.mauthescreolecreamcheese.com

Creole Mustard and Spices

Zatarain
P.O. Box 347
Gretna, LA 70053
504-367-2950
www.zatarain.com

Falernum

www.native-treasures.com

Hispanic Products

Goya Foods

Jerk Seasoning and Jamaican Condiments

www.23degreesnorth.com

Pimenton and Other Spices

Dean & Deluca
560 Broadway
New York, NY 10012
800-221-7714

Rennet

www.traderjoes.com
www.caprinesupply.com

Spices and Spice Blends

Adriana's Caravan
409 Vanderbilt Street
Brooklyn, NY 11218
800-316-0820

Kalustyan's
123 Lexington Avenue
New York, NY 10016
212-685-3451
www.kalustyans.com

Penzeys, Ltd.
P.O. Box 933
Muskego, WI 53150
414-679-7207

Zingerman's
422 Detroit Street
Ann Arbor, MI 48104
888-636-8162
www.zingermans.com

Appetizers

Roast Corn (Jamaica)

Chorreadas — Corn Pancakes (Costa Rica)

Cerviche de Mango — Mango Cerviche (Costa Rica)

Stamp and Go — Jamaican Codfish Fritters (Jamaica)

Buljol — Flaked Saltfish (Trinidad)

Solomon Gundy — Salt Herring Paste (Jamaica)

Chiquetaille de Morue — Flaked Saltfish (Martinique and Guadeloupe)

Féroce d'Avocat — Avocado and Saltfish Paste (Martinique and Guadeloupe)

Texas Caviar — (United States)

Oeufs Mayonnaise aux Crabes — Crab-stuffed Eggs (Guadeloupe)

Deviled Eggs (United States)

Crab Backs (Trinidad and Tobago)

Scallop *Cebiche* (Peru)

Jicama Chips with Pimentón (Mexico)

Calaouangue—Green Mango Salad (Guyane Française)

Souskai de Mangues Vertes—Marinated Green Mangoes (Martinique)

COUNTRY DRIVIN'
Jamaica 2000

ONE OF MY FAVORITE THINGS to do when I'm in Jamaica is drive around the streets with my friends Maria and Norma. I do everything but hang my head out of the car window like an overzealous Labrador retriever, sniffing the air, watching the sights, and convincing my friends to stop for treats from the various small vendors who set up umbrellas and stands along the roadside.

In this manner, I've been to yam plaza where, in season, roasted yams are sold. I've tasted sugar-sweet sugarloaf pineapples pulled off even stacks, sliced, and scarfed down by hungry passersby. I've ruined more than one white t-shirt by dribbling ice-chilled coconut water down the front, and learned about the nibbles and street foods of the island that I have come to love.

On short excursions, we might stop at the section of Kingston that the *cognoscenti* refer to as Harrod's. Located near the embassies, it boasts a few street stalls where the produce is always the freshest, but is reputed to cost almost as much as the delicacies purveyed by the venerable British institution. If I beg and plead, they might let me go rafting. This activity—being poled down one of Jamaica's rivers on a bamboo raft—is decidedly a tourist one, but one that allows me to see what the folks are selling on the riverbank. In this manner I discovered *janga,* small river shrimp that are cooked to peppery doneness and sold in sacks, and truly understood the delights of a river-chilled Red Stripe beer.

Heading to the north coast from Kingston, we might detour to Boston Beach for a lunch of jerk. There, at the jerk center, we'd have a word or two with one of the island's pit masters. I learned that there are two secrets to true jerk: a small bit of the blood of the slaughtered animal is frequently a part of the jerk sauce and second, there is no real jerk in Jamaica that is not cooked over a fire of pimento wood. (Several years after that, I realized that *pimento* was Jamaican for allspice!)

My most recent discovery is roast corn. A brazier, a pot of boiling water, and a bucket holding pieces of coconut signaled the stop to my friend Norma. We pulled to the side and she ordered two pieces of roast corn. The woman deftly removed one of the cooked ears that had been grilling on the flame, wrapped it in a twist of paper, plopped a piece of coconut on the top, and handed it to Norma. After the requisite haggling over price and

The acra vendor, Guadeloupe.

an extra piece of coconut as *lagniappe* we drove off, exercising our teeth on the alternance of the chewy sweet of the coconut and the creamy sweetness of the corn. It was a perfect Jamaican day. Back at Norma's, I remembered that appetizers are not a part of the meal in much of my African-Atlantic world. Instead, the street snacks that are a part of the nations of nibblers that comprise the Creole world often head to the table disguised as appetizers. I wonder how roast corn will make a formal appearance on someone's table?

Roast Corn

(Jamaica)

Roast corn is a common street food in many parts of the Caribbean; it is hawked by ladies who plant themselves and a brazier under the shade of a large tree or umbrella and grill away. I was driving along the streets in Kingston, Jamaica, with my friend Norma Shirley, when we spotted a lady selling this snack and I was surprised to note that she not only was selling the corn with which I was familiar, she was giving each patron a piece of fresh coconut along with the corn. The idea is to gnaw the corn and then have a bite of the coconut for a mix of sweet and savory, and the surprise of two different textures. Try it.

SERVES 4 TO 6

Olive or vegetable oil, for grilling
6 ears fresh corn, shucked and cleaned
6 2-inch pieces fresh coconut, peeled

Preheat the broiler or outdoor grill. Spray a grill rack with a light coating of olive or vegetable oil. Place the corn on the rack and cook for five to seven minutes turning frequently. Serve the corn hot, with the coconut pieces on the side.

Chorreadas

Corn Pancakes

(Costa Rica)

These pancakes are eaten as a street snack, which are called bocas, *or mouthfuls.*

MAKES ABOUT 20 PANCAKES

2 cups corn kernels, fresh or frozen
½ cup sugar
¼ cup flour
2 eggs
2 tablespoons butter
½ cup milk
½ teaspoon vanilla extract
Oil, for frying
Cream cheese or sour cream, for serving

Place all the ingredients in the bowl of a blender and process until a thick paste forms. It will be lumpy because of the corn kernels. Heat the oil in a heavy skillet and pour enough of the batter into the skillet to form a silver-dollar–sized pancake. Fry for 1 minute on each side, turning once, or until they are golden brown on each side. Serve warm topped with cream cheese or sour cream.

Cerviche de Mango

Mango Cerviche

(Costa Rica)

While those in the North tend to prize the luscious juiciness of a perfectly ripe mango and disregard green fruit, those in sunnier climes know that there is no such thing as an unusable mango. Green mangoes turn up in the souskai *of the French-speaking Caribbean, and in chutneys and condiments of Jamaica and Trinidad, and wherever Indian immigrants have left their culinary mark. In this recipe, they are treated as an appetizer and served in a savory marinade.*

SERVES 8 TO 10

5 green mangoes, pitted and minced
1 tablespoon ketchup
¼ teaspoon hot Dijon mustard
1 tablespoon minced onion
1 teaspoon Worcestershire sauce
Salt and freshly ground black pepper, to taste

Mix all the ingredients together in a nonreactive bowl. Cover with plastic wrap and chill for at least one hour. Serve with crackers or toast points as an hors d'oeuvre.

Stamp and Go

Jamaican Codfish Fritters

(Jamaica)

Codfish, sometimes called saltfish, is a Caribbean staple. Centuries ago it was slave food and the sustenance of seafarers. Today, although expensive and a luxury item for some, it is an ingredient that is indispensable to the Jamaican fritter known as stamp and go. *No one is sure how it got the name, but wags suggest that it is because the fritters were prepared so that they could be eaten on the run and the individual could stamp and go.*

SERVES 6 (ABOUT 24 FRITTERS)

½ pound salt codfish
2 small scallions, minced
⅓ cup minced red bell pepper
½ teaspoon minced Scotch bonnet chile, or to taste
2 cups flour
2 teaspoons baking powder
Salt and freshly ground black pepper, to taste
Oil, for frying

Remove the salt from the codfish by soaking it overnight in several changes of cold water. Place the codfish in a saucepan with water to cover, and bring to a boil over low heat. Drain and remove all the skin and any small bones. Flake the codfish with a fork or fingers. Heat the oil to 375 degrees in a heavy saucepan or Dutch oven. Mix the codfish, scallions, red bell pepper, chile, flour, baking powder, and salt and pepper, adding about 1 cup water to create a slightly sticky batter. Drop the mixture into the heated oil by the teaspoonful, a few at a time, and fry until golden brown. Drain and serve immediately.

Buljol

Flaked Saltfish

(Trinidad)

This is a traditional Trinidadian accompaniment to drinks. The name comes from the French brule gueule, *which means to burn your mouth. This lets you know that the dish is supposed to be served on the fiery side. Popular in other parts of the Caribbean, where it is called* pickup saltfish, *it's delicious served with crackers and slices of ripe avocado.*

SERVES 4

½ pound boneless saltfish
2 tablespoons freshly squeezed lime juice
1 English cucumber, peeled and diced
1 medium onion, diced
2 teaspoons minced garlic
2 tablespoons minced green bell pepper
2 medium tomatoes, peeled, seeded, and chopped
2 tablespoons minced parsley
½ Scotch bonnet chile, seeded and minced, or to taste
3 tablespoons olive oil

Desalt the saltfish by boiling it in water for five minutes, discarding the water, and boiling it again for an additional five minutes. Discard the water, drain the fish, and flake it with a fork or your fingers, discarding any bones. Place the fish in a medium nonreactive bowl. Add the lime juice, cucumber, onion, garlic, green bell pepper, tomatoes, parsley, and Scotch bonnet; mix well. Gradually drizzle in the oil. Check the seasoning, cover with plastic wrap, and refrigerate for at least two hours. When ready to serve, mound the buljol in the center of a platter, surround it with crackers and avocado slices, and serve.

Solomon Gundy

Salt Herring Paste

(Jamaica)

This Jamaican dish is a cousin of the Trinidadian buljol, *and harks back to British colonial days. Here, the salted fish of preference is herring. Some think the name harks back to the nursery rhyme about Solomon Grundy, born on Monday. In reality, it goes back to the old English term* salmagundi, *meaning a dish composed of chopped meat, anchovies, eggs, and onions, oil, and a condiment paste, which* Oxford English Dictionary *cites as first appearing in print in 1674.*

SERVES 4 (ABOUT ¾ CUP)

¾ pound salt herring
¼ cup rum, warmed
1 tablespoon minced onions
4 allspice berries, crushed
⅓ cup cane vinegar
2 tablespoons vegetable oil
¼ Scotch bonnet chile, seeded, or to taste

Desalt the herring by placing it in a bowl with water to cover for 1 hour. Change the water and repeat the process. Place the herring in a fireproof bowl, pour the warmed rum over it, and light it to roast the herring. When the flames subside, skin and flake the herring. Place it in the bowl of a food processor. Add the onion, allspice, vinegar, oil, and chile and pulse until you have a thick paste. Cover and refrigerate for 1 hour. Serve at room temperature with crackers or rounds of toasted bread.

Chiquetaille de Morue

Flaked Saltfish

(Martinique and Guadeloupe)

This is a French Antilles version of the dish, similar to the buljol *of Trinidad. Here, the vegetables are lightly cooked before they are added to the flaked codfish.*

SERVES 4 TO 6 (ABOUT 1¼ CUPS)

1 pound saltfish
1 tablespoon olive oil
1 small onion, minced
3 scallions, minced
3 cloves garlic, minced
2 medium tomatoes, peeled, seeded and coarsely chopped
¼ teaspoon minced habanero chile, or to taste
1 branch fresh thyme, stripped
1½ tablespoons red-wine vinegar

Desalt the saltfish by boiling it in water for 5 minutes. Change the water, and boil it for an additional 5 minutes. Discard the water, drain the fish, and flake it with your fingers, discarding any bones. Place the flaked fish in a medium nonreactive bowl. Heat the oil in a heavy skillet and sauté the onion, scallions, garlic, tomatoes, chile, and thyme over high heat for 2 to 3 minutes. Add the vinegar and pour the vegetable mixture over the flaked codfish. Mix well; check the seasonings. Serve immediately, with crackers or toasted French bread.

Féroce d'Avocat

Avocado and Saltfish Paste

(Martinique and Guadeloupe)

This paste is a typical appetizer of the French-speaking Caribbean. It's called féroce *because it is usually ferociously hot with chile. You may adjust to suit your own taste.*

SERVES 4 TO 6 (ABOUT 2 CUPS)

2 large, ripe avocados
1 recipe *Chiquetaille de Morue* (p. 76)
⅔ cup cassava meal

Split the avocados in half lengthwise, remove the meat, and set the empty shells aside. Mix avocado with the *chiquetaille*. Sprinkle the top with the cassava meal. Mix well. Fill the avocado shells with the mixture. Serve immediately with bread or crackers.

CARMELITA JEANNE
Guadeloupe

"Adieu Foulards/Adieu Madras"

"BONJOU, DOUDOU" (Hello, sweet), she said, smiling. I knew I was in Guadeloupe. I have known eighty-one-year-old Carmelita Jeanne for little more than a decade, but I have known women with her fierce determination all my life. I first met her when dining with a group of friends at *La Nouvelle Table Créole,* her restaurant in St. Félix, Guadeloupe. Later, I had spent time with her in her home and in her kitchen while writing *Sky Juice and Flying Fish* and several articles about food in the Caribbean. In the course of our conversations, I discovered her wit, her humanity, and her ferocious devotion to the classic Creole cooking of Guadeloupe.

Over the years, I have watched Madame Jeanne as she readies herself for market, tying her hair up in a bright madras headscarf and striding forth majestically on astonishingly high-heeled clogs that are one of her indications of great coquetry. On one of our early meetings she gave me one of her dresses from Guadeloupe's *cuisinières* and I was delighted to find that it fit and have worn it at more than one Caribbean food demonstration.

I have traipsed through Pointe-à-Pitre's market with her, learning about fruits whose names I know only in French: *monbin, pomme cythère, surette.* I know her large restaurant kitchen so well that I am able to tell when she has purchased something new. A few years back, upon discovering that she has only sons, I wangled an "adoption" into the family, and now I call her "Mama Guadeloupe." I have even taken my real mother to meet her, and delighted in their ability to communicate fluently through the language of food. Anyone who has ever been to market with her or watched her cook knows that food is Madame Jeanne's life. The ease with which she hefts heavy industrial pots speaks of a life spent in the kitchen, as does her dexterity with a paring knife and her ability with a chef's blade. Indeed, her mother ran a restaurant as did her sister, who is now a caterer. She's precise and meticulous; when she says chop the garlic this way, she means it. Yet she measures all ingredients into her hand, adjusting a pinch of this and a dab of that. Food is tasted constantly as it's cooked, seasonings adjusted and added at the appropriate moments. When the dish is ready, she shoos me into the restaurant to sit down and sample. I do, savoring the inventiveness of French Creole cooks and their ability to meld two cultures on one plate.

Texas Caviar

(United States)

Most folks forget the role that African Americans played in the opening of the West. This dish celebrates the Black presence in the West, from the cowboys to the chuck wagon cooks to the homesteaders. Here, we find the African black-eyed pea transformed into something rich, an appetizer to be eaten on its own, with crackers, or even rolled up in lettuce leaves. Texas caviar is what it's called in the Lone Star State.

SERVES 8 TO 10

2 16-ounce cans black-eyed peas
⅓ cup minced green bell pepper
⅓ cup minced red bell pepper
5 scallions, minced, including the green part
½ cup extra-virgin olive oil
3 tablespoons balsamic vinegar
1 clove garlic, minced
1 teaspoon cumin powder
1 teaspoon minced jalapeño *chile,* or to taste (for extra bite, use a smaller
    amount of minced habanero)

Drain the black-eyed peas and place them in a nonreactive bowl. Add green and red bell pepper, scallions, olive oil, vinegar, garlic, cumin, and chile. Mix well. Cover with plastic wrap and refrigerate for at least 5 hours.

Serve chilled or at room temperature with crackers or with green leaf lettuce. Let your guests wrap a spoonful of the "caviar" in individual leaves.

Oeufs Mayonnaise aux Crabes

Crab-stuffed Eggs

(Guadeloupe)

This fancier version of the traditional deviled egg recipe uses lump crabmeat to fill the eggs.

MAKES 16 DEVILED EGGS

8 hard-boiled eggs
3 tablespoons mayonnaise
¼ pound fresh lump crabmeat
Black pepper to taste
Minced parsley, for garnish
Mild paprika, for garnish

Carefully remove the eggs from the shells. Slice each in half lengthwise. Remove the yolks. Arrange the whites on a dish (or a deviled egg plate, a Southern must). Place the yolks in a small bowl with the mayonnaise, crabmeat, and salt and pepper. Mash with a fork until smooth. Gently spoon a bit of the yolk mixture into each of the whites. Cover with plastic wrap and refrigerate for at least 1 hour. Serve chilled or at room temperature, garnished with minced parsley and a dusting of paprika.

Deviled Eggs
(United States)

While this dish may not seem terribly Creole to most folks, stuffed eggs do turn up in cookbooks of the Caribbean and beyond, and they played a major role in the spread of the foods of the African-American South. During the period of the great migrations, African Americans left the South by the thousands for jobs and refuge from Jim Crow in the North. They traveled not knowing when their next meal would be. They often brought a shoebox of food with them: their last tastes of the South. The shoebox inevitably held a deviled egg or two, along with fried chicken, a slab of pound cake, and a cool drink. In this way, deviled eggs have ridden the roads and the rails into pride of place in the foodways of African Americans in the United States. I've added the pimentón for a nontraditional but delicious smokey taste.

MAKES *16* DEVILED EGGS

8 hard-boiled eggs
3 tablespoons mayonnaise
1 tablespoon Dijon mustard
⅓ teaspoon chile powder
¼ teaspoon pimentón, plus additional, for garnish (*see* Note)
Salt and freshly ground black pepper, to taste

Carefully remove the eggs from the shells. Slice each in half lengthwise. Remove the yolks. Arranged the whites on a dish (or a deviled egg plate, a Southern must). Place the yolks in a small bowl with the mayonnaise, mustard, chile powder, pimentón, and salt and pepper. Mash with a fork until smooth. Gently spoon a bit of the yolk mixture into each of the whites. (You can be fancy and pipe the yolk in with a

Preparing dinner, Mexico.

pastry bag.) Cover with plastic wrap and refrigerate at least 1 hour. Sprinkle with pimentón before serving, chilled.

Note: Pimentón is smoked hot Spanish paprika. It adds a zap of chile heat and a wonderful smoky taste. If unavailable, you may use hot paprika.

Crab Backs

(Trinidad and Tobago)

Throughout the coastal United States, the Caribbean, and Latin America, crab turns up on tables in many guises. One way is stuffed. Called casquinha de siri *in Brazil,* crabes farcies *in Martinique and Guadeloupe, and crab backs in much of the Caribbean, they are simple to prepare and take on the flavorings of their country of origin. This recipe, from Trinidad, is a basic version that lets the flavor of the crab shine through.*

SERVES 4

4 crab shells
1 pound lump crabmeat, picked over
1 teaspoon minced onion
1 teaspoon minced flat-leaf parsley
Salt and freshly ground black pepper, to taste
3 tablespoons olive oil
½ cup breadcrumbs
4 tablespoons butter

Combine the crabmeat, onion, parsley, and salt and pepper in a medium bowl. Add 3 teaspoons of the olive oil and mix well. Place the remaining olive oil in a heavy skillet and gently sauté the mixture over low heat, stirring constantly, for 3 to 4 minutes. Preheat the broiler. Remove the mixture and place it into well-cleaned crab shells. Sprinkle with breadcrumbs, dot with butter, and place on a rack in the broiler until lightly browned. Serve hot.

Scallop Cebiche

(Peru)

This is considered by many to be the national dish of Peru. There are two theories of the origin of the word cebiche or ceviche, which is also spelled cerbiche or cerviche. Some feel that it goes back to the Incan tradition of eating salted fish or fish marinated in chicha of some type. The Quechua word for this dish was sivichi. Others believe that it has Moorish origins and dates back to the Spanish conquest, taking its name from the Arabic word cisbech, meaning "a pickled thing." Whatever the origin, it is a simple dish and can only be made with the freshest ingredients. Don't even think about attempting this away from the ocean, as the ingredients have to be floppin' fresh. It should be eaten immediately after preparation as the lime juice will cook the fish as soon as it is poured on, and the flavor will be at its best. Boiled corn on the cob and slices of boiled sweet potato traditionally accompany it.

SERVES 4 TO 6

1½ pounds diver scallops
1 medium red onion, thinly sliced
Salt, to taste
½ red *aji limo* or bird pepper, minced
½ yellow *aji limo* or bird pepper, minced
Juice of 14 Key limes
1 ear boiled corn on the cob, cut into 1" slices
1 boiled sweet potato, cut into ½" slices

Place the scallops and the onion in a nonreactive bowl. Wash well and drain. Season with salt and the *aji limo*. Add the lime juice and toss quickly. Refresh the ceviche by adding a few ice cubes. Mix them in, then remove them before they have a chance to melt. Serve immediately, accompanied by corn and sweet potato slices.

Jicama Chips with Pimentón
(Mexico)

Jicama is one of my favorite of the new ingredients. Its mild, sweet taste is perfect to balance the bite of chile. It's also delicious, with a squeeze of fresh lime juice and a sprinkle of the smoked paprika called pimentón. *Try this for a quick snack instead of the usual fried chips.*

SERVES 4 TO 6

6 teaspoons hot pimentón
1 teaspoon coarse sea salt
1 medium jicama
6 teaspoons freshly squeezed lime juice

Mix the pimentón and salt together. When ready to serve, peel the jicama and cut it into thin slices. (This will be easier if you use a mandoline or similar cutting device.) Arrange the slices on a platter and sprinkle with lime juice. Serve immediately with the pimentón dip.

Calaouangue

Green Mango Salad

(Guyane Française)

This refreshing salad is prepared as an appetizer and as a condiment to accompany meat stews in the former French Guyana. It is reputed to be one of the dishes that children love the best. When serving it for family, some folks leave the mango pit in the center of the salad so that one lucky mango lover will not be deprived of the joy of sucking all of the meat from it.

SERVES 4

4 small green mangoes
1 scallion, minced
2 garlic cloves, minced
⅛ teaspoon minced hot chile
2 tablespoons peanut oil
Juice of 1 lemon
Salt and freshly ground black pepper, to taste
1 tablespoon minced parsley, for garnish

Peel the mangoes, and slice them thinly. Place them in a salad bowl and add the onion, garlic, chile, and peanut oil. Drizzle in the lemon juice until the salad is well seasoned. Mix well. Cover with plastic wrap and refrigerate for 1 to 2 hours. Garnish with minced parsley. Serve chilled.

Souskai de Mangues Vertes

Marinated Green Mangoes

(Martinique)

There are over sixty different varieties of mango in Martinique. In Jamaica, a local saying implies that, in mango season, cooks can turn over their pots because everyone's eating their fill of the luscious fruit. Throughout the Caribbean, they are picked and enjoyed by all. Those who do not like the taste of ripe mangoes, and there are a few, will enjoy the tartness of a green mango. In Martinique, green mangoes are used as vegetables, as in this recipe.

SERVES 4

4 small green mangoes
Juice of 2 limes
1 clove garlic, minced
⅛ teaspoon minced hot chile, or to taste
4 tablespoons peanut oil

Peel the mangoes and cut into medium dice. Place them in a salad bowl with the lime juice, garlic, and chile. Mix well. Slowly add the peanut oil. Mix well. Cover with plastic wrap and allow the souskai to marinate in the refrigerator for one to two hours. Serve as an appetizer.

Soups and Salads

Soupe aux Pois Rouges — Kidney-Bean Soup (Haiti)

Pepperpot Soup with Seafood and Pumpkin (United States)

Jean d'Costa's Jamaican Pepperpot Soup (Jamaica)

Dumplings for Jamaican Pepperpot (Jamaica)

Sopa de Elote — Aztec Corn Soup (Mexico)

Sopa de Frijol Negro — Black-Bean Soup (Cuba)

Pozole — Hearty Hominy Soup (Costa Rica)

Sopa de Mani — Peanut Soup (Ecuador)

Sopa de Ajo — Garlic Soup (Cuba)

Pumpkin Soup (Dominica)

Green Banana *Escabeche* — Vinegared Green Bananas (Puerto Rico)

Soupe de Gombos—Okra Soup (French Caribbean)

Jicama Cole Slaw (United States)

Red, White, and Blue Potato Salad (United States)

Maryse's Salade Mixte—Maryse's Mixed Salad (Guadeloupe)

Maryse's Salade Verte—Maryse's Green Salad (Guadeloupe)

Pineapple and Cabbage Salad (Cuba)

Yuca en Salsa—Manioc in Sauce (Cuba)

Roquette—Arugula Salad (New Orleans)

Vinny's Arugula Salad (United States)

Salade de Christophine—Shaved Chayote Salad (Guadeloupe)

Creole Tomato and Vidalia Onion Salad (New Orleans)

THE HEALER'S MARKET
Mexico City 1980

MEXICO CITY IS ONE of the places that I have not visited enough. I've only made a few trips, and each one seemed too brief as I discovered more and more about the fascinating, multilayered town and its environs. What I discovered was not at all what folks thought I should or would. In Mexico City, I discovered Mexico's connection with the African world in the unlikeliest spot: the *Mercado Sonora,* which includes the *Mercado de las curanderas*—the healers' market.

I don't remember where the market is located, but it took us several wrong turns to find it. We'd been to the main tourist market and I'd loaded up with *rebosos* in bright colors, baskets, and even a China *poblano* that has remained in my closet—a silent rebuke for my spendthrift ways. As we arrived at the *Mercado Sonora,* the items for sale amazed me: beautiful pottery with green and black glazes, mortars and pestles, and grinding stones for preparing corn for tortillas. These items seemed more ancient and more real than those that had been available in the morning's market. As we stepped into the *Mercado de las Curanderas,* the atmosphere changed. There was a more ancient look to the market, a more serious and profound aura. This was a market like the ones that I'd known on the West African coast, with stalls laden with leaves and branches. Betty, the guide who had become my friend and confidante during the trip, pointed out *copal,* the resin that was used as an incense by the Aztecs; we sniffed its musky fragrance, which was not unlike a lighter version of frankincense. I saw rosemary and thyme and many of the herbs utilized not only in the kitchen, but also in beauty and religious rituals. We rounded a corner and there were even candles for the seven African powers of Santeria—Shango's smiling face grinning from the brilliant red one, Saint Lazarus's hobbled figure offering solace and healing from the nearby brown one, and Yemanya, placidly and regally glowing from the blue one. I was astonished. This was not the Mexico that I knew from tourist brochures, but rather a place whose roots intersected with my own. "You see," said Betty, "Mexico is a country of mixing of many cultures. We are *meztiso* and we know the religions of many ancient civilizations: the European, naturally, but also the Indian and even the African." Betty was more forward-thinking than many, but the intervening years have proved her right. Not only in the *Mer-*

Vegetable hawker, Barbados.

cado de las Curanderas, but also in its music and in foods, like the *carne de chango* and *mariquitas,* or deep-fried plantain chips, of Veracruz and the bordertown peanut patties knows as *prasle de cacahuatl,* the country is a vibrant, if often unheralded, part of the African-Atlantic world.

Soupe aux Pois Rouges

Kidney-Bean Soup

(Haiti)

From the red beans and rice of New Orleans to the red-pea soup with spinners of Kingston, these legumes are turned into soups and composed rice dishes. In Jamaica, in Haiti, in New Orleans, and even in the part of Cuba that is nearest to Santiago, the red bean reigns supreme. Here's one Haitian way with soup.

SERVES 4 TO 6

1 pound dry kidney beans
½ cup finely chopped scallions
2 sprigs flat-leaf parsley, minced
2 sprigs fresh thyme, minced
¼ cup minced celery
2 tablespoons minced garlic
2 chicken bouillon cubes
Salt and freshly ground black pepper, to taste
6 tablespoons Haitian dark rum, for garnish
Minced onion, for garnish

Pick over beans and soak in cold water to cover, overnight. The next day, drain, place in stockpot with 2 quarts water, scallions, parsley, thyme, celery, garlic, and bouillon cubes. Cover and bring to a boil, then lower heat and simmer for 30 minutes, or until beans are tender. Put bean mixture through a food mill or mash through a wide sieve and return to pot. Add the boiling water, whisk, and adjust seasonings. Garnish each serving with a tablespoon of dark Haitian rum and minced onion. Serve hot.

Pepperpot Soup with Seafood and Pumpkin

(United States)

I have long been intrigued by the history of Philadelphia as a Creole city. Many think that the coming together of Africa and Europe in the Americas is a New Orleans phenomenon, or at the very least, a Southern thing. Years ago, when I was writing The Welcome Table, *food historian and heirloom gardener William Woys Weaver started me thinking about the Northern seaports, particularly Philadelphia, as Creole cities. In the ensuing years, I became more convinced of the cultural connections between Philadelphia and the Caribbean. Nowhere is the connection more apparent than in Philadelphia's pepperpot soup. When the time came to write* Beyond Gumbo, *I penned an e-mail to my adopted culinary "cousin," Chef Fritz Blank of Deux Cheminées restaurant in Philadelphia, and asked him if he would be so kind as to send his pepperpot soup recipe for inclusion. This is the missive that I received in return:*

> *Cuz Jess:*
>
> *Here it is, along with some introductory notes: Philadelphia Pepperpot has an interesting and little known evolutionary history. Its beginnings are seventeenth century and arise from the West African–Caribbean–Philadelphia slave trade triangle. Turtle rather than tripe was the original meat found in Philadelphia pepperpot. Fou-fou dumplings made from plantain or wheat flour are* de rigeur *for any pepperpot. (At* Deux Cheminées, *we use spätzle.) Also required is a liberal jolt of Habanero peppers to put the pepper into the pot. (Yes, Habaneros were readily available in Colonial Philadelphia.)*
>
> *1. It's a lot of work.*
> *2. I use fresh killed local snapping turtle, but frozen raw out-of-the-shell*

continued on next page

> *meat is available if you give a fish dealer a couple of day's notice to get it for you.*

2a. *To cook turtle or veal, use a mix of white wine, white wine vinegar and water in equal portions. Use veggies, herbs and spices as for chicken stock, but include a shot of whole allspice berries. If using veal, use veal shanks—the cartilage in turtle and/or veal yields a distinct mouth feel in the final pepperpot.*

2b. *Cook it for a long time so the turtle becomes tender.*

3. *Fish stock is a white wine base fumet. My recipe is available if you need it.*

Astonished, but not surprised by his generosity, I am including the recipe as sent. It makes a lot, but it's so good you'll want to put some by for later.

1 cup clarified butter
½ gallon sliced leeks, white part only
6 quarts raw, peeled, and seeded crookneck pumpkin or butternut squash, cut into 1" cubes
2 cups raw converted rice (Uncle Ben's, for example)
¼ cup salt
2 tablespoons grated fresh ginger root
2 tablespoons finely minced fresh habaneros
2 cups roasted red sweet bell peppers, cut en brunoise*
⅓ cup tomato paste
3 gallons rich fish fumet
2–3 quarts turtle stock, or substitute Minors turtle stock base
2–3 cups heavy cream
Salt & pepper to taste
Ground mace or nutmeg

*Brunoise: Very fine dice.

3–4 pounds cooked turtle meat cut into ½" cubes
   (or substitute poached veal)
5 pounds assorted raw shellfish such as shrimp, scallops, shucked oysters,
   and/or cooked seafoods such as crabmeat or lobster meat, all cut into
   ¾-inch cubes
Fresh nasturtium blossoms, for garnish
Toasted pine nuts, for garnish

1. Fill the bottom of a large stockpot with clarified butter. Add the leeks and sweat until limp but not browned.

2. Add the raw pumpkin or squash, rice, ginger, hot peppers, bell peppers, tomato paste, and then the fish and turtle stocks.

3. Bring to a full boil over high heat. Adjust to a simmer, and cook for 30 to 45 minutes, or until the pumpkin is tender.

4. Purée the soup using a food mill or fine sieve.

5. Reheat the puréed soup and add heavy cream.

6. Season with salt, pepper, and a hint of mace.

7. Add cooked turtle meat, then the raw seafood. Bring to a boil just to cook the shellfish. Serve hot, garnished with fresh nasturtium blossoms and/or toasted pine nuts.

Jean d'Costa's Jamaican Pepperpot Soup

(Jamaica)

Just in case you thought that my "cousin" Fritz was the only one who knew his pepperpot, here is a recipe that was given to me by my good friend Marcella Martinez from Jamaica. She's no slouch in the kitchen, but she decided to go to an expert and got the following recipe from her friend Jean d'Costa and swears it is the best Jamaican pepperpot soup that she's tasted. Jamaican pepperpot, like the pepperpots from the northern Caribbean, as distinguished from those of the southern region, are hearty soups, rich with ground provisions, as the Jamaican refer to root vegetables, and flavored with coconut milk and Scotch bonnet chile. Preparing the soup takes about three hours, but the pepperpot may be made weeks ahead and frozen, or made two days ahead and refrigerated.

The pepperpots of the southern Caribbean are more akin to the traditional South American Indian stews and are usually flavored with casareep, *a condiment prepared from cassava.*

SERVES ABOUT 8

2 pounds beef shin bones, cut in 2" sections

1 pound beef stew meat

2 tablespoons vegetable oil

2 large onions, coarsely chopped

2–6 cloves garlic, chopped, or to taste

2 plum tomatoes, coarsely chopped

8 cups water

1 teaspoon whole allspice and 1 teaspoon whole cloves (wrapped in cheesecloth or placed in a tea infuser)

¼ pound salt pork (as lean as possible), sliced into 1" cubes

1 cup freshly made thick coconut milk (p. 32), or the equivalent amount
   canned coconut milk, or prepared from powdered concentrate

1 pound yellow yam, peeled and cut horizontally into 1" slices

2 Jamaican cocoes (about 5" long), peeled and cut into 1" slices (*see* Note)

2 1-pound packages frozen chopped spinach or 1 bunch fresh *calalou*,
   stripped and chopped

1 pound fresh okra, topped, tailed, and chopped, or 1 1-pound package
   frozen okra, prepared in the same way

1 small green bell pepper, seeded and chopped

1 fresh Scotch bonnet chile, pricked with a fork (*see* Note)

2 to 4 cloves garlic, chopped

1 recipe dumplings, optional (p. 100)

2 pounds small shrimp, peeled, or 16 large shrimp, two per serving, optional

Brown the beef bones and stew meat in the vegetable oil, over moderate heat, with the onion, garlic, and tomato, about 15 to 20 minutes. Remove to a stockpot and add 8 cups water, and the allspice and cloves. Bring to rolling boil, reduce to a simmer, and cook for 2 to 3 hours, until reduced by one quarter.

When done, remove the bones and add the salt pork, coconut milk, yam, cocoes, spinach or calalou, okra, green pepper, Scotch bonnet, and a bit more garlic, if desired. Simmer for 30 minutes, reducing slightly. To thicken the soup, remove the stew meat, the hot pepper, the yam, and coco, and purée the remaining soup in a blender or food processor. Return the puréed soup to the saucepan with the reserved vegetables. Add dumplings if you wish. Adjust all seasonings. Cool and store or set aside for serving. When ready to serve, bring soup to a boil and drop in the peeled shrimp. Cook for 3 minutes. Serve hot, placing a serving of shrimp in the middle of each soup bowl, along with bits of yam and coco, and a dumpling or two, if desired.

Note: Cocoes are Jamaican roots; you may substitute any type of yam, or, in a pinch, white potatoes.

Be sure to prick the Scotch bonnet with a fork to make sure that it does not burst and make the soup too hot.

Dumplings
for Jamaican Pepperpot

1 cup flour
2 tablespoons water
1 teaspoon salt

Mix ingredients together until you have a thick dough. Roll cut dough into 2" dumplings. Drop them into the simmering soup.

Sopa de Elote

Aztec Corn Soup

(Mexico)

The importance of corn in the Aztec diet is inestimable. Young tender ears were known as elote *and eaten in many forms. The following recipe is one of their ways with soup, which uses many ingredients from the Aztec pantry, yet seems amazingly contemporary.*

SERVES 6 TO 8

2 tablespoons vegetable oil
½ cup minced onions
3 poblano chiles, roasted, deveined, and thinly sliced
2 cups corn, freshly cut from the cob
4 tomatoes, peeled, seeded, mashed, and sieved
7 cups chicken stock
4 sprigs parsley
Salt and freshly ground black pepper, to taste

Heat the oil in the bottom of a saucepan and cook the onion until golden. Add the chile and corn and cook, stirring occasionally, for 5 minutes. Add the tomato and continue cooking and stirring for an additional 5 minutes, or until well blended. Add the chicken stock and parsley and simmer for 10 minutes. Serve hot.

Sopa de Frijol Negro

Black-Bean Soup

(Cuba)

The black bean is thought of by many as being the hallmark of the food of the Spanish-speaking Caribbean. However, they are used only in some areas, specifically around Havana in Cuba and in parts of the Dominican Republic. Puerto Rico shows a preference for pigeon peas or gandules, *while Santiago, Cuba, prefers kidney beans, as do its Haitian and Jamaican neighbors. One thing is certain: black-bean soup is Cuba's classic entrant in the soup dishes of the Creole world.*

SERVES 4 TO 6

1 pound dried black beans
¼ cup olive oil
1 medium onion, minced
1 small green bell pepper, seeded and minced
1 red bell pepper, seeded and minced
¼ teaspoon minced Scotch bonnet chile, or to taste
1 stalk celery, minced
4 garlic cloves, minced
1 smoked ham hock
3 strips thick sliced bacon
2 tablespoons tomato paste
2 teaspoons powdered cumin
2 teaspoons Italian oregano
1 bay leaf
Salt and freshly ground black pepper, to taste
1 tablespoon dark rum
1 cup cooked white rice, for garnish

2 tablespoons minced cilantro, for garnish
1 tablespoon minced onions, for garnish
2 tablespoons sour cream, for garnish

Pick over the beans and soak them according to package directions. When ready to cook, drain the beans and set them aside. In a stockpot, sauté the onion, bell peppers, chile, celery, and garlic in the olive oil at medium heat for 15 minutes, or until the onion is sweated and translucent but not crisp. Add the beans, ham hock, bacon, and water to cover. Add the seasonings one at a time, and bring to a boil over medium heat. Cover and simmer for 2 hours. Remove half the soup and purée it in a blender. Return the puréed mixture to the stockpot and cook for 5 minutes. Add the rum and serve garnished with a spoonful of white rice. Serve cilantro, onions, and a small bowl of sour cream on the side.

Pozole

Hearty Hominy Soup

(Costa Rica)

Pozole is a large-grained hominy, known as samp *in some parts of the American South. A processed form of corn, its use goes back to pre-Colombian days. It turns up often in soups and stews in the Hispanic world. Although this dish is called a soup, it is hearty enough to be eaten as a main course and is often served as one in Costa Rica.*

SERVES 12

1 pound lean beef, cut into ½" cubes
1 pound lean pork, cut into ½" cubes
1 tablespoon vegetable oil
1 large onion, minced
2 cloves garlic, coarsely chopped
Salt and freshly ground black pepper, to taste
1 teaspoon minced parsley
2 tablespoons tomato paste
4 large tomatoes peeled, seeded, and coarsely chopped
1 pound can yellow hominy

In a heavy saucepan, sauté the beef, pork, onion, garlic, and seasonings in the oil, stirring occasionally, over medium heat for about 5 minutes or until the onion is translucent. Add enough water to cover, lower the heat, cover the saucepan, and simmer for 30 minutes, or until the meat is tender. Add the tomato paste and tomatoes with their liquid, and cook for about 20 minutes. Add the hominy and its liquid and cook for an additional 15 minutes over low heat, stirring occasionally. Add more water if the soup is too thick and adjust the seasonings. Serve hot.

Sopa de Maní

Peanut Soup

(Ecuador)

Peanut soups are another hallmark of the Creole world, appearing in tureens from Savannah, Georgia to Bahia, Brazil. Many feel that peanut butter can be substituted for the peanuts, but I feel that if you want a bit of crunch with your soup, you should begin with your own roasted nuts. However, you may replace the finely minced peanuts with three-quarters of a cup of chunk-style peanut butter if you wish.

SERVES 6

2 tablespoons peanut oil
1 small onion, minced
2 garlic cloves, minced
1 small red bell pepper, seeded and minced
1 teaspoon minced jalapeño chile, or any minced hot chile, to taste
2 large tomatoes, peeled, seeded, and coarsely chopped
1 cup finely ground dark-roasted peanuts
6 cups chicken stock
2 tablespoons minced cilantro leaves, for garnish

In a heavy skillet, sauté the onion, garlic, bell pepper, and chile in the oil at medium heat for 5 minutes, or until they are soft. Place mixture into the bowl of a food processor, add the tomatoes, and pulse until you have a thick liquid paste. Place the ingredients in a heavy saucepan, add the peanuts, and cook over low heat for 5 minutes. Add the stock, cover, and cook for 15 minutes, stirring occasionally. Serve garnished with the minced cilantro.

Sopa de Ajo

Garlic Soup

(Cuba)

An Eastern European saying suggests that garlic is as good as twelve mothers. Certainly, with dishes like Guyana's garlic pork and this garlic soup from Cuba, the Creole world is no stranger to the stinking weed. Try making this soup for some garlic-loving friends.

SERVES 6

5 cloves garlic, crushed
1 tablespoon olive oil
Salt and freshly ground black pepper, to taste
3 cups cubed stale French bread
2 eggs

Sauté the garlic in the olive oil in the bottom of a heavy saucepan at medium heat until golden. Add 3 cups water and season to taste. Bring to a boil, and cook for 5 minutes over medium heat. Meanwhile, in a heavy skillet, brown the bread cubes in the remaining olive oil. Beat the eggs in a small bowl, fold in the bread and place about a ½ cup of the egg and bread mixture in the bottom of each soup bowl. Pour ½ cup of the boiling garlic water in each soup bowl. Serve immediately.

Pumpkin Soup

(Dominica)

There are myriad versions of pumpkin soup in the Creole world, from Jamaica's hearty, chunky version to a creamy velouté from the French Caribbean. This recipe, from Dominica, combines the bland sweetness of the pumpkin with the sweet taste of coconut milk.

SERVES 6

2 pounds calabaza, peeled and cubed
2 cups milk
2 cups coconut milk
2 tablespoons butter
1 medium onion, chopped
2 scallions, minced, including the green tops
2 chives, minced
Salt and freshly ground black pepper, to taste

Place calabaza in a saucepan with 2 cups water and cook for 20 minutes, or until soft. Remove from the heat and add the milk and the coconut milk. In a second saucepan, sauté the onion, scallions, and chives in the butter for 10 minutes, or until soft. Add them to the calabaza mixture. Cover, and simmer over medium heat, stirring occasionally for about 10 minutes, until heated through. Season to taste. Serve hot.

Green Banana Escabeche

Vinegared Green Bananas

(Puerto Rico)

This dish from my friend Chef Patricia Wilson shows the Moorish influence in Spain, and by extension, Spanish colonial cooking. The etymology of the escabeches *of the New World, including the* ceviches *of South America, comes from the Arabic word* cisbech, *which, in turn, comes from the Persian* siquisbe, *meaning pickled food. Dishes in which the food is pickled with a hot marinade, then served at room temperature abound in North Africa and can also be found in Spain. On this side of the Atlantic, dishes like the* escabeche *of Cuba, the* escovitched *fish of Jamaica, and this dish testify to the Spanish culinary presence in this hemisphere.*

SERVES 6 TO 8

12 green bananas
3 tablespoons salt
1 cup extra-virgin olive oil
½ red bell pepper, julienned
½ yellow bell pepper, julienned
1 Spanish onion, julienned
⅓ cup white-wine vinegar
4 tablespoons capers
1 tablespoon fresh thyme leaves

Slit the green banana skins lengthwise. Place in a large pot, add the salt and cover with cold water. Bring to a boil and cook for 30 to 40 minutes, or until tender. (The skins will turn dark.) Drain, refresh under cold water, drain again, cool, and peel. Slice the bananas into ½" slices and place in a mixing bowl. Heat the olive oil in a sauté pan, add the peppers and onion and cook until soft, about 10 minutes. Add the vinegar. Strain the mixture over the bananas, reserving the peppers and onion. Add the capers, thyme, and salt to taste. Mix well. Mound on a serving platter or in a bowl. Top with the pepper–onion mixture. Serve at room temperature.

NORMA SHIRLEY
Jamaica

"Pass de Dutchie on de Left-Hand Side"

NORMA SHIRLEY IS A WOMAN with a mission. Trained as a surgical nurse in Scotland, she's had a career as tortuous as a winding road through the Blue Mountains. She's been a caterer, a nurse, a restaurateur, a celebrity chef, and more. Now, she's taken on the entire Jamaican food establishment. From her restaurant at Devon House in Kingston, she's working to upgrade the training of chefs, the quality of service, and the entire Jamaican dining experience not only in her own place, Norma's on the Terrace, but in the entire country!

It's no mean feat, but Norma is making progress, slowly encouraging chefs to use Jamaican products, and to celebrate the bounty and culinary traditions of their island home rather than to look to the United States or Europe for inspiration. If anyone can do this, Norma can. She's single-handedly transformed the Kingston food scene, convincing people to dine out, and providing them with a setting in which they can. Norma's food is not classical Jamaican; rather, the traditional tastes of the island are filtered through her experience of world travel and her extraordinary aesthetic sense. A starter of smoked marlin, using fish from the folks that she encouraged to go into business, arrives dotted with capers and topped with a blanket of thinly sliced onions. A Cornish game hen arrives as a ship under sail, with a mast and full sheets of fried breadfruit.

Norma feels that cooking is for everyone, and a means of artistic expression. Her chef can man the kitchen successfully in her absence, yet is unlettered in more traditional ways. Waiters beg to work in her restaurant, and she submits them to stunning on-the-job training, roundly badgering them into perfection with a smile and a tease. In her own kitchen, she's a martinet, demanding that things be done just so. Threatening to box ears and "clart" folks in a manner that they all greet with knowing smiles as they hurry to do her bidding, they know that Mrs. Shirley suffer fools neither gladly nor lengthily. Norma's generosity often goes unnoticed among her peers who wonder how she commands such loyalty. Anyone who has watched her as she thinks of her staff while on trips and as she makes sure that they are well fed and housed and get to and from work safely, understands that she is someone who knows that loyalty cannot be bought—it must be earned.

Norma's restaurant has had astonishing success,

and has won accolades from publications in the United States and Europe and made Norma a culinary ambassador for the food of Jamaica and the entire Caribbean. Her Creole food hints at the way of the future, blending the tastes of the past with the aesthetics of the present to remind everyone that Creole food is not static, but an ongoing and ever-evolving art.

Soupe de Gombos

Okra Soup

(French Caribbean)

This simple and easy-to-prepare soup is not a gumbo in the traditional sense of a soupy stew. Rather, it is a thin broth to which okra, tomato, and rice are added.

SERVES 4

2 cups chicken stock
2 dozen okra pods, topped, tailed, and cut into rounds
3 medium tomatoes, peeled, seeded, and coarsely chopped
¾ cup rice

Place the stock and 2 cups water in a heavy saucepan and bring to a boil. Add the okra and cook for 10 minutes at low heat, stirring regularly. Place the tomato in a blender and pulse until you have a frothy liquid. Add tomato mixture to the okra and stir until well mixed. Drizzle in the rice and cook for 20 minutes over medium heat, stirring occasionally. Serve hot.

Jicama Cole Slaw
(United States)

Cole slaw is a staple of many a summer picnic. Somehow, though, I never liked the cole slaw that is made with raisins and a creamy dressing. I prefer a bit of bite to mine and came up with this recipe, which has the surprising addition of jicama.

1 large head cabbage, cored and shredded
½ head red cabbage, cored and shredded
1 large jicama, peeled and grated
2 medium carrots, grated
¾ cup mayonnaise
1 tablespoon buttermilk
1 tablespoon apple-cider vinegar
1½ tablespoons sugar, or to taste
Salt and freshly ground black pepper, to taste

Place the cabbages, jicama, and carrots into a medium glass bowl and fluff with a fork so that the strips are separated. Mix the jicama, carrots, mayonnaise, buttermilk, vinegar, sugar, and salt and pepper in a small bowl. Adjust seasonings and pour the dressing over the slaw. Cover with plastic wrap and refrigerate for at least 1 hour. Serve chilled.

Red, White, and Blue Potato Salad

(United States)

Every once and a while, I do feel patriotic—usually in the summer time when bunting is out and flags are flying. One year, I took advantage of the new bounty of potatoes that are available and concocted this red, white, and blue potato salad to dazzle some of my young cousins. It's perfect for the Fourth of July.

SERVES *6 TO 8*

1 pound small **Red Bliss potatoes**
1 pound **Yukon Gold potatoes**
½ pound blue potatoes (also called **Peruvian purple potatoes**)
2 large celery ribs, minced
1 small onion, minced
¼ cup minced red bell pepper
1 cup mayonnaise
Salt and freshly ground black pepper, to taste

Wash the potatoes and place them in a saucepan with water to cover. Bring to a boil over high heat, then lower the heat and cook until fork tender, but not mushy, about 20 minutes. Drain the potatoes and allow them to cool. Place the celery, onion, and bell pepper into a large bowl. When the potatoes have cooled, cut them into chunks, leaving the skins on, and add them to the onion mixture. Add the mayonnaise a bit at a time until the salad is well coated, but not too wet (you may not need the entire cup). Add the salt and pepper and mix well. Cover with plastic wrap and refrigerate. Serve chilled.

Maryse's Salade Mixte

Maryse's Mixed Salad

(Guadeloupe)

My friend Maryse Pochot has been my entrée to things Guadelopean since I first met her when I was travel editor for Essence *magazine in the 1970s. Needless to say, we've had many a culinary adventure since that time. We were inducted into the* Association des Cuisinières *in the same year, and we have crisscrossed the island doing everything from attending the ceremonies for Miss Guadeloupe, a hoot of an occasion, to sharing meals with Madame Carmelita Jeanne, a second-generation cook I refer to as "Maman Guadeloupe." When Maryse entertains at home, she shows the same quickness of preparation and thought for good taste that have made her a sought-after hostess in Guadeloupe. This is a dish that she can always whip up by combining a few cans from her larder and a bit of aesthetic ingenuity. Don't turn up your nose at canned corn. Trust me, in Guadeloupe it's better canned.*

SERVES 4 TO 6

1 small head green leaf or Bibb lettuce
1 cup corn, off the cob or canned
1 cup cubed beetroot, drained
1 cup finely grated carrots
2 medium ripe tomatoes, sliced
1 small sweet onion, thinly sliced
Maryse's Vinaigrette (p. 136)

Arrange the lettuce on the bottom of a small platter. Arrange the remaining ingredients artistically—that's the trick—on top of the lettuce. Drizzle with the vinaigrette and serve. It's simple, but folks love it.

Maryse's Salade Verte

Maryse's Green Salad

(Guadeloupe)

I know from my six-and-one-half-year stint as a restaurant reviewer that sometimes the simplest things are the most difficult to make. I am constantly amazed at just how much difference something like a small pinch of salt can make. From Maryse Pochot, again, I learned a few Guadeloupean tricks of the salad trade. The raw garlic is finely minced and added to give the salad a heartiness that works well with the climate.

SERVES 4

2 heads fresh green leaf or Bibb lettuce
2 cloves garlic, finely minced
Pinch of salt and freshly ground black pepper, to taste
Maryse's Vinaigrette (p. 136)

Make sure that the lettuce is well chilled. Wash it and separate the leaves. Pat them dry with absorbent paper. Place lettuce in a glass or ceramic salad bowl. Dress with vinaigrette.

Pineapple and Cabbage Salad

(Cuba)

This salad is unusual in that the pineapple is blanched, which softens it.

SERVES 6 TO 8

1 small ripe pineapple
1 small green cabbage
¼ cup mayonnaise
1 small head Boston lettuce

Peel the pineapple and cut it into quarters. Blanch the pineapple by plunging it into boiling water for 3 minutes, then plunging it into a bath of ice water. Drain, cut it into small pieces, and reserve. Remove the tough outside leaves and the core from the cabbage and shred it. Place the cabbage strips and the pineapple in a bowl, toss with the mayonnaise, cover with plastic wrap, and refrigerate for 1 hour. (You may need a bit more mayonnaise but remember, the salad should only be lightly coated.) When ready to serve, line a serving platter with the lettuce leaves and mound the cabbage and pineapple on top. Serve chilled.

Yuca en Salsa

Manioc in Sauce

(Cuba)

This is one way that the tubers and roots of the Creole world make their way to the table—as salads or as cold marinated vegetables.

SERVES 4 TO 6

1 pound sweet cassava tubers, peeled and cut into 2" pieces
1 tablespoon salt
4 cloves garlic, chopped
1 tablespoon olive oil
⅓ cup *Mojo Criollo* (p. 152)

Place the peeled cassava into a heavy saucepan. Add salt and water to cover. Bring to a boil and cook for 30 minutes, or until tender. Remove, dice, and set aside. Heat the olive oil in a heavy skillet and sauté the garlic over medium heat until brown. Add the *mojo criollo* and pour the warm sauce over the cassava. Serve warm or at room temperature.

Roquette

Arugula Salad

(New Orleans)

I can remember when arugula became a regular staple in my house, and how hard it was to find even in New York City. I was surprised to find it listed as one of the favorite salad greens of New Orleans Creoles in the 1901 edition of the Picayune Creole Cookbook. *This is an arugula salad that serves as a reminder that there is nothing new under the culinary sun.*

SERVES 4

2 bunches fresh arugula
1 small Vidalia or other mild onion, thinly sliced
2 tablespoons vinaigrette (p. 136 or p. 137)

Wash the arugula, remove any woody stems, tear it into pieces, and place in a glass salad bowl. Add the onion and vinaigrette and serve.

Vinny's Arugula Salad

(United States)

These garlic cloves don't come from the Creole world, but they're a part of my creolized cooking which borrows flavors from everywhere. This recipe was inspired by the fantastic salad that Chef Vincent Scotto prepares. I wheedled and begged and, finally, he gave me the recipe, so that when I can't make it to Gonzo, his wonderful Manhattan restaurant, I can at least marinate some garlic cloves and think of him.

SERVES 4

1 cup peeled garlic cloves
Balsamic vinegar (if the vinegar is pungent, you may wish to add
    ½ teaspoon or so dark-brown sugar)
2 bunches arugula
Freshly grated Parmesan cheese, to taste
Olive oil
Salt and freshly ground black pepper, to taste

Prepare the garlic cloves by removing the ends and any blemished spots. Place them in a small nonreactive saucepan with balsamic vinegar to cover. Bring the vinegar to a boil, then lower the heat and simmer, stirring occasionally, until the vinegar becomes syrupy and the garlic cloves soften. Remove from heat, cool, and pour into a glass canning jar or container.

Make the salad by washing the arugula, removing any tough stems and discolored spots, and placing in a salad bowl with 2 tablespoons of the drained garlic cloves. Sprinkle the grated cheese on top, drizzle with balsamic vinegar and olive oil and add salt and pepper to taste. Serve chilled. The remaining garlic will keep in a jar in the refrigerator for 2 weeks.

Salade de Christophine

Shaved Chayote Salad

(Guadeloupe)

This salad is an unusual way of serving the chayote squash, known as christophine, *in the French-speaking Caribbean and* mirliton *in New Orleans.*

SERVES 4 TO 6

2 small chayote
Vinaigrette (p. 136 or p. 137)
1 head Boston lettuce

Peel the chayote and grate it into a nonreactive bowl on the large holes of a grater. Add the vinaigrette, toss, cover with plastic wrap and chill for 1 hour. When ready to serve, arrange the inner leaves of the Boston lettuce on a platter. Mound the chayote on top of the leaves. Serve chilled.

Creole Tomato and Vidalia Onion Salad

(New Orleans)

There is no more natural pairing than the sweet taste of a Georgia Vidalia onion with the lush acidity of a fresh New Orleans Creole tomato. Combining them demands a simplicity that will let the flavors speak for themselves.

SERVES 4

3 large ripe Creole tomatoes
2 Vidalia or other mild onions, thinly sliced
Vinaigrette (p. 136 or p. 137) to taste

Slice the tomatoes and arrange them on a platter. Interleaf the onion slices with the tomato slices or mound the onion slices in the middle of the tomatoes. Drizzle with your favorite vinaigrette. For each diner, serve a bit of the tomatoes and some of the onions. Yum!

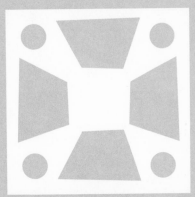

Condiments and Sauces

Creole Tomato Chutney (New Orleans)

Mango Chutney (Barbados)

Hot Sauce (United States)

Caribbean Pepper Sauce (Caribbean)

Passion Fruit–Peach Salsa

Mojo Criollo—Creole Sauce (Cuba)

Rub for Pork (Jamaica)

Peanut *Aji*—Peanut Sauce (Colombia)

Picklises—Preserved Vegetables and Chiles (Haiti)

Sauce Chien (Martinique)

WOMEN'S WORK
Bridgetown Barbados, 1976

I'VE BEEN HEADING to the island affectionately known as Bimshire (for being so British) for
almost three decades. I made my first visit as a
fledgling travel editor at *Essence* magazine in the
1970s, and have virtually commuted in recent
years, as a culinary consultant for Almond Resorts,
a small chain of all-inclusive properties. I've
watched tourism boom, and seen the island grow
ever more prosperous. I've seen the country become increasingly aware of its African heritage, and
watched as Crop Over, the end of harvest festival,
grew from a small tourist board event to a carnival
of international proportions. Throughout my years
of going to Barbados, I've had one constant—a
small shop at the end of Bridgetown's main street
called Women's Self Help.

Located on the ground floor of an old wooden
building, Women's Self Help was an organization
that seemed to be left from the earlier part of the
twentieth century. Slightly musty and definitely
old-fashioned, glass display shelves overflowed with

hand-crocheted doilies, lovingly made baby clothes, rag dolls dressed in bright colors, cut tropical bouquets in rusty juice tins, and even a section of consignment wares that could include everything from bakelite jewelry to bone china. I loved rummaging through all of these, but the reason that I really loved the Women's Self Help was that there was an entire section devoted to homemade preserves and condiments. It was at Women's Self Help that I first learned about Barbadian fruits like golden apple and Barbados cherry that, up until very recently, never turned up on a hotel table. My first bottle of the mossy green mix known as *Bajan seasoning* came from the shop's shelves long before there were professionally bottled jars for sale at every hotel gift shop and department store. I sampled spicy pepper jelly and turmeric-hued hot sauce, and found a mango chutney that I still dream about. There were peppers in sherry or vinegar and an entire range of confections, including tart tamarind balls with shiny black seeds inside, and a ginger fudge so sweet that a few bites was all I could manage.

A visit to the shop was a trip to times past, when parts of Barbados resembled English countryside villages more than neighboring Caribbean islands. The ladies who ran the store were unfailingly polite and ready to discuss the merits of one item over another, and the myriad uses to which they could be put. The check-out system was archaic—a chit written up in great detail was presented at a window with your cash, and then you returned to the counter to pick up the wrapped merchandise—all in a space the size of a tiny New York apartment. Business was slow, and I always tried to visit Women's Self Help early in a trip as the process alone demanded that I slow down and give up my New York brusqueness. Urban renewal has come to Bridgetown and the building in which the Women's Self Help was housed was torn down to make way for a bank. I miss it.

My work at Almond has ended, and I no longer visit the island as often as I did. I've heard though that Women's Self Help has found another spot in the city and I know that, when I return to one of my favorite places in the Caribbean, one of my first questions will be what's happened to Women's Self Help. I'll also leave extra room in my suitcase; I'm just about out of mango chutney.

Sofrito

(Puerto Rico)

This is Puerto Rico's passe partout *seasoning. It is added to soups, stews, and other dishes. There are numerous ways to prepare* sofrito, *which can also be purchased ready-made.*

MAKES ABOUT 2 CUPS

2 green bell peppers, seeded and coarsely chopped
2 medium tomatoes, peeled, seeded, and coarsely chopped
1 medium onion, chopped
4 cloves garlic, crushed
3 sprigs cilantro
1 sprig flat-leaf parsley
2 tablespoons Annatto Oil (p. 135)
¼ pound Virginia ham, trimmed of fat and minced
¼ pound salt pork, minced
1 teaspoon dried oregano, crushed, optional
1 tablespoon minced pimento-stuffed olives, optional

Place the vegetables in the bowl of a food processor and process until a smooth paste forms. (The paste can be kept in the refrigerator in a sterilized glass jar.) When ready to prepare the dish, sauté the vegetable and herb mixture in the annatto oil along with the ham, salt pork and optional ingredients, if using. Be sure to sauté and not fry as you want the ingredients only lightly cooked. The sofrito is used as a starter sauce for many Puerto Rican dishes.

Green Sofrito

(Puerto Rico)

My friend Patricia Wilson and I once did a demonstration of Caribbean tastes for the Chef des Chefs seminars put on by the American Culinary Federation. She was demonstrating sofrito, *and the entire hall smelled like an aromatic green forest, thanks to the masses of* culantro *that they had brought in.* Culantro *is the main ingredient in this classic mix, used to flavor sauces throughout the island. Although you can purchase prepared* sofrito *from Goya, the best way is to make your own.* Culantro, *(which is* not *cilantro), is available fresh in many Hispanic markets. It is also called* Shadow Benny *in the southern Caribbean. If you can't find fresh* culantro, *make do with the Goya version.*

MAKES 1½ CUPS

1 onion, peeled
1 head garlic, separated into cloves and peeled
1 bunch coriander
8–12 leaves culantro
2 Italian peppers or 1 large green bell pepper, seeded
½ pound *ajies dulces*, seeded, optional

Blend all of the ingredients in the food processor. Freeze in ice cube tray and use a cube at a time to season stews, soups, or rice.

Bajan Seasoning

(Barbados)

This verdant paste of herbs, garlic, and chile is the hallmark of good Bajan home cooking. Each housewife has her own version. I used to purchase mine at the late, lamented Women's Self Help, a small shop on the main street in Bridgetown. There, churchwomen kept the nineteenth century alive. Their goods, ranging from intricately crocheted doilies and baby clothes to put-up preserves like golden apple chutneys and pepper wines, were some of my favorite gifts. I still dream about mango chutney made by Number 56. (I broke the code once, met her daughter, and returned to New York laden with chutney.) I never did find out who made my favorite version of seasoning. This recipe from a friend is as close as I've gotten.

MAKES ½ CUP

1 medium onion, sliced
3 cloves garlic
3 chives
3 scallions, including the green tops
½ Scotch bonnet chile, or to taste
3 sprigs fresh thyme, leaves stripped from branches
4 sprigs flat-leaf parsley
1 sprig fresh marjoram
2 sprigs cilantro
3 allspice berries
½" piece ginger, peeled
Juice of 1 lime
1 teaspoon vegetable oil
½ teaspoon salt

Peanuts galore, United States.

Place all the ingredients in the bowl of a food processor and pulse until a thick paste forms. Place the mixture into a sterilized bottle and refrigerate. It will keep for 1 month, and is used in dishes like Baxter's Road Fried Chicken (p. 208).

Cilantro Paste

(Curaçao)

This is a simplified Curaçaoan version of the Hispanic sofrito *or Bajan seasoning. It is used to add an intense cilantro flavor and green coloring to dishes like Green Rice (p. 270).*

MAKES ½ CUP

¾ **cup stripped cilantro leaves**
¼ **cup water, as needed**

Place all the ingredients in the bowl of a food processor, drizzle in the water, and pulse until a thick paste forms.

Annatto Oil

Achiote Oil

(Puerto Rico)

Annatto, which is also called achiote *or* roucou, *goes way back in the history of the Caribbean. Native peoples used to color their bodies with the reddish berries, which are still used to color items like lipstick. However, most of the uses of annatto are culinary. The oil gives color and a slight flavor to many dishes in the Hispanic world. I got a hint that this might have something to do with the unavailability of the palm oil, used for the same purpose in the food of parts of West Africa, when I was working on my book,* Tasting Brazil. *Then, I discovered an oil that is used in the transitional state of Espiritu Santo, where the Afro-Brazilian cuisine of Bahia filters into the more European food of Rio de Janeiro. It is used in places where* dende *or red palm oil would be used in Bahia and olive or vegetable oil would be used in Rio. It is called* azeite de urucum *and is, simply, annatto oil.*

MAKES 1 CUP

1 cup olive oil
3 tablespoons achiote seeds

In a sauté pan, add the seeds to olive oil and heat gently until red color is released. Allow the oil to cool. Strain. The oil can be used in rice dishes, *pasteles,* and in marinades.

Maryse's Vinaigrette

(Guadeloupe)

Wherever I am in the world, I seem to crave a daily salad, and alternate between rich creamy avocados slathered with a thick vinaigrette in Mexico and crunchy leaves of a lettuce that I find only in France and in the French Caribbean. When I stay with my friend Maryse in Point à Pitre, she's always got a head or two in the fridge and I indulge. I suspect that one of the reasons I like it so much is her own way with vinaigrette, which is mustardy and filled with minced pieces of raw garlic. Not classic, but just perfect for the heartiness of Guadeloupean food.

MAKES ¼ CUP

2 tablespoons olive oil
2 teaspoons red-wine vinegar
½ teaspoon minced fresh garlic
½ teaspoon Dijon mustard

Combine all of the ingredients together in a small bottle and shake to mix well. Serve over salad greens.

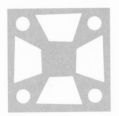

Passion Fruit Vinaigrette

(Barbados)

While working at Almond Resorts in Barbados, we tried to think of innovative ways to use some of the fruits and vegetables of the Caribbean region. This salad dressing is wonderful with fresh passion fruit, if it can be found (mash the pulp in a sieve to separate liquid from the seeds). If not, there are passion fruit pulps available that are just fine. Look for one that is not overly sweet, such as the one made by Goya products.

MAKES ABOUT ¾ CUP

1 tablespoon passion-fruit liquid
¼ cup red-wine vinegar
Salt and freshly ground black pepper, to taste
⅛ teaspoon Dijon mustard
½ cup extra virgin olive oil

Combine all of the ingredients in a small nonreactive bowl, and whisk well. Gradually drizzle in the olive oil, continuing to whisk, until the dressing is well mixed. Serve immediately.

Browning

(All Caribbean)

When we outlanders attempt to achieve the rich dense flavor of a Caribbean stew we are at first, baffled. I know I was, until I watched my girlfriends in their Caribbean kitchens a few times. I soon realized that there were several steps in each operation that never made it into the recipes, one of them was browning. The stew meat can be browned in the pan in a mix of oil and sugar, or you can use your own homemade browning to give the stew a homecooked flavor.

MAKES ABOUT 1¼ CUPS

1 pound sugar

Place the sugar and 2 tablespoons water in the bottom of a heavy skillet and cook, stirring constantly, until the sugar turns a deep, dark brown. Be careful not to burn the sugar, as this will ruin the taste. Gradually add 1½ cups cold water and bring the mixture to a boil, stirring constantly, until a syrup forms. Allow to cool, and pour it into a sterilized bottle. It will keep in the refrigerator for several months. Use in soups and stews for additional flavor.

Rum-Pineapple Mustard

(United States)

The foods of the Creole world are evolving every day, as new ingredients are rediscovered and the world shrinks via television and other media. I was fortunate enough to spend several months as the on-air culinary historian on Sara Moulton's Cooking Live Prime Time *cooking show on the on the Television Food Network. Each week, I would work with an ingredient that was germane to the week's recipes and guest chef and I would explain its history. This is the Caribbean-flavored recipe that I came up with when the discussion turned to mustard. This hot mustard was inspired by the champagne mustards of France.*

MAKES ABOUT ⅓ CUP

2 tablespoons yellow mustard seeds
1 tablespoon brown mustard seeds
1½ tablespoons mustard powder
¼ cup crushed fresh pineapple
1 teaspoon fresh thyme leaves
Salt, to taste
Small pinch dried Scotch bonnet chile, to taste
2 teaspoons dark-brown sugar
6 tablespoons dark rum (the amount will vary depending on the thickness desired)

Mix all the ingredients except the rum in the bowl of a food processor and slowly pulse until a paste forms. Gradually drizzle the rum while pulsing until you have the thickness desired. Serve with ham or pork.

Chef Patricia Wilson
Puerto Rico

"Cocinando Suave . . . Cocinando."

PIG WAS WHAT PATRICIA WILSON and I were looking for as we headed out into the Puerto Rican *campo*. Chef, restaurateur, radio commentator, and now chef/instructor at Johnson and Wales University, Patricia has been my secret weapon about Puerto Rican food for almost a decade. She has since moved to Miami but, in the days when she was the owner of the gone-but-not-forgotten *Bistro Gambaro* in Old San Juan, I would visit and we'd take to the hills on Sunday searching for *lechon*, the Puerto Rican roast pig that is a sublime use of swine.

Usually we let our noses act as our guides. Soon our olfactory senses detected the unmistakable aroma of roasting pig. We'd found our spot; it was off in the countryside, surrounded by a few houses, with a shady dining area punctuated by a few tables with umbrellas. We entered salivating, and found that the pig was ready. One pound of pork and a few beers would do the trick as long as there was enough crackling that we didn't fight in the car.

Cleavers came out and the pork was hacked to pieces and packaged in brown paper, while icy Medalla beers were retrieved from the cooler. Then it was back into the car and we were on our way again. As we journeyed into the hills of Puerto Rico selecting pieces of sweet juicy pork, gnawing on bones, and taking long gulps of refreshing beer parked brazenly in the cup holders, we said a silent thank you to the Spaniards who brought the pigs to this hemisphere and to the island that Patricia jokingly calls Puerco Rico.

Back in San Juan, after the nap that is obligatory after a pig gorge, it was time to prepare for dinner. Patricia donned her cook's whites, which consisted of a hand-embroidered chef's jacket with a lace-edged, long, flounced, white skirt and headed down the hill to the restaurant. This outfit is one of the things that first endeared Patricia to me as it reminded me of the dresses worn by my religious "sisters" at Casa Branca in Bahia, Brazil. A creolized garment, it combines the severity of the French chef's jacket, albeit personalized with Patricia's multihued embroidery, with the femininity and fantasy of the lace-edged skirts that women of the Creole world have worn for centuries. It's practical, comfortable, functional, and woman friendly in ways chef's pants are not. Thus clothed, Patricia headed into her tiny kitchen where she ruled. Soon, the candlelight flickered on the patio in the

Picking allspice, Jamaica.

soft breeze, and the writers, scholars, and members of the Puerto Rican art crowd who made the Bistro Gambaro their hangout assembled to dine on innovative spins on traditional dishes under the velvet Puerto Rican night.

Molho Brasileiro

Brazilian Sauce

(B r a z i l)

This lime-based sauce is so popular in Brazil that it is simply called Brazilian sauce. It is eaten with grilled meats and with roasts. I like it drizzled over stewed vegetables or served with my sautéed greens called couve. *It's simple to prepare and will keep for a few days in the refrigerator.*

MAKES ABOUT 3 CUPS

Juice of 3 limes
Salt and freshly ground black pepper, to taste
2 teaspoons minced flat-leaf parsley
2 teaspoons minced onion
1 teaspoon minced fresh cilantro
Minced preserved *malagueta* pepper, to taste

Place all the ingredients in a small nonreactive bowl. Stir to mix well. Cover with plastic wrap and allow to stand for ½ an hour while the flavors blend. Serve at room temperature.

Watermelon Rind Pickle

(United States)

The watermelon is a touchstone of African-American cooking. It was part of the African diet before the Europeans arrived and, during the trials of enslavement, it provided thirst-quenching coolness in the heat of the day. I'm not a great lover of watermelon, but, I dote on watermelon rind pickles. I spend most summers scheming to beg rind from various friends, so that I can have my pickle without having to eat my way through tons of melon.

MAKES ABOUT 2 PINTS

9 cups watermelon rind, cut into ¾" cubes
½ cup salt
1¾ cups cider vinegar
½ cup balsamic vinegar
2 cups sugar
1 lemon, sliced thin
2 sticks cinnamon, crushed
1 teaspoon whole cloves
2 teaspoons cracked allspice

Remove the green skin and all but a small amount of the red meat from the watermelon rind.

Place the prepared watermelon in a large bowl and soak overnight in a brine made from the salt and 2 quarts water. The next day, drain the watermelon, wash it with fresh water, and drain. Place the rind in a large nonreactive saucepan with water to cover, and simmer until it is fork-tender. Place the remaining 2 cups water and the vinegars, sugar, lemon, cinnamon, cloves, and allspice in another large nonreactive pan, bring to a boil, and simmer for 15 minutes or until a thin syrup forms. Drain the watermelon rind and add it to the syrup. Continue to simmer until the rind becomes translucent, 15 to 20 minutes. Place the watermelon rind pieces in hot sterilized jars, cover with the (unstrained) syrup, and seal them according to proper canning procedures. The pickle will keep for several months.

Creole Tomato Chutney

(New Orleans)

There's nothing that can match the taste of a ripe Louisiana Creole tomato. I discovered them even before I became a part-time resident of New Orleans, and now I bring carefully carried boxes of them back on the plane. Once, when I had more than I could eat, I decided to make a chutney using some of the fresh bird chiles that grow in my backyard, and are staples in my New Orleans kitchen. The result was super. This chutney is particularly good with grilled meats or roasted chicken or turkey. If you're not lucky enough to live in or near New Orleans, this chutney is just fine with other tomatoes—just be sure to get the ripest juiciest tomatoes that you can find.

MAKES ABOUT 6 8-OUNCE CANNING JARS

6 large ripe Creole tomatoes
2 1" pieces fresh ginger, peeled
4 bird chiles, or to taste
2 large onions, quartered
2 cloves garlic, minced
½ cup dark raisins
1 cup firmly packed brown sugar
1 cup distilled white vinegar

Peel and slice the tomatoes. Place them with the ginger, chiles, onions, garlic, and basil in a food processor and pulse until the ingredients are the consistency of a thick liquid. Place the mixture in a heavy, nonreactive saucepan with the remaining ingredients and stir well. Place the saucepan on the stove at medium heat and bring to a boil. Lower the heat and continue to cook, stirring occasionally, for about 1½ hours, or until the mixture reaches a jamlike consistency. Remove from heat and pour into scalded 8-ounce canning jars. The chutney should be served immediately, but will keep in the refrigerator for up to 2 weeks.

Note: Larger batches can be made for canning for those who have bumper crops of tomato, but proper canning procedures should be followed and the jars should be processed in a hot water bath.

Mango Chutney

(Barbados)

After the Emancipation of the African slaves in the British Caribbean, indentured ser-
vants were brought in from China and the Indian subcontinent to work the canefields.
They brought their foodways with them and again the cooking was transformed, with
curries and a wide array of condiments, including a range of chutneys, added to the diet.
This mango chutney is an Anglo-Indian one, similar to the one that I found years ago at
Women's Self Help in Barbados.

MAKES ABOUT 5 CUPS

4 large green mangoes, peeled and coarsely chopped
1 medium onion, diced
2 tablespoons Caribbean Pepper Sauce (p. 150)
1 tablespoon puréed garlic
1 1" piece fresh ginger, peeled and grated
¼ cup dark raisins
¼ cup currants
1 cup apple-cider vinegar
1 cup firmly packed brown sugar
2 teaspoons Angostura bitters
1 teaspoon Coleman's mustard powder
Salt, to taste

Place all the ingredients in a large nonreactive saucepan, stir well, and bring to a
boil. Reduce the heat to low and simmer, stirring occasionally, for 35 to 40 minutes,
or until the mixture thickens. Continue to stir, until the mixture becomes a dark
caramel color. Pour into sterilized jars and process according to canning directions,
or refrigerate and serve within 3 days.

Hot Sauce

(United States)

Hot sauce is indispensable to any well-set African-American table. In truth, though, most African Americans do not prepare their own hot sauces as do our cousins in the Caribbean and Brazil, instead, we rely on commercial brands. A few hardy souls like their hot sauce homemade, and even grow their own chiles. Fresh hot chiles, though, are easier to find in markets than ever before, so preparing your own hot sauce is a snap. Here's a recipe that approximates the taste of the sauce in those long thin bottles that are a hallmark of good African-American cooking.

MAKES ABOUT ⅔ CUP

24 tabasco chiles
2 garlic cloves
1 teaspoon prepared horseradish
2 teaspoons sugar
¼ teaspoon salt
½ cup apple-cider vinegar

Place the chiles and garlic in a small nonreactive saucepan, cover with water, and cook until soft. Place the mixture in a food processor and pulse, until you have a thick liquid. Add the horseradish, sugar, salt, and vinegar to the liquid and stir well. Pour into a sterilized jar and refrigerate until ready to use. The mixture will keep for several weeks. Use sparingly.

Caribbean Pepper Sauce

(Caribbean)

From Castries Market in St. Lucia and Georgetown market in Grenada to the markets of Port-of-Spain and the duty-free shops of Barbados, pepper sauce is the thing that most visitors to the Caribbean crave. This mustard-hued version is a good substitute until you head to the local supermarket, where many are now available, or until your next trip to the Caribbean. Use sparingly—this one is hot!

MAKES ABOUT 2½ CUPS

½ cup chopped scallions, including the green tops
½ cup minced chives
¼ cup minced shallots
4 large onions, chopped
1 tablespoon minced garlic
1 tablespoon turmeric
1 tablespoon dried mustard
1 tablespoon salt, or to taste
1½ cups water
1½ cups distilled vinegar
3 habanero chiles, stems and seeds removed, or to taste

Place all the ingredients in a food processor and pulse until smooth. Pour the mixture into a medium, nonreactive saucepan and bring to a boil over medium heat. Reduce the heat to low, cover, and simmer for 30 minutes. (Beware of the cooking fumes; they're intense.) Remove from the heat, cool, and pour into sterilized bottles. Top with nonreactive covers and allow to stand for 1 week before using.

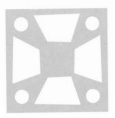

Passion Fruit—Peach Salsa

There is no complex food history to this salsa; it's one that I came up with to go with a passion fruit glazed pork roast. I like it so much that I use it with almost anything.

MAKES ABOUT 2½ CUPS

1½ cups diced fresh, slightly underripe peaches
¼ cup California-style dried apricots, minced
1 small red onion, minced
1 tablespoon minced green bell pepper
2 teaspoons passion fruit nectar
1 tablespoon balsamic vinegar
1 tablespoon freshly squeezed lemon juice
1 tablespoon minced cilantro leaves
1 jalapeño chile, seeded and minced, or to taste

Combine all the ingredients in a nonreactive bowl and mix well. Cover with plastic wrap and refrigerate for 1 hour. Serve chilled or at room temperature.

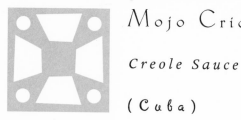

Mojo Criollo

Creole Sauce

(C u b a)

This sauce is such a Cuban classic that it is even bottled and sold in shops. The trick is to find the sour oranges. If you cannot, try this version, which uses regular orange juice, cut with the tartness of fresh lime juice.

MAKES ABOUT 1 CUP

¼ cup freshly squeezed lime juice
½ cup freshly squeezed orange juice
½ cup olive oil
1 teaspoon dried oregano
6 garlic cloves, minced
Salt and freshly ground black pepper, to taste

Place all the ingredients in a small jar, cover and shake vigorously for 2 minutes. Adjust seasonings, and use as a marinade for meats.

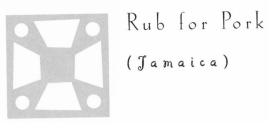

Rub for Pork

(Jamaica)

I first came across the pork rub as a packaged mix in a Jamaican supermarket, and was delighted by the taste it gave to my traditional New Year's roast pork. I was distressed when the package was empty, and I was unable to find more, so I decided to examine the ingredients and come up with my own variation.

MAKES ABOUT ½ CUP

4 tablespoons Bell's Poultry Seasoning
3 tablespoons dark-brown sugar
1 teaspoon dried onion flakes
1 teaspoon garlic powder
1 teaspoon allspice berries
Salt and fresh black peppercorns, to taste

Place all the ingredients in a spice mill and pulse until you have a coarse mixture. Pour into a small jar and mix well. Seal with a stopper and store in a cool, dry place until ready to use. The rub will keep for several months.

Peanut Aji

Peanut Sauce

(Colombia)

This peanut sauce accompanies appetizers in the Gran Cauca region of Colombia. The area is noted for its mix of cultures and, the colonial period was one during which Indians, Africans, and Europeans mixed freely. The peanuts, therefore, may be a result of the Andean influence, or a hint of African hands in the pot.

MAKES ABOUT 1 CUP

½ cup chicken stock
⅓ cup chunk-style peanut butter
1 small ripe tomato, peeled, seeded, and coarsely chopped
2 scallions, minced, including the green part
⅛ teaspoon minced hot chile, or to taste
2 teaspoons minced cilantro
1 hard-boiled egg, chopped
Juice of 1 lemon
Fried green bananas, for serving

Place all the ingredients in a small bowl and whisk to mix well. Serve at room temperature with fried green bananas to dip in the sauce.

Picklises

Preserved Vegetables and Chiles

(Haiti)

The food of Haiti has a complex relationship with the Creole dishes of New Orleans. Although words like mirliton *may be the same, there's no equivalent for dishes like* griots de porc *and* mamba. *I have, however, spied some pickled vegetables in the weekly Farmer's Market, with a tell-tale red of hot chile peeking out, which looked remarkably like* picklises.

MAKES ABOUT 4 CUPS

1 cup blanched French-cut string beans
1 cup shredded cabbage
½ cup green peas
1 cup julienned carrots
1 large onion, thinly sliced
1 Scotch bonnet chile, seeded and quartered
2 cups apple-cider vinegar

Place all the ingredients except the vinegar and one of the chile quarters into a medium sterilized canning jar. Heat the remaining chile quarter and vinegar in a small saucepan over medium heat. Pour it into the jar to cover the vegetables. Cover and store in a cool, dry place for 1 week, to pickle. Serve with roasted or grilled meats.

Sauce Chien

(Martinique)

In the years since I first discovered this sauce, I've tasted many different versions, but I've still not found the etymology for it. I guess I'll have to continue thinking that it's a sauce that's so good you could eat roast dog covered with it.

MAKES ABOUT ⅓ CUP

1 small onion, minced
3 scallions, minced, including green part
1 small tomato, peeled, seeded, and minced
1 clove garlic, minced
3 sprigs flat-leaf parsley
Juice of 1 lime
2 teaspoons white-wine vinegar
¼ teaspoon minced Scotch bonnet chile, or to taste
3 tablespoons olive oil

Place all ingredients, except the olive oil, in a small nonreactive bowl and whisk together. Continue to whisk while drizzling in the olive oil. Serve immediately.

Vegetables

Creole Tomatoes and Olives (New Orleans)

Giraumonade — Calabaza Purée (Guadeloupe)

Caribbean-Style Zucchini (Guadeloupe)

Fruit à Pain Fondu — Melted Breadfruit (Haiti)

Soused Breadfruit (Barbados)

Fried Breadfruit (Guadeloupe)

Beignets de Gombo — Okra Fritters (Guadeloupe)

Arepita di Pampuna — Pumpkin Fritters (Curaçao)

Baked Ripe Bananas (Guadeloupe)

Epinards et Bananes Vertes — Spinach and Green Bananas (Guadeloupe)

Bananes Jaunes — Boiled Plantains (Guadeloupe)

Mignan de Ti-Figue — Mignan of Green Bananas (Martinique)

Plátanos Empanizados — Breaded Plantains (Costa Rica)

Tostones — Fried Plantains (Puerto Rico)

Fufu — Mashed Plantains (Belize)

Exquites — Nahuatl-Style Sweet Corn (Mexico)

Creole String Beans (New Orleans)

Maquechou (New Orleans)

Guiso de Maíz — Corn Stew (Costa Rica)

Creole Okra (New Orleans)

Okra, Corn, and Tomatoes (United States)

Okra (United States)

Quiabo — Blanched Okra (Brazil)

Panned Lettuce (New Orleans)

Aubergines Farcies — Stuffed Eggplant (New Orleans)

Couve a Mineira — Greens Mineira Style (Brazil)

CREOLE LOVE APPLES
New Orleans, 1989

NOT EVERYONE CAN SAY that they know a grown man who owns a tomato-red tuxedo. I do. My friend Lou Costa has a bright red-velvet suit that he used to don once a year to lead the tomato parade. Lou, used to be the head of New Orleans' French Market commission and, as such, he was responsible for publicizing market events at one of the city's, and indeed the country's, most venerable city markets. The tomato festival celebrated the joys of Creole tomatoes.

I am a tomato lover; I can eat tomatoes in anything and refuse to chomp down on the ones that are odorless, colorless, and cottony, so I wait for summer tomatoes with the anticipation of a crusader in quest of the Holy Grail. I was ignorant of Creole tomatoes until I began to travel to New Orleans. Sure, I knew about farm-fresh tomatoes from New Jersey and the rich roseate delights of my Martha's Vineyard summers, but the Creole tomato was not on my horizon. Then, one year, I was asked to speak at a conference centered around the Tomato Festival and I was brought face to face with the love apple of my dreams.

Creole tomatoes are large and firm and would seem, at first glance, to be just another one of those *bocce* balls that pass for tomatoes in so many supermarkets. But when you slice into one and taste it, you know it's different. Juicy, but not watery; meaty, but not tough; and dense with the sweet-tart flavor of a vine-ripened tomato, they are bliss. Their flavor and their fine and almost unique combination of heft and taste are unique. No one's been able to give me a satisfactory explanation for why this should be, so, I chalk it up to another of the Crescent City's mysteries and wait until late May or early June rolls around again and pig out.

In Lou's days at the French Market, the vendors would vie for the earliest and tastiest tomatoes. Now, things seem to happen with a little less fanfare, but the city's cognoscenti all know when to begin to think of cooling salads tossed with a light vinaigrette or fried green tomatoes prepared from the unripened fruit. I've now joined them and know to leave room for a box of tomatoes in my carry-on luggage—no mean feat for someone like me who suffers from pack-mule syndrome.

Several years after my love at first sight meeting with the Creole tomato, I purchased a painting called "Creole Love Apples," by Mississippi artist Blair Hobbs. It's a smiling Creole woman with ripe,

Street market, Richmond, Virginia.

luscious red tomatoes as breasts. She hangs over my bed in New Orleans, reminding me not only of the connections between tomatoes and sensuality—it is not without reason that they were called love apples—but also of the promise of love apples each year.

Creole Tomatoes and Olives

(New Orleans)

Creole tomatoes are a New Orleans phenomenon. Luscious and firm on the outside, they are juicy within. They appear in the Crescent City Farmer's Market and in the French Market around June, and I try to make it my business to get some. I've hand-carried many a box to New York, where there's nothing like them. This is a savory dish that plays off the tomatoes' sweetness with the meatiness of ripe olives.

SERVES: 4 TO 6

6 large ripe Creole tomatoes, peeled and sliced
2 tablespoons salted butter
1 teaspoon dried Italian oregano
1 cup minced ripe olives

Sauté the tomatoes in the butter until lightly browned. Sprinkle on the oregano and add the olives. Cook about 3 minutes, or until heated through. Serve hot.

Giraumonade

Calabaza Purée

(Guadeloupe)

This purée of calabaza is one way that cooks from Guadeloupe keep their plates from turning into a study in brown. It adds color to the plate and adding cassava meal before serving gives it texture.

SERVES 4 TO 6

1 pound calabaza
1 small onion, minced
2 tablespoons minced parsley
3 branches fresh thyme, leaves stripped
¼ cup olive oil
3 cloves garlic, minced
Salt and freshly ground black pepper, to taste
1 cup cassava meal

Peel and seed the calabaza and cut it into ½" dice. Place it with the onion in a skillet with the oil. Add the thyme leaves and parsley. Cook over medium heat, stirring constantly, until the onion is light brown. Add the garlic and the calabaza and continue to cook, stirring constantly, for 8 to 10 minutes or until the calabaza becomes a purée. Serve hot, with the cassava meal. Diners should sprinkle a bit of the meal on the purée before eating.

Caribbean-Style Zucchini

(Guadeloupe)

Although the zucchini is not native to this hemisphere, this method of cooking the squash can be applied to other squashes and no doubt was.

SERVES 4 TO 6

1 pound zucchini
2 tablespoons butter
2 tablespoons olive oil
3 branches fresh thyme, stripped
2 tablespoons minced flat-loaf parsley
1 tablespoon minced chives
1 clove garlic, crushed
Salt and freshly ground black pepper, to taste

Peel the zucchini, slice lengthwise, remove the seeds, and cut into small pieces. Place the zucchini in a saucepan with the butter and oil and cook over medium heat, until lightly browned. Add the remaining ingredients, cover, lower the heat and cook for 5 to 8 minutes, mashing the zucchini with a spoon until it has the consistency of a thick paste. Serve hot.

Fruit à Pain Fondu

Melted Breadfruit

(Haiti)

Breadfruit was brought to the Caribbean at the end of the eighteenth century to provide food for the enslaved Africans by the infamous Captain Bligh, on the H.M.S. Bounty. Bligh paid more attention to his breadfruit saplings than to the crew, particularly in matters of water, and the result was the notorious mutiny on the Bounty. Bligh survived the mutiny and returned to the South Seas for more breadfruit plants, which he eventually took to the islands. A descendant of the first sapling can be seen in the botanical gardens in Saint Vincent.

SERVES 4 TO 6

1 small breadfruit
4 tablespoons butter
3 tablespoons dark Haitian rum
3 tablespoons milk
½ teaspoon freshly grated nutmeg

Preheat the oven to 350 degrees. Core the breadfruit and place the butter, rum, milk, and nutmeg in the center. Wrap in aluminum foil and bake for 45 minutes to 1 hour. When done and the breadfruit has softened, remove the aluminum foil, slice, and serve.

Soused Breadfruit

(Barbados)

For six years I worked with the chefs at Almond Resorts in Barbados, creating dishes using traditional Caribbean ingredients and based on Barbadian classics. Once, when we were trying to come up with a vegetarian alternative for a menu, the executive chef of Almond Beach Village, Paul Hamilton, suggested that we use breadfruit instead of the traditional pig parts in a souse. *The result was a hit. When served with a sweet potato pudding, it is a vegetarian version of the traditional Saturday feast of pudding and* souse. *Alone, it is just grand.*

SERVES 6 TO 8

1 medium breadfruit
3 cloves garlic, minced
1 onion, minced
1 medium cucumber, peeled, seeded, and thinly sliced
¼ cup minced red bell pepper
¼ cup minced green bell pepper
2 sprigs flat-leaf parsley, minced
½ habanero chile, seeded, and minced, or to taste
1½ cups freshly squeezed lime juice
Salt and freshly ground black pepper, to taste
Parsley, for garnish

Peel the breadfruit and cut it into quarters. Core the fruit and slice it into ½-inch cubes. As you dice the breadfruit, place it into a bowl of salted, cold water, so that it will not discolor. Drain the breadfruit and drop it into boiling salted water for 20 to 25 minutes or until fork tender. The breadfruit will initially float, but will sink in the

Women vegetable vendors, Charleston, South Carolina.

water as it cooks. Remove the breadfruit, drain it and place it in a nonreactive bowl. Mix the chile, lime juice, and salt and pepper. Pour the mixture over the breadfruit, cover, and refrigerate for five hours or overnight so that the flavors marry. Serve slightly chilled, and garnish with parsley.

Fried Breadfruit

(Guadeloupe)

Breadfruit prepared in this manner can be served as a snack, as a vegetable, or used to garnish a dish. Norma Shirley of Jamaica brings roasted Cornish hens topped with a sail of fried breadfruit to the table of her Kingston restaurant.

SERVES 8 TO 10, AS A SNACK

1 medium breadfruit
Vegetable oil, for frying

Peel the breadfruit and cut it into thin slices on a mandoline or with a sharp knife. Heat the oil to 375 degrees in a heavy saucepan or Dutch oven. Place the breadfruit slices, a few at a time, into the oil and fry for about 2 minutes on each side, turning once or until they are nicely browned. Drain on absorbent paper and serve hot.

Note: If using the breadfruit as a vegetable, you may wish to cut the breadfruit into fries.

Beignets de Gombo

Okra Fritters

(Guadeloupe)

There is a fritter tradition still alive in the African-Atlantic world of Creole food. They may be savory like the akara *of Nigeria or the* acaraje *of Brazil, or sweet like the pineapple and dessert fritters that are found in the southern United States. Early cookbooks from New Orleans show how fritters were frequently used as a tasty way to get rid of leftover food.*

SERVES 4 TO 6

½ pound fresh okra, topped and tailed
Juice of 1 lemon
2 tablespoons olive oil
Salt and freshly ground black pepper, to taste
Fritter batter (p. 315)
Oil, for frying
Lemon slices, for garnish

Wash the okra and place it in a small saucepan of boiling salted water. Cook for 3 minutes, drain, and place in a marinade prepared from the lemon juice, oil, and salt and pepper. Allow to sit for 1 hour. When ready to fry, heat the oil to 375 degrees in a heavy saucepan or Dutch oven. Drain the okra and dip it in the fritter batter. Gently place it in the oil and fry for 3 minutes or until golden brown. Remove and drain on absorbent paper. Serve hot with slices of lemon and hot sauce.

Arepita di Pampuna

Pumpkin Fritters

(Curaçao)

Curaçao's food is some of the most imaginative and least known in the Caribbean region. The cooking of the island is some of the hemisphere's original fusion food, as a result of its diverse history. It was settled by the Dutch, who had left Pernambuco in Brazil; has a strong presence of Sephardic Jews, who have had a community on the island for over 300 years; and a large population of African descent, resulting from its position as a "seasoning" point for slaves in the Caribbean. Here the calabaza, or West Indian cooking pumpkin, meets the West African fritter tradition and the Dutch love for fried goodies.

MAKES ABOUT 30 FRITTERS

2 cups boiled, mashed calabaza
¾ cup flour
¼ cup milk
1 egg
1 teaspoon cinnamon
⅛ teaspoon freshly ground nutmeg
2 tablespoons sugar
Pinch salt
½ teaspoon vanilla
1/16 teaspoon baking powder
Oil, for frying

Place all the ingredients in the bowl of a food processor and pulse until a thick paste forms. Heat 2" of oil to 375 degrees in a heavy skillet or Dutch oven. When the oil is ready, drop tablespoons of batter into the oil, a few at a time, and fry for 2 minutes on each side, or until golden brown. Remove and drain on absorbent paper.

Baked Ripe Bananas

(Guadeloupe)

The residents of French islands, defying all thoughts of hot weather, have a love for heavy dishes served with a cheesy topping of grated Gruyère.

I've discovered the Japanese breadcrumbs known as panko. *Try them for a nice crunchy topping.*

SERVES 4 TO 6

6 ripe bananas
3 tablespoons salted butter
¼ cup grated Gruyère cheese
½ cup breadcrumbs

Heat the oven to 400 degrees. Peel the bananas and slice them lengthwise. Place them in an ovenproof baking dish. Melt the butter and drizzle it over the bananas. Sprinkle with a mix of breadcrumbs and cheese. Bake for 15 minutes. Serve hot.

GÉRARD VIRGINIUS
Martinique

TALL AND INTENSE, Gérard Virginius can at first be an intimidating presence—a chef in the traditional French manner. Then he smiles, and the tropical sun of his Caribbean birth seems like the sun breaking through the clouds. I first met Gérard over a decade ago, in his small restaurant, *La Canne a Sucre* which, with the neighboring antique shop run by author Simone Schwartz-Bart, are my two favorite places in Pointe à Pitre, Guadeloupe. I'd spend money in the first and chat with Simone, then hurry to *La Canne à Sucre* to snag one of the forty-five seats for lunch. The small-frame colonial house on a back street in the heart of the city was a haven of calm with swirling ceiling fans and bentwood furniture; it was an upscale Antillean version of the mom-and-pop restaurant. Gérard ran the kitchen while his French wife, Marie-Claude, manned the front of the house, greeting all with a ready smile and regulars by name.

Gérard is the epitome of the new Creole chef. He trained at *Le Nôtre* and *Dalloyau* in Paris and applies his savoir faire to the dishes of his home. He could be found in the local market at 6 A.M. with the traditional cooks shopping for the same fresh produce but, when they appear on his table, they're a more sophisticated presentation. His innovations include taking fillets of the traditional red snapper and saucing them with lemongrass, red wine, and chocolate and serving them over a mousseline of white yams, or grilling them and serving them in a scallion butter. His curried clams are quite simply the stuff of legend.

I'd lost touch with Gérard over the years and only recently found him again, this time in Martinique. I made a reservation in another name, wanting to surprise Gérard and Marie-Claude and see if they remembered me as fondly as I did them. My friend and I arrived, climbing the steps to the small restaurant that I was pleased to note maintains the same swirling fans and bentwood furniture that made *La Canne à Sucre* a haven of informal calm. I stepped across the threshold to be transported into the past and when Marie-Claude greeted me with the same ready smile, followed by a look of astonishment and a hearty "Jessica," I knew that the venue had changed, but the welcome had not. I settled in, had my usual 'ti punch and began to look at the menu. I realized that, although some of my old favorites had disappeared, Gérard still continues to work his culinary magic. A bottle of wine, a fantastic meal and a postprandial rum later, Gérard had finished service and came out of the kitchen to join us at the table. We sat reminiscing about times past and comparing gray hairs and weight gains. Finally, it was time to go, and I reluctantly headed off, vowing never again to lose touch with Virginius who years ago vowed to be the first Michelin-starred, Black Caribbean chef. If they're watching the region, he may yet make it.

Epinards et Bananes Vertes

Spinach and Green Bananas

(Guadeloupe)

One of the hallmarks of the Caribbean section of the Creole world is its use of the banana, in all of its degrees of ripeness. Here, green bananas are cooked, then served with spinach, which is a good substitute for the leafy greens like malanga *and* callaloo, *which are not readily available.*

SERVES 4 TO 6

2 pounds green bananas
3 pounds spinach
4 cloves garlic, minced
Juice of 1 lemon
3 scallions, minced
1 habanero chile, pricked with a fork

Peel the bananas according to the instructions on page 21. Cut the bananas in rounds and simmer them in water to cover for 30 minutes. Add the spinach, garlic, lemon juice, scallions, and chile, lower the heat, and continue to cook for 10 minutes. Remove the chile. Serve hot.

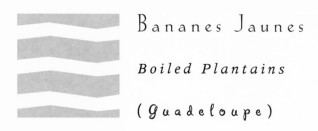

Bananes Jaunes

Boiled Plantains

(Guadeloupe)

While plantains come to the table at every state of ripeness, these boiled yellow ones are the standard starch on many a Caribbean table.

SERVES 4 TO 6

4 large yellow plantains
2 tablespoons butter

Cut the ends off the plantains and slit them lengthwise. Place in a saucepan with water to cover, bring to a boil, and cook until the skins open, about 10 minutes. Serve hot, topped with the butter.

Mignan de Ti-Figue

Mignan *of Green Bananas*

(Martinique)

This is a dish of the poor in the French Caribbean. In the film Sugar Cane Alley, *based on the book by Martinician novelist Joseph Zobel, it figures prominently in a scene in which young Jose and his friends wreak havoc at a neighbor's hut.*

SERVES 4 TO 6

2 pounds green bananas
½ pound salt codfish, soaked and flaked according to the directions on p. 54
2 tablespoons olive oil
3 scallions, minced
3 cloves garlic, minced
4 branches fresh thyme, stripped
2 tablespoons minced parsley
Salt and freshly ground black pepper, to taste

Peel the bananas and cut each into 3 or 4 pieces. Place the banana pieces in a medium saucepan with the codfish in water to cover, and cook over medium heat for 15 minutes, or until bananas are fork tender. Remove, put through a food mill, and reserve. Place the oil in a saucepan and lightly brown the scallions, garlic, thyme leaves, parsley, and salt and pepper. Add the reserved puree, adjust the seasoning, cover, and cook for an additional 5 minutes. Serve hot with meat or fish.

Plátanos Empanizados

Breaded Plantains

(Costa Rica)

Fried plantains are a way of life in the tropical section of the Creole world. They turn up in as many guises are there are grandmothers. This recipe is a recent addition to the Costa Rican culinary repertoire, as witnessed by the use of relatively modern, American crushed cornflakes as breading.

SERVES 4 TO 6

Vegetable oil, for frying
1 egg, beaten
¾ cup evaporated milk
Salt to taste
4 ripe plantains
1¼ cups cornflakes, crushed

Pour the oil into a heavy skillet, to a depth of 2", and heat to 375 degrees. Beat the egg in a small bowl and add the evaporated milk and salt. Peel the plantains and cut into 1" rounds. Dip the plantain slices into the egg mixture, then roll them in the cornflakes and fry for 3 minutes or until golden brown. Drain on absorbent paper. Serve hot.

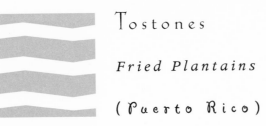

Tostones

Fried Plantains

(Puerto Rico)

Fried plantains are typical of the Caribbean region. They're sort of like the region's French fries, and are eaten with almost all dishes. Tostones *are particularly traditional with dishes like* asopao *(pp. 202–5).* Haiti's *bananes vertes pesées and Colombia's patacon pisao are somewhat similar; they, too, use the frying, smashing, and refrying method. Here, from my friend Patricia Wilson, is Puerto Rico's take.*

SERVES 4

3 green plantains
2 cups vegetable oil, for frying
Salt, for serving

Cut green plantains in 1½ to 2" chunks. Slit the skin and peel. Fry them in at least 2" of oil until tender inside, about 3 to 4 minutes. Remove from fat and smash with the bottom of a plate. When ready to serve, refry the *tostones* until golden. Drain on absorbent paper, sprinkle with salt, and serve immediately.

Fufu

Mashed Plantains

(Belize)

Another of Africa's culinary influences on the hemisphere is the use of pounded plantain known by its West African name, fufu. Fufu *is made by pounding boiled green plantains in a mortar until they become a doughlike mass. The dough is then formed into balls, which are eaten in soups and stews. The word* fufu *comes from the Twi language of Ghana. In Trinidad the dish is called* pound-plantain; *it is also known as* hudut *in parts of Belize. While the West African* fufu, *or* foofoo, *can be prepared from mashed yams or mashed cassava, the New World* fufu *almost always applies to mashed plantains. The Caribs, who can still be found in Dominica, prepare a version of* fufu *called* pong plantain, *which is prepared in the same manner using fire-roasted plantains.*

SERVES 4

4 green plantains
2 tablespoons salted butter

Place the plantains in water to cover, and boil for 25 to 30 minutes. Remove the skin and place the flesh in the bowl of a mortar and pound away. You will have to moisten the pestle from time to time, as plantains are very sticky. The plantains are ready when the paste is smooth and creamy. Remove the plaintains from the mortar and place in a serving bowl, top with butter, and serve. You may also add the butter, then form small meatball-sized balls of the *fufu* with wet hands. Serve these warm with soups or stews.

Exquites

Nahuatl-Style Sweet Corn

(Mexico)

The pre-Hispanic Mexicans had several gods of vegetation. One of the most important ones was the Aztec goddess Chicomecoatl, who was called the goddess of sustenance by the ancient chroniclers. She was also known as the Seven Ears of Corn and was represented with her face and body painted red, and ears of corn in her hands. One of the sixteenth-century descriptions of corn is from Fray Bernardino who writes, "They also used to eat seeds which were like fruit; one kind is called xilotl which means tender, edible cooked cobs; others are called elotl and are also tender cobs which have been prepared and cooked." This dish dates to the pre-Columbian era.

SERVES 4 TO 6

5 cups fresh corn kernels
2½ cups pulque (see Note)
3 slices poblano chiles
1 sprig epazote (see Note)
Salt to taste

Place the corn and the pulque in a small saucepan and cook over medium heat until the liquid has been almost absorbed. Add the chile and epazote and continue to cook until the mixture is almost dry. Season to taste with the salt and serve. Traditionally this dish is served on cornhusks.

Note: If you cannot obtain the milky liquor known as pulque, you may substitute tequila for a different, but still delicious, dish. If you cannot find epazote, you may substitute flat-leaf parsley.

Creole String Beans
(New Orleans)

The word Creole *has been applied to many dishes that use tomatoes and onions, from Creole rice to the ubiquitous Shrimp Creole, in a way that has made the word a culinary cliché. Here, though, the recipe for these Creole string beans actually has a New Orleans origin. In the 1960s version of the classic recipe, the beans are cooked with a piece of salt meat for a lengthy period, then combined with ketchup and chile sauce. This updated version shortens the cooking time, but keeps much of the flavor.*

SERVES 6 TO 8

1 pound fresh string beans
3 strips slab bacon, cut into 1" pieces
1 tablespoon olive oil
2 large onions, chopped
3 large tomatoes, peeled, seeded, and coarsely chopped
Dash Tabasco, or to taste
White rice, for serving

Prepare the string beans by cutting off the stem end and cutting into 2" pieces. Blanch the string beans in boiling water, then shock them by placing them in a bowl of iced water to stop the cooking process. Fry the bacon pieces in a large skillet until they are crisp. Add the olive oil to the rendered bacon fat. Add the onion and cook for about 5 minutes or until golden. Add the tomatoes and Tabasco, and cook for an additional 5 minutes. Finally, add the string beans and cook for 2 to 5 minutes. (They should still have a bit of crunch to them.) Serve hot with white rice.

Maquechou

(New Orleans)

No one is really sure of the origin of this dish, traditional to southern Louisiana. Some feel that it is Spanish in origin and that the name originated with the Spanish machica, composed of toasted cornmeal and sweetened with sugar and spices. Others think that it came from the French maigrichon, which means a thin child, as the dish was originally soupier and thinner. Others think it is related to a dish originally made with cabbage, and that it means maque choux, or false cabbage. Take your pick, but this dish of corn and pimentos has become a Creole classic.

SERVES 4 TO 6

4 cups fresh corn kernels
2 tablespoons butter
1 pint light cream
2 tablespoons minced pimientos
2 large onions, minced
Dash Tabasco, or to taste
Salt and freshly ground black pepper, to taste

Sauté the corn in the butter for 2 to 3 minutes or until tender. Add the onions and cook for 5 minutes, stirring occasionally. Heat the cream in a small saucepan and gradually add it to the corn and onion mixture, stirring occasionally. Cover, lower the heat, and simmer for 10 minutes. Add the pimento pieces, Tabasco, salt, and pepper. Cook for an additional 2 to 3 minutes. Adjust seasoning, and serve hot.

Guiso de Maíz

Corn Stew

(Costa Rica)

Corn was one of the staple dishes throughout the Creole world. It was considered sacred by many of the Indian peoples, and turns up in virtually every part of a meal, from appetizers to desserts to beverages.

SERVES 6

2 cups fresh corn kernels
1 cup diced *chayote*
½ cup milk
¼ cup chicken stock
2 tablespoons minced cilantro
1 tablespoon sugar, or to taste
1 tablespoon salted butter
Salt and freshly ground black pepper, to taste

Place all the ingredients in a saucepan over medium heat and cook, uncovered, stirring occasionally, for about 7 minutes, until the vegetables are tender. Serve hot.

Creole Okra

(New Orleans)

Okra is one of the hallmarks of the food of the Creole world. It turns up in everything from the gumbos of New Orleans to the soups of the Caribbean to the caruru of Brazil. This dish is one of the ways that it is used in southern Louisiana. It makes use of that area's culinary holy trinity: celery, bell pepper, and tomato.

SERVES 6 TO 8

3 large onions, chopped
1 tablespoon olive oil
1 stalk celery, minced
½ cup minced red bell pepper
1 tablespoon tomato paste
3 large tomatoes, peeled, seeded, and coarsely chopped
Dash Tabasco, or to taste
1 pound fresh okra, topped and tailed
White rice, for serving

Sauté the onions in the olive oil until they are translucent. Add the celery, bell pepper, and tomato paste and cook for 5 minutes. Add the tomatoes and Tabasco and cook until you have a thick sauce. You may have to add up to 3 tablespoons of additional water at this point. Finally, add the okra and cook for 10 minutes. Adjust the seasonings. Serve hot with white rice.

Okra, Corn, and Tomatoes

(United States)

This dish is a standby on many tables of the American South. Its ingredients are emblematic of the fusion that has occurred naturally there. One of the attractions of the dish is that it can be prepared all year. In the summer, it benefits from the freshest of ingredients, while in the winter it loses little in being prepared from vegetables that have been put up. I add a bit of habanero chile to give it a bit of heat, but that is strictly optional.

SERVES 6 TO 8

6 large, ripe tomatoes, peeled, seeded, and coarsely chopped
2 cups fresh corn kernels
1 pound fresh okra, topped, tailed, and cut into ½" rounds
1 habanero chile, pricked, optional

Place all of the ingredients in a medium saucepan. Add 1½ cups of water. Bring to a boil, then lower the heat, cover, and cook for 20 minutes, until well mixed and cooked through. Remove the chile when the dish has the desired spiciness. Serve hot.

Okra

(United States)

With the possible exceptions of rice and sesame, no food from Africa has been as widely embraced as okra, which was one of the first African plants to be adapted and adopted on this continent. While today we think of the vegetable as purely southern, if not relegated to African Americans alone, in the mid-1800s it was widely used. An okra recipe appears in the 1828 The Virginia Housewife *under the simple title "Gumbs, a West India Dish," and cookbook author Eliza Leslie published several mid-nineteenth century okra dishes, one of which I've adapted here.*

SERVES 4 TO 6

3 pounds okra, minced
3 pounds ripe tomatoes, peeled, seeded, and coarsely chopped
1 large onion, minced
2 tablespoons unsalted butter
Salt and freshly ground black pepper, to taste
5 cups cooked white rice, for serving

Combine all the ingredients, except the rice, in a large saucepan and simmer, covered, for 1 hour. Ms. Leslie suggests serving over toast points, but I find that rice is better, and probably more indicative of the way the dish would have been eaten in the slave cabins in the Carolina rice-growing areas.

Quiabo

Blanched Okra

(Brazil)

Wherever okra is seen, Africa has touched that region. The tiny green pods are indigenous to Africa, and came to the New World, both north and south, to feed the slaves. In Africa, okra is prized for its thickening properties. In much of the New World, though, okra's slipperiness is disliked. This dish, in which the okra is simply blanched, cuts down on the slime and can only be prepared when the okra pods are small and tender. The trick to remember with okra is the more you cut it, the slimier it gets. Here, a squeeze of lemon juice is added at the last minute of cooking to cut the pod's mucilaginous properties.

SERVES 4

1 pound small unblemished okra pods, topped and tailed
2 teaspoons freshly squeezed lemon juice
Salted butter, for serving

Place 2 cups water in a large saucepan and bring to a boil over medium heat. Plunge the okra into the water and allow it to cook for 3 to 5 minutes. Add the lemon juice at the last minute. Remove the okra, drain, and serve hot with a pat of butter.

Panned Lettuce

(New Orleans)

Lettuce, although usually thought of only in salads in most of North America, is braised in the French style in New Orleans and called panned lettuce.

SERVES 4

2 heads Boston lettuce
2 tablespoons salted butter
¼ cup boiling chicken stock
2 hard-boiled eggs, for garnish

Wash the lettuce, remove the core, and break the leaves into pieces. Melt the butter in a small saucepan, add the lettuce, and cook for 2 minutes until a bit browned on the bottom. Add the chicken broth and continue to cook until the lettuce has wilted and the broth is almost absorbed. Serve hot, garnished with slices of hard-boiled egg.

Aubergines Farcies

Stuffed Eggplant

(New Orleans)

While it seems, at times, that the Creole world was not one that favored vegetables as any-thing more than occasional accompaniments or ways to add brilliance to a plate, in New Orleans, Creole cooks delighted in a wide range of vegetables using their northern advan-tage. Eggplant is deep fried and served as appetizers in esteemed Creole eateries like Gala-toire's and Antoine's, and turns up in menus elsewhere, stuffed with everything from crabmeat and shrimp to savory bread mixtures. This version is a vegetarian adaptation of the classic dish.

SERVES 6

3 large eggplant
½ loaf day-old French bread
1 large tomato, peeled, seeded, and coarsely chopped
1 small onion, minced
1 clove garlic, minced
1 sprig fresh thyme, stripped and leaves minced
2 sprigs flat-leaf parsley, minced
4 tablespoons butter
½ cup breadcrumbs

Wash the eggplant, cut in half lengthwise, and place in a saucepan with water to cover. Cook for ½ hour over medium heat or until tender. Drain and cool. When cooled, remove the seeds and discard. Remove the meat, leaving a thin shell of skin; set aside. Mince the eggplant and reserve. Crumble the bread into a separate bowl. Soak with water, squeezing until you have about a cup of moist bread. Place the onion in a frying pan with 2 tablespoons of butter and cook over medium heat until lightly browned. Add the tomato and its liquid and cook for 5 minutes. Add the garlic, herbs, reserved minced eggplant, and bread and cook for 5 minutes. Adjust the seasoning and remove from heat. Preheat the oven to 350 degrees. Fill the eggplant shells with the bread mixture, top with breadcrumbs, and dot with the remaining 2 tablespoons of butter. Place the shells on a shallow baking dish and bake for 20 minutes, or until the tops are nicely browned. Remove and serve hot.

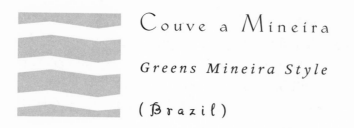

Couve a Mineira

Greens Mineira Style

(Brazil)

This side dish traditionally accompanies feijoada, *Brazil's national dish, as well as dishes from the northeastern Brazilian region of Minas Gerais. However, for people who are looking for a new way with green vegetables, it becomes a vegetable dish. Traditionally prepared with young kale, this can also be prepared with broccoli rabe or green cabbage. My favorite way, though, is with collard greens, which become wonderfully green and cook rapidly.*

SERVES 4 TO 6

2 pounds fresh young kale or collard greens
3 tablespoons pure olive oil
1 medium onion, minced
2 cloves garlic, minced
Hot Sauce (p. 149) or *Molho Brasileiro* (p. 143), for serving

Wash the kale thoroughly, and bunch together. Take each bunch, roll it tightly, and cut it crosswise into thin strips. Wash the strips and drain them thoroughly. Heat the oil in a large, heavy skillet over medium heat and cook the onion and garlic, stirring them until they are lightly browned. Add the kale strips and cook, stirring, for 5 minutes. The greens should be soft, but retain their bright green color. Serve hot, with the hot sauce of your choice.

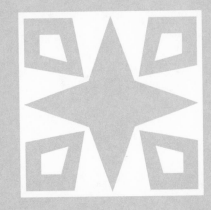

Main Dishes

Roast Leg of Pork (Puerto Rico)

Roast Pork with Passion Fruit Sauce (Dominican Republic)

Chile-Rubbed Ribs (United States)

Pork Souse (Barbados)

Guyanese Pepperpot (Guyana)

Anticuchos de Corazon — Beef Heart Brochettes (Peru)

Caldo Santo — Fish Poached in Coconut Milk (Puerto Rico)

Escovitched Fish (Jamaica)

Redfish *Courtbouillon* (New Orleans)

Courtbouillon de Poisson (Martinique)

Rundown (Jamaica)

Rundown — Stewed Conch (Colombia)

Bagre Frito — Fried Catfish Steaks (Colombia)

Aunt Sweet's Seafood Gumbo (New Orleans)

Sopa de Guingambo — Okra Soup (Puerto Rico)

San Antonio Gumbo (United States)

Grammy's Okra Gumbo (New Orleans)

Julie Tronchet Masson's Okra Gumbo (New Orleans)

Gerri Elie's Creole Filé Gumbo (New Orleans)

Four-Generation Filé Gumbo (New Orleans)

Asturia's *Guingambo* with *Mofongo* (Puerto Rico)

MAKIN' GROCERIES
New York, New Orleans, and the World, 2002

I FIRST FELL IN LOVE with markets in Paris, where every Sunday morning my French "father" and I would head off to the *Marché de Neuilly* to *faire le marché*. He'd gather up dew-dapped bunches of leeks and sniff Cavaillon melons, while I'd gaze in wonder at the artfully arranged abundance that changed with the seasons. I honed my market love wandering ankle deep in pig swill; in open air markets from Guadeloupe to Abidjan to Old Delhi, talking to the vendors, challenging my cast iron stomach, and learning to poke, pick, and bargain with the best of them. Returning to the United States, I missed the everyday ordinariness of the open-air markets. New York's farmer's markets are somehow too Birkenstock precious, and the supermarkets in my Brooklyn neighborhood are filled with double-wide women in stretch pants buying steaks, industrial quantities of potato chips, and grape soda. I contented myself with the city's fancy-food emporia designed for the gastronomically sensitive where each precious plum is swaddled like the baby Jesus.

I rediscovered my fascination in the supermarkets of the South. My first inkling came when a brief stop at an Atlanta Publix transformed me into an aficionada. No provincial purveyors these; not only were there the grits and souse meat, pickled okra and pork rinds, Alaga syrup, and Octagon soap that had punctuated my up-North–down-home childhood, mangoes and jalapeños, coconuts and jerk sauce also lined the bins and shelves in silent witness to a new cultural diversity. Items were available in one shop it would take hours of criss-crossing New York's ethnic neighborhoods to locate. I was hooked.

Subsequent visits and a second home in New Orleans have transformed me into a supermarket sociologist. I've learned that Morton's is to the South what Diamond Crystal is to the North, Hellman's is the *ne plus ultra* of mayonnaise, fifty-pound bags of rice are the norm for the Low Country, grits come without a Quaker on the package, and there are too many types of corn meal to count. I've discovered raw peanuts, Creole tomatoes, and a ginger ale that comes in three strengths.

Each chain has its own personality as well. In Houston, aisles are flagged by country and I can pick up basmati rice and mint chutney mix in one, Pickapeppa and cassava meal in the next, and lo-

Going to sell the pig, Jamaica.

cate British brown sugar cubes for tea in a third, all
in the same trip. Charleston's Harris Teeter amazes
and amuses with its tubs of pimento cheese and
benne wafers at a fraction of their souvenir shop
tab a few blocks away; I fill my cart and my larder.
My friend Ellen Sweet says that she makes her living transporting food across state lines and I certainly try to emulate her, totin' boxes and cartons

and brown paper shopping bags on and off planes. The French *faire le marché* that got me started in my love of markets translates into creolized English as makin' groceries in New Orleans, where I am fortunate enough to spend time. There, Dorignac's has turduckens at Thanksgiving, Foodie's has picked up some of the slack from the late lamented Spice Inc., and Whole Foods reveals its West Coast origins with more than a hint of California's organic ethos and the fresh produce is just dandy, when I can't find it in season at the farmer's market in the Warehouse District. I've even discovered friends who will ferry me across the river for fresh Creole tomatoes or satsumas in season. As I wander the South, I remind folks that I brake for markets. Winn Dixie still feels a bit politically charged to me as a transplanted Black Yankee, but just saying Piggly Wiggly makes me smile.

Pasteles

(Puerto Rico)

Pasteles are the food of celebration. They are typically served for Christmas and Three Kings Day (January 6), but they now show at Thanksgiving and special parties. Making pasteles *was traditionally a community affair. Several people grated the root vegetables or* viandas, *others made the filling, and, finally, all sat around a table and wrapped them into bundles made of plantain leaves and a special* pastele *paper (available from Goya Foods). This recipe came from my friend Patricia Wilson, a Puerto Rican culinary whiz.*

MAKES ABOUT 60 PASTELES

6 pounds pork (or chicken), chopped in small pieces and fat removed

2 tablespoons Annato Oil (p. 135)

1 large onion, diced

¼ cup *Sofrito* (p. 130)

¼ cup capers

¼ cup sliced pitted olives

⅓ cup raisins plumped in rum

1 cup tomato sauce

1 cup cooked garbanzo beans (optional)

12 pounds green bananas

3 or 4 *yautias* (*malanga*)

2 green plantains

1 wedge calabaza (Caribbean pumpkin) (about 1 pound)

1 can unsweetened coconut milk (or 1¼ cup chicken or meat broth)

Salt, to taste

continued on next page

Pasteles (*cont.*)

4 or 5 large banana leaves (*see* Note)
1 package pastele paper or parchment paper (*see* Note)

Brown the pork in annatto oil. Add onion and cook until wilted. Add sofrito, and mix to coat. Add capers, olives, raisins, tomato sauce, and garbanzo beans. Remove from heat and let cool.

Grate the bananas, yautias, plantains, and calabaza, and mix well. Add salt, coconut milk (or broth), and annatto oil to color. Place a piece of softened banana leaf over the pastele paper. Brush with annatto oil. Place ¼ cup of the grated vegetable mixture on the leaf and 3 tablespoons of the meat mixture in the middle. Fold and tie into a packet. Boil in salted water for 30 to 40 minutes, or until the pasteles float.

(Pasteles can be frozen. That's how Puerto Ricans transport them to New York, Philadelphia, and Chicago, among other places. If frozen, boil for one hour, then serve.)

Note: Goya sells the banana leaves and the pasteles paper and they are available in Latin America markets.

Arroz con Pollo

Chicken and Rice

(Puerto Rico)

This recipe, another dish from Patricia Wilson, is simply a Puerto Rican classic.

SERVES 4 TO 6

2½ to 3 pound frying chicken, cut into serving pieces
Salt and pepper, to taste
2 tablespoons Annatto Oil (p. 135)
4 links *longaniza* (Puerto Rican pork sausage), sliced
4 ounces slab bacon, diced
1 onion, diced
1 red pepper, diced
2 tablespoons Green Sofrito (p. 131)
2 tablespoons capers
2 cups long-grain rice
4½ cups chicken broth or water

Wash the chicken, pat it dry, and season it with salt and pepper. Heat annatto oil. Brown the chicken pieces in the oil. When the chicken is golden, remove and set aside. Brown the *longaniza* and bacon. Drain off the fat, leaving approximately 3 tablespoons. Add the onion and cook until wilted. Add the red pepper and the sofrito, and stir well. Add rice and stir to coat. Add chicken, broth or water, and salt to taste. Bring to a boil. Lower heat to simmer. Cover and cook for 20 minutes. Adjust seasonings. Serve hot.

Asopao de Pollo

Chicken and Rice Stew

(Puerto Rico)

Several years ago, I wrote an article on asopao, *Puerto Rico's soupy version of Spain's paella. My buddy Patricia and I headed off to explore. We began at* La Mallorquina, *the pink restaurant in Viejo San Juan where businessmen, grandmothers, and those who enjoy good Puerto Rican lunch have been consuming vats of the stuff under the ceiling fans for more than a century. We visited with Alfredo Ayala, the dean of Nueva Cocina Puertoriquena, listened to his tales of the old-fashioned three-can* asopao—*a can of pimento, a can of asparagus, and a can of peas. We tasted his divine version that used the freshest ingredients, garnished with roasted red peppers and slender stalks of asparagus. Finally, one day, at a friend's house deep in El Yunque, Patricia pulled out all of the stops at lunch and made her own classic version. This is it.*

SERVES 4 TO 6

1 chicken, cut into 10 pieces, skin removed from breast and thighs
2 tablespoons Annatto Oil (p. 135)
1 onion, diced
4 tablespoons Green Sofrito (p. 131)
2 tomatoes, peeled, seeded, chopped
1½ cups long grain rice
6 cups chicken stock
2 tablespoons capers
2 tablespoons salt
Black pepper, to taste
1 teaspoon dry oregano leaves
1 cup frozen peas

Tostones (p. 179), **for serving**
Hot Sauce (p. 149), **for serving**

In a heavy saucepan, brown the chicken pieces in the Annatto Oil. Set aside. Add the onion and cook until wilted. Add the green sofrito and the tomatoes. Cook over low-to-medium heat until the vegetables are soft. Add the rice, the chicken stock, the capers, the chicken pieces, salt, and oregano. Simmer for 35 to 45 minutes, or until the chicken is just cooked through. About 10 minutes before the *asopao* is done, add the peas. Taste for salt and pepper. Serve hot, with *Tostones,* and pass the Hot Sauce.

Note: To peel tomatoes, cut an "x" on one end and place in boiling water for 30 seconds. Remove with a slotted spoon, place in ice water, then peel and cut in half. Squeeze out the seeds and chop or mince.

Asopao de Pollo II

Chicken and Rice Stew

(Puerto Rico)

This is a more elaborate version of the asopao; *it's great for fancier entertaining.*

SERVES 6 TO 8

1 teaspoon dried oregano
1 garlic clove, minced
Salt to taste
3 to 4 pounds chicken, cut into serving pieces
2 thick slices slab bacon
2 medium tomatoes, peeled, seeded, and minced
1 medium onion, minced
1 medium bell pepper, seeded and minced
1 tablespoon drained capers
¼ cup diced pimento-stuffed olives
2 cups medium-grain rice
1 cup fresh peas
4 pimentos, thinly sliced, for garnish
½ cup freshly grated Parmesan cheese, for garnish

Combine the oregano, garlic, and salt in a small bowl and rub on the chicken. Cook the bacon in a heavy casserole until it has rendered its fat; crumble and reserve. Brown the chicken in the bacon fat, a few pieces at a time, over medium heat. Return all the chicken to the pan. Add the bacon, tomatoes, onion, and green bell pepper. Cover and simmer over low heat for 25 minutes, or until the chicken is cooked through. Let cool.

Remove the chicken meat from the bones and return to the pan. Add 6½ cups of water, capers, and olives and simmer for 5 minutes. Add the rice and simmer for an additional 15 minutes, or until the rice is tender. Add the peas during the final 5 minutes of cooking. When done, adjust the seasonings, and serve at once in soup bowls garnished with strips of pimento and the Parmesan.

Colombo de Poulet

Chicken Curry

(Guadeloupe)

Martinique and Guadeloupe surprise visitors with their French tone, as well as with their diversity of ethnic groups. Few can imagine why there is so much curry for sale in the open market that is one of the photographers' favorite morning stops in Pointe-à Pitre, *until they drive down a road in the south of* Basse Terre *between* Capesterre *and* Sainte-Marie. *They'll come across a place called* Changy, *which is the location of a Hindu temple devoted to the veneration of the deity known as* Maliemin, *complete with traditional statues of the gods made by a Tamil sculptor who came over from India. The curry that turns up on the tables of Guadeloupe and Martinique comes with good reason. Following the emancipation of the enslaved Africans in 1848, indentured workers from India were brought over to work the cane fields. They left their culinary mark with dishes like* Colombo, *which takes its name from the name of the former capital of Sri Lanka.*

SERVES 4 TO 6

1½ teaspoons coriander seeds
1½ teaspoons allspice berries
2 teaspoons cumin seeds
1 teaspoon black peppercorns
¼ teaspoon turmeric
2 tablespoons freshly squeezed lime juice
Salt and freshly ground black pepper, to taste
2½- to 3-pound frying chicken, cut into serving pieces
2 tablespoons unsalted butter
2 tablespoons olive oil
1 onion, coarsely chopped
2 scallions, including the green part

1 shallot, minced
1 garlic clove, minced
2 tablespoons flat-leaf parsley, minced
2 fresh thyme sprigs, stripped
2 medium tomatoes, peeled, seeded and coarsely chopped
1 medium chayote, peeled and cut into 1" chunks
1 small eggplant, peeled and cut into 1" chunks
2 medium potatoes, peeled, and cut into large dice
1 Scotch bonnet chile, pricked with a fork
White rice, for serving

Prepare the curry powder by toasting the coriander, allspice, cumin, and pepper-corns in a heavy skillet over high heat, until fragrant. Transfer to a plate to cool. Pulverize in a spice grinder, then stir in the turmeric.

Lime wash the chicken by placing it in a large bowl with 2 tablespoons of the lime juice and salt and pepper. Cover and let stand for 15 minutes. Heat the butter and oil in a cast-iron casserole, add the chicken, and cook over moderate heat until the chicken is browned. Add the onion, scallion, shallot, reserved spice mixture, garlic, parsley, and thyme leaves, and continue to cook for about 8 minutes. Add the remaining tablespoon of lime juice and 2 cups water, to barely cover the chicken. Lower the heat and simmer for about 30 minutes. Add the tomatoes, chayote, eggplant, potatoes, and chile, and cook for an additional 30 minutes. Remove the chicken and place on a serving plate, remove the chile, and boil the *colombo* over moderately high heat for about 4 minutes, until the liquid is slightly reduced. Return the chicken to the casserole, adjust the seasoning, and serve hot with white rice.

Baxter's Road Fried Chicken

(Barbados)

During my tenure at Almond Resorts in Barbados, I was in charge of two restaurants devoted to Barbadian food, one called Enid's. One menu favorite was always available: chicken fried in the Barbadian (Bajan) style. It takes its name from the women that used to appear at Baxter's Road in Bridgetown in the evening, frying chicken and fish, and selling it to those looking for substantial fare after an evening out. The fragrant chicken and the delicious surprise of Bajan seasoning is one of my first memories of Bajan cooking. Made fragrant with the luscious verdant condiment known as Bajan Seasoning, it is simply scrumptious. Traditionally served hot, it is also good at room temperature. Baxter's Road got a bit too seedy in the late nineties, and now the ladies oversee the pots at Oistin's, but the taste of crunchy fried chicken seasoned just right will always mean Baxter's Road to me.

SERVES 4 TO 6

3-pound frying chicken, cut into pieces
2 tablespoons freshly squeezed lime juice
Salt to taste
2 cups vegetable oil, for frying
¼ cup or more of Bajan Seasoning (p. 132)
½ cup all-purpose flour
2 teaspoons Bell's Poultry Seasoning
Salt and freshly ground black pepper, to taste

Wash the chicken with the lime juice and salt, and pat dry. Heat the oil to 375 degrees in a cast-iron skillet. With a sharp knife, score the chicken pieces and fill each slash with the Bajan seasoning, pushing it well into the chicken. Mix the remaining ingredients in a paper bag. Add the chicken pieces and shake until well coated. Put the chicken pieces in the hot oil and cook, turning, until golden brown and cooked through, 35 to 40 minutes. Remove the chicken and drain. Serve hot.

Aji de Gallina

Quechua-style Chicken Stew

(Peru)

A type of chicken existed in Peru in pre-Columbian days called hualpa *in Quechua. The last of the ruling Inca emperors was named for the chicken, Atahualpa. In Incan times, the bird was cooked with* aji *chiles in a rich stew. The dish has survived, and is one of Peru's most popular examples of the fusion of Spanish and Quechua ingredients. Some would argue that the use of ground nuts is a Spanish addition, but they probably forget that Spain was colonized by the Moors for over 700 years. Looking at the cooking of northeastern Brazil, it is possible that the use of the groundnuts as a thickener in the sauce may indicate an African presence in the pot as well.*

SERVES 8 TO 10

Two whole 2½ to 3 pound frying chickens
1 bouquet garni (1 bayleaf, 3 sprigs thyme, and 4 sprigs parsley wrapped in
   cheesecloth)
1 small onion, cut into quarters
1 carrot, cut into large pieces
1 stalk celery, cut into large pieces
9 slices white bread, crusts removed
½ cup milk
½ cup vegetable oil
1½ cups minced red onion
2 cloves garlic, minced
1 cup *aji amarillo* paste (p. 20)
2 tablespoons *aji mirasol* paste (p. 20)
1 teaspoon oregano
Pinch cumin

Pinch cilantro
1 cup freshly grated Parmesan cheese
½ cup walnuts, shelled and pulverized
1½ cups evaporated milk
Rice, for serving
4 to 5 small boiled new potatoes, for garnish
4 to 5 sliced hard-boiled eggs, for garnish
½ cup pitted black olives, for garnish
½ cup chopped walnuts, for garnish

Place the chickens, bouquet garni, onion, carrots, and celery in a large stockpot and bring to a boil. Lower the heat and simmer for 30 minutes, or until the chicken is cooked. Remove from the heat; let cool, and set aside. Strain off the cooking liquid and reserve ½ cup. Discard the rest of the vegetables and the cooking liquid. Strip the chicken meat from the bones. Discard the bones and the skin.

Soak the bread in a mixture of milk and ¼ cup of the chicken's cooking liquid until it can be mashed into a thick paste. Meanwhile, heat the oil in a heavy saucepan and sauté the red onion and garlic for about 3 minutes. Add the seasonings and continue to cook for an additional 10 minutes. Add the bread mixture to the saucepan and cook for 2 minutes. Add the chicken, Parmesan, and nuts. Add more chicken stock if the mixture is too thick. Continue to cook for about 2 minutes, stirring frequently. Add the evaporated milk and cook on low heat, making sure that the mixture does not come to a boil. Serve hot over rice garnished with potatoes, hard-boiled egg halves, pitted black olives, and a sprinkle of chopped walnuts.

Pecan-Crusted Fried Chicken

(United States)

Every once and a while, I like to see what's in the larder and play around with foods that I like. My mother adored nuts in her food; I find them intrusive. This is a dish she never got to taste, but I suspect she'd have liked it.

SERVES 4 TO 6

2½ to 3 pound frying chicken, cut into pieces
Vegetable oil, for frying
½ cup flour
¼ cup white cornmeal
½ cup pulverized pecans
1½ tablespoons Bell's Poultry Seasoning
Salt and freshly ground black pepper, to taste

Wash the chicken thoroughly and pat dry with paper towels. Heat the oil to 375 degrees in a cast-iron skillet. Place the remaining ingredients in a brown paper bag and shake to mix well. Add the chicken pieces to the mixture, a few at a time, and shake to ensure that each piece is well coated.

Place the chicken pieces in the skillet and fry, uncovered, for 20 minutes, turning once, or until the chicken is golden brown and the juices run clear when the chicken is pricked with a fork. Remove and drain on paper towels. Serve warm. (Traditionally, chicken is drained on brown paper bag.)

Note: The pecans can be pulverized by placing them in a coffee grinder or food mill and processing briefly—too long and you will have pecan butter.

Chicken-and-Andouille Etouffée

(New Orleans)

My friend Ken Smith is the executive chef at Upperline restaurant at the Garden District of New Orleans. There he reigns supreme in the kitchen, turning out inspired variations of classic Creole dishes while, in the front of the restaurant, owner Joann Clevenger creates a salon that sparkles with the wit and magic for which the Crescent City is known. Upperline is off the tourist track and an insider's secret, but it's one of the must stops for me on any visit to my second home. One of the menu items that I always request is a helping of the sublime duck-and-andouille etouffée *that is one of the signatures of the restaurant. This chicken version is a variant of that dish.*

SERVES 4 TO 6

1 cup oil
1 cup flour
1 cup chopped celery
2 cups chopped onions
½ cup chopped green peppers
½ pound andouille sausage, cut into ½" rounds
5 cups chicken stock
Salt, freshly ground black pepper, white pepper, dried thyme, and minced
    garlic, to taste
3 cups cooked chicken, cut into pieces

Prepare a roux by combining the flour and oil in a cast-iron 10" skillet. Heat over low-to-medium heat and cook, stirring constantly, until it is a dark rich chocolate brown. Add the celery, onions, and bell pepper. Cook in roux for 5 minutes. Add the

continued on next page

Catching terrapin, Savannah, Georgia.

Chicken-and-Andouille *Etouffée* (*cont.*)

andouille and cook for 3 minutes. Add the chicken stock and season to taste with the salt, black pepper, white pepper, thyme, and minced garlic. Continue to cook, stirring occasionally, for 45 minutes or until the etouffée becomes a thick, rich gravy. You may need to add more stock or water. Just before serving, add the chicken. Serve hot over white rice.

Curried Lamb

(Trinidad)

The curries of the Creole world are varied; everything shows up in the pot, from shrimp and Trinidad's cascadura, *or trunkfish; to Jamaica's curried goat and the black-bellied lamb of Barbados (a local cross between the African hair sheep and the European wool sheep). This version is one of Trinidad's most popular.*

SERVES 4 TO 6

Juice of 1 lime
1 lime, cut into quarters
1 tablespoon coarse salt
3 pounds lamb roast, cut into 1" cubes
½ cup Bajan seasoning
4 tablespoons Madras curry powder
3 tablespoons vegetable oil
1 tablespoon garam masala
1 teaspoon grated fresh ginger
1 teaspoon minced garlic
3 medium onions, thinly sliced
3 medium potatoes, peeled and cut into 1" dice
3 large tomatoes, peeled, seeded, and coarsely chopped
2 cups vegetable stock
Salt and freshly ground black pepper, to taste
White rice, for serving

Lime and salt the lamb by placing it and 2 cups water into a large, nonreactive bowl, adding the lime juice, pieces of lime, and salt. Cover and allow to sit for 30

continued on next page

minutes. Remove the lamb pieces, pat dry, and season with the Bajan seasoning and 2 tablespoons curry powder. Heat the oil in a medium saucepan, add the remaining curry powder and garam masala and cook for 2 minutes, stirring occasionally. Add the ginger and the garlic and cook for an additional 2 minutes, stirring well. Brown the seasoned lamb in the spices. Add the onions and potatoes, stirring well to make sure that they are coated with the curry mixture. Add the tomatoes, salt and pepper, and stock, and bring to a boil over medium heat. Reduce the heat, cover, and cook for 1 hour. When ready to serve, adjust the seasonings and serve hot over white rice.

Piñon

(Puerto Rico)

This Puerto Rican way with ground beef is somewhat similar to the Curaçaoan dish keshy yena, *in that they both combine cheese and ground beef in a baked dish. Some think that they may have originated with the Sephardic Jews, who were some of the first settlers in the region, even though Jewish dietary laws do not allow the mixing of meat and dairy.*

SERVES 6

6 very ripe plantains
Vegetable oil, for frying
1 tablespoon olive oil
1 pound ground round beef
1 onion, diced
2 tablespoons *Sofrito* (p. 130)
½ cup tomato sauce
Salt and freshly ground black pepper, to taste
2 eggs, beaten
1 cup grated mozzarella, Swiss, or Edam cheese

Peel the plantains and slice lengthwise into 4 or 5 strips. Fry in vegetable oil for about 2 minutes on each side or until light gold and cooked through. Drain on absorbent paper. Heat the olive oil, brown the beef, and drain off the excess fat. Add the onion and cook until the onion is wilted about 5 minutes. Add the sofrito and tomato sauce and cook for about 5 minutes.

Line a baking dish with the plantains. Cover with the meat mixture. Pour half the beaten eggs over the meat. Cover with remaining plantains. Pour the remaining egg on top. Sprinkle with the cheese and bake at 350 degrees for 35 to 40 minutes. Serve hot.

Roast Leg of Pork

(Puerto Rico)

My friend Patricia Wilson, from whom I begged all my Puerto Rican recipes, is a wonder woman when it comes to the foods of her adopted Puerto Rico. Born in Canada, she was raised in Arecibo, Puerto Rico, and the island has been a part of her heart ever since. For many years, she was the chef-owner of the renowned Bistro Gambaro *in Old San Juan. Today, she is a chef-instructor at Johnson & Wales in Miami, where she's teaching a new generation of chefs about the tastes of the rich port that is her culinary home.*

SERVES 8 TO 10

1 head garlic
2 tablespoons cumin powder
2 tablespoons dried oregano
2 tablespoons salt
1 tablespoon freshly ground black pepper
⅓ cup Annatto Oil (p. 135)
¼ cup bitter orange or lime juice
7½ pound fresh bone-in ham, with skin

Place the garlic, cumin, oregano, salt, pepper, oil, and juice in a food processor and purée. Make incisions in the pork skin and fill with the spice mixture. Rub the entire pork leg with the seasoning mixture, cover, and marinate for 24 to 48 hours. Preheat the oven to 325 degrees. Roast for approximately 6 hours. The skin should be crisp, and the internal temperature reads 175 degrees.

Roast Pork with Passion Fruit Sauce

(Dominican Republic)

This is a recipe I came up with one day while playing around with several of my favorite tastes. It's not traditional, but it's too good to leave out.

SERVES 8 TO 10

5 pounds pork shoulder, with skin
1 cup Goya *mojo criollo*
1¼ cup Goya pineapple–passion fruit nectar
2 tablespoons poultry seasoning
2 teaspoons salt
Freshly ground black pepper, to taste
2 teaspoons minced garlic, or to taste
½ teaspoon cumin powder
2 tablespoons olive oil
1 cup passion fruit preserves
½ teaspoon minced jalapeño pepper, or to taste

Score the skin of the pork shoulder in a criss-cross pattern. Mix the *mojo criollo* and 1 cup nectar, and rub into the meat. Cover and refrigerate for 1 hour. Preheat the oven to 450 degrees. Mix the poultry seasoning with the salt, pepper, garlic, and cumin. Remove the meat from the marinade, lightly pat dry, and rub olive oil over meat and cover it with the seasoning mix. Roast for 30 minutes. Lower oven to 350 degrees and continue to cook for 4½ hours, or until a meat thermometer reads 175 degrees. Place the passion fruit preserves, ¼ cup remaining pina, parcha nectar, and jalapeño in a small saucepan and simmer over low heat, stirring occasionally. Serve meat with sauce on the side.

Note: Goya products are readily available at supermarkets.

Chile-Rubbed Ribs

(United States)

I usually leave all things related to barbecue to my friend Lolis Eric Elie, whose book, Smokestack Lightning, is a 'cue lover's tour of the country. A few years back, though, I was asked to do an article about Juneteenth, the Texas African-American emancipation holiday, for B. Smith's magazine, and it would have been impossible not to celebrate the Texas holiday with a form of barbecue. I came up with this nontraditional, but tasty, recipe. (And, yes, I do know that pork is usually not the preferred form of barbecue in Texas!)

SERVES 6 TO 8

6 pounds baby-back pork ribs, in one piece
1½ cups apple-cider vinegar

DRY RUB
¾ cup light-brown sugar
¼ cup salt
¼ cup lemon pepper (I use Lawry's)
1 tablespoon coarsely ground black pepper
1 tablespoon onion powder
1 tablespoon garlic powder
1 teaspoon powdered ancho chile
1 teaspoon chile powder
½ teaspoon cayenne pepper
1 teaspoon cumin powder
Barbecue sauce (recipe follows)

Wash the ribs, trim them, and place in a large stockpot with water to cover, and the vinegar. Parboil for 30 minutes, remove, drain, and pat dry with paper towels. Prepare the dry rub by mixing all the ingredients in a plastic bag. Rub the ribs with the dry rub and place on a preheated barbecue grill. Cook for about 15 minutes on each side, turning once. Serve hot, with barbecue sauce.

Note: These ribs can be prepared indoors or out, but they are better if grilled over an aromatic wood like hickory, pecan, or Texas mesquite.

BARBECUE SAUCE
½ cup beer
1½ cups ketchup
¼ cup apple-cider vinegar
2 tablespoons salted butter
2 tablespoons brown sugar
1 tablespoon chile powder
2 tablespoons Worcestershire sauce
2 tablespoons Busha Browne's Planter's Sauce (available in most
    supermarkets, online, or via mail order)
1 medium onion, minced
1 clove garlic, minced
Salt and freshly ground black pepper, to taste

Place all the ingredients in a medium saucepan, and bring to a boil over medium heat. Lower heat, and simmer for 35 minutes or until thick. Adjust seasonings. Serve warm with the ribs.

LEAH CHASE
New Orleans

"That's My Blood Down There"

I WILL ALWAYS REMEMBER the first time
that I met Leah Chase, almost fifteen years ago. She
was walking out the door of the Hermann Grima
historic house in New Orleans. We were both attending a conference on Creole food ways and I
knew that she would be speaking. I took one look
at her and decided that we had to be family. My
first words to her were, "You look too much like
my relatives for me to feel comfortable calling you
Mrs. Chase, and I could never be so informal as to
call you by your first name. May I call you 'Aunt'
Leah?" She acquiesced with her usual generosity
and "Aunt" Leah she's been ever since.

My "Aunt" Leah is made of stern stuff and will
brook no challenge to her knowledge of Creole
food, not that anyone would ever question her au-
thority. She wields a mighty cleaver in her kitchen
and is the undisputed *doyenne* of the African style
of Creole cooking in the Crescent City. Like some
of my older aunts, she's a terrific tease and one of
her running jokes is to insist that I can't cook. I fi-

nally rose to the bait and the first person invited to dinner when I bought my house in New Orleans was "Aunt" Leah. My meal was simple—roasted chicken and vegetables—but I was gratified and knew I'd done well when I saw "Aunt" Leah heading back for a second helping.

As time has passed, my mother, "Aunt" Leah, and I forged a bond that goes beyond cooking. I was pleased to watch as my mother and "Aunt" Leah formed their own friendship, one that grew out of shared experiences of being black women of a certain age. I basked in their company, listening and taking mental notes as their conversations meandered across subjects ranging from personal to political.

Although I was not born into the culinary traditions of New Orleans, I now know the special piquancy of "Aunt" Leah's *daube glacée;* I find it in the flavors of Guadeloupe. The slow-cooked taste of her okra creole parallels that of my Tennessee grandmother's, albeit with different seasonings. No one, though, can duplicate her wonderful way with grits and *grillades* and the taste of her bread pudding. A bowl of her *gumbo z'herbes* is worth the trip to the Crescent City on Holy Thursday—the one day of the year that she prepares industrial-sized vats of it for folks who call from around the country to reserve their portion. I love the way she loves to entertain, selflessly inviting old and new friends to celebrate the glories of Creole cooking in her art-filled private dining room. I'm tickled that she's always up for a new taste experience, although she'll be quick to judge the results. Most of all, I love her fierce determination to document, celebrate, and maintain the high standards of the Black Creole cooking of New Orleans.

Pork Souse

(Barbados)

Pudding and souse *is a traditional Saturday dish in Barbados. I've tasted many a version of the dish, but my favorite* souse *is the one that is prepared by Letsie, who owns a small bar* cum *restaurant off the Oistin's fishmarket on the southern coast of the island. There, you can pull up a plastic chair, grab a cold Banks beer, and on Saturday, sit and pick your way through a plate of* souse *in no time flat—if you've been lucky enough to get there before it's all gone! Traditionally,* souse *is served with sweet potato pudding but I like it just fine by itself as a nibble. Folks who have given up swine, for whatever reason, find that the dish is almost as good when prepared with chicken.*

SERVES 4 TO 6

2 pounds pig's feet, cut into small pieces
2 pounds pork loin, cut into 1" pieces
1 tablespoon salt
1 large onion, thinly sliced
3 teaspoons minced garlic
1 Scotch bonnet chile, seeded, and minced, or to taste
1 cup freshly squeezed lime juice
2 cucumbers, peeled and thinly sliced
Salt and freshly ground black pepper, to taste

Place the pig's feet into a large saucepan with salt and water to cover. Cook over medium heat for 1 hour. Add the pieces of pork loin and cook for 30 minutes, or until the meat is cooked through and tender. Remove the meat and place it in a non-reactive bowl. Add the onion, garlic, chile, lime juice, 3 cups water, cucumber, and salt and pepper and stir well. Cover with plastic wrap and refrigerate for 12 to 24 hours. Serve at room temperature with sweet potato pudding or crusty bread.

Guyanese Pepperpot

(Guyana)

The pepperpot of the southern Caribbean is different from its northern relative. The pepperpots of Jamaica (p. 98), and even those of Philadelphia (p. 95), are hearty soups served with dumplings of some sort. The pepperpot of the southern Caribbean is a mixed meat stew that harkens back to the Amerindians. One of the hallmarks of the southern Caribbean pepperpot is the use of cassareep, *a cassava-based seasoning. If you can't find it, don't even try to make this recipe.* Cassareep *allows this stew to remain on the back of the stove virtually indefinitely if brought to a boil each day. Additional* cassareep *is added each time more meat is added. For many years, Betty Mascoll in Grenada was reputed to have a pepperpot that was kept in this manner for over a century. When I tasted the centenarian dish, it was a rich, dense stew in which all of the ingredients had coalesced into a tasty darkness.*

SERVES 8 TO 10

2 pounds oxtail, cut into pieces
1 pound salt beef
2 calf's feet, cut into small pieces
2 pounds beef stew meat, cut into 1" cubes
2 pounds pork loin, cut into 1" cubes
Juice of 1 lime
1 tablespoon coarse salt
1 cup *cassareep*
1 cup brown sugar
2 teaspoons minced garlic
1 small onion, thinly sliced
2 Scotch bonnet chiles, pricked

1 2" piece cinnamon
3 whole cloves
White rice, for serving

Lime and salt the oxtail, salt beef, calf's feet, stew meat, and pork loin according to the directions on p. 215. Place the oxtail, calf's feet, and salt meat in a stockpot or large saucepan with water to cover. Add the *cassareep* and bring to a boil. Lower the heat and simmer for 2 hours. Sprinkle the sugar evenly over the bottom of a skillet and allow it to caramelize until it is the color of chocolate fudge. Add the stew meat and pork loin, garlic, and onion, and gently simmer until the meat has browned. Add to the other meat mixture. Add the chiles, cinnamon and cloves, reduce the heat, and cook until the meat is cooked through. When the pepperpot has attained the desired spiciness, remove the pricked chiles. Serve hot with white rice.

Anticuchos de Corazon

Beef Heart Brochettes

(Peru)

With the exception of cebiche, *no appetizer is more Peruvian than these brochettes, grilled over an open fire and served with corn on the cob and slices of boiled sweet potato. It is surprising for many, then, that these typical dishes owe their origin to Peru's enslaved Africans. They were the cooks in the kitchens of the vice royalty, and it is to them that many of the* criollo *dishes of South America's western coast owe their origin.*

SERVES 6 TO 8 AS AN APPETIZER

1 beef heart, cleaned, trimmed, and cut into ½" pieces
1 cup red-wine vinegar
3 cloves garlic, minced
½ teaspoon cumin powder
2 tablespoons *pasta de aji mirasol* (p. 20)
Salt and freshly ground black pepper, to taste
Vegetable oil, if necessary
Boiled corn on the cob cut into 1" pieces and slices of boiled sweet potato,
    for serving

Wash the beef heart, making sure that all of the fat and sinew has been removed. Prepare a marinade from the remaining ingredients, and marinate the heart pieces overnight. When ready to cook, heat a broiler or outdoor grill. Thread the pieces onto presoaked wooden skewers and grill quickly, about 3 minutes per side, over high heat, basting, if necessary, with vegetable oil. Serve hot, with corn and sweet potato.

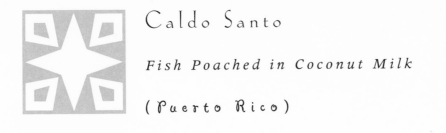

Caldo Santo

Fish Poached in Coconut Milk

(Puerto Rico)

Another winner from Patricia. This recipe is called Holy Broth *because it was tradition- ally served during Holy Week, when strict Roman Catholics did not eat meat. It is said to originate in* Loiza Aldea, *a town on Puerto Rico's north coast noted for its African reten- tions, both cultural and culinary.*

SERVES 4

For the fish broth:
1 pound red snapper bones, tail, and head
1 onion, roughly chopped
3 cloves garlic
2 bay leaves
2 sprigs fresh thyme
4 whole black peppercorns
¾ cup unsweetened coconut milk
4 red snapper fillets
1 ripe tomato, seeded and chopped

Place the fish bones, onion, garlic, bay leaves, thyme, peppercorns, and water to cover in a large saucepan and simmer for 30 minutes. Strain the broth, and reserve 2 cups. Pour the reserved broth and coconut milk in a pan large enough to hold the fish fillets, and bring to a simmer. Add the fish and poach for about 5 to 8 minutes, depending on thickness, or until the fish is firm and cooked through. Add the tomato during the last 2 minutes of cooking. Serve in shallow soup bowls with a lit- tle broth.

Escovitched Fish

(Jamaica)

This dish owes its name and some of its technique to the Spanish occupation of Jamaica. It is also prepared in the Spanish-speaking parts of the Caribbean and called pescado en escabeche. *The* escabeche *is a pickled marinade that harks back to the Moorish occupation of Spain, and can be traced back to Persia. It can be prepared with fish fillets or with whole, small fish.*

SERVES 4 TO 6

2 pounds small red snapper, cleaned, with the heads on
½ cup freshly squeezed lime juice
Salt and freshly ground black pepper, to taste
2 cups flour
2 eggs, beaten
Vegetable oil, for frying
1 cup cane vinegar
1 cup water
3 large onions, thinly sliced
1 teaspoon cracked allspice berries
1 tablespoon sugar
1 small red bell pepper, julienned
½ chayote, julienned
2 carrots, julienned
Minced Scotch bonnet chile, to taste

Wash the fish in the lime juice and pat dry. Mix the salt, pepper, and flour in a small bowl. Heat the oil in a heavy skillet. Dip the fish into the beaten egg, then into the seasoned flour. Fry for 5 minutes, or until crisp and cooked through, turning once. Set the fish aside. Place the vinegar, water, onions, allspice, sugar, and salt into a nonreactive saucepan and bring to a boil over medium heat. Add the bell pepper, chayote, carrots, and chile, lower the heat, and simmer for 8 minutes, or until the vegetables are cooked but crisp. Place the fish on a deep platter, top with the vinegar marinade, and let sit for at least 1 hour. Serve at room temperature.

Redfish Courtbouillon

(New Orleans)

This courtbouillon *is nothing like the French poaching liquid of the same name. Rather, it is a New World kin of the* courtbouillon *of the French Caribbean and creolized fish dishes like Mexico's* huachinango a la Veracruzana. *The addition of wine, red or white, makes for a hearty sauce that is much appreciated by locals, who call it* coor-be-yon.

SERVES 6

1 tablespoon vegetable oil
2 tablespoons flour
1 teaspoon allspice powdered
3 sprigs fresh thyme
3 sprigs flat-leaf Italian parsley
3 sprigs marjoram
1 bay leaf
1 clove garlic, minced
1 large onion, minced
5 large tomatoes, peeled, seeded, and chopped, with their liquid
¼ cup dry red wine
Salt and freshly ground black pepper, to taste
3 pounds red snapper fillets
2 teaspoons lemon juice

Heat the oil in a cast-iron skillet. Prepare a *roux:* by stirring the flour into the oil, stirring constantly until the mixture is caramel in color. When the roux is ready, add the allspice, thyme, parsley, marjoram, bay leaf, garlic, onion, tomatoes, water, and wine, and bring to a boil. Season to taste, and cook over medium heat for 5 minutes. Add the fish fillets, one at a time. Add the lemon juice and cook for 5 to 7 minutes, remove, and serve hot. Some folks serve this with French fries, but I prefer rice.

Courtbouillon de Poisson

(Martinique)

SERVES 4

¼ cup freshly squeezed lime juice
1½ cups dry white wine
2 to 3–pound red snapper, scaled and cleaned with the head on
3 blades chives
5 scallions, including the green tops
2 medium tomatoes
1 medium onion
¼ cup olive oil
¾ cup hot water
Bouquet garni: 1 bay leaf, 3 allspice berries, 2 branches fresh thyme,
    ½ Scotch bonnet chile, wrapped in cheesecloth
White rice, for serving

In a nonreactive bowl, prepare a marinade with all but 1 tablespoon of the lime juice and ¾ cup white wine. Place the fish in the marinade and marinate for 1 to 2 hours. Pulse the chives, scallions, tomatoes, and onion in a food processor until a thick paste forms. Heat the oil in a heavy skillet, add the vegetable mixture and cook for 5 minutes, stirring occasionally. Add the fish and cook for about 10 minutes, until cooked through. Add the boquet garni along with the remaining white wine and lime juice. Cook for 5 more minutes. Serve hot over white rice.

Rundown

(Jamaica)

This dish, called rundown *in Jamaica,* oildown *in Barbados, and* metagee *in Guyana, is a Creole way of cooking fish in coconut milk. In Jamaica, it's traditionally served with roast breadfruit or boiled green bananas.*

SERVES 6

¼ cup freshly squeezed lime juice
2 pounds mackerel fillets (other oily fish, such as bluefish, may be
    substituted)
3 cups coconut milk
1 large onion, minced
1 Scotch bonnet chile, seeded and minced, or to taste
3 garlic cloves, minced
3 large tomatoes, peeled, seeded, and coarsely chopped
1 tablespoon apple-cider vinegar
2 sprigs fresh thyme, stripped
Salt and freshly ground black pepper, to taste
Roast breadfruit, for serving

Place the lime juice in a nonreactive bowl, add the fish, and marinate for 15 minutes. Pour the coconut milk into a heavy skillet and cook over medium heat for 5 minutes, or until it begins to turn oily. Add the onion, chile and, garlic and cook for 5 minutes, or until the onion is translucent. Stir in the tomatoes, vinegar, thyme, salt, and pepper. Add the fish. Cover, lower the heat, and cook for about 10 minutes, or until the fish flakes with a fork. Serve hot with roast breadfruit.

Rundown

Stewed Conch

(Colombia)

In coastal Colombia, the name rundown is given to conch stew. It differs from its Jamaican counterpart in that it is rich with plantains, breadfruit, and root vegetables slowly cooked in coconut milk, along with salted pork and tenderized conch meat.

SERVES 8

2 pounds fresh conch meat
Salt and freshly ground black pepper, to taste
1 pound salt pork, cut into small cubes
7½ cups coconut milk
2 green plantains, peeled and sliced
1 pound yuca, peeled and cut into 1" pieces
1 pound yam, peeled and cut into 1" pieces
½ pound sweet potatoes, peeled and diced
½ pound breadfruit, peeled and cut into 1" pieces
1 tablespoon minced fresh basil
1 tablespoon minced fresh oregano

Tenderize the conch meat by pounding it with a meat mallet. Place in water to cover with salt and pepper and simmer for 10 minutes. Drain and cut into small pieces. In a separate pan, cook the salt pork in water to cover for 20 minutes, to remove the salt. Place the conch and salt pork in a heavy saucepan with the coconut milk and bring to a boil over medium heat. Lower the heat to a simmer and add the plantain, cassava, yam, and sweet potato, and cook for 25 minutes. Add the breadfruit, adjust the seasonings, and cook for an additional 20 minutes. Add the basil and oregano, stirring to mix well, and adjust the seasonings. Serve hot.

Bagre Frito

Fried Catfish Steaks

(Colombia)

To most of us, catfish is a dish emblematic of the American South. I was delighted to find that it is also eaten in coastal Colombia, where it is known as bagre. *There, it is cut into steaks and batter fried in much the same way it is in the South. The difference in texture, though, between the fillets that are eaten in the United States and the thick steaks used in Colombia is amazing.*

SERVES 4

2 pounds catfish steaks, about ¾" thick
2 tablespoons freshly squeezed lemon juice
Salt and freshly ground black pepper, to taste
Vegetable oil, for frying
2 eggs
2 tablespoons flour
1 tablespoon flat-leaf parsley, minced
Lemon wedges, for garnish

Season the catfish steaks with the lemon juice, salt, and pepper and place them in a nonreactive bowl. Marinate for 1 hour in the refrigerator. When ready to cook, heat the oil to 375 degrees in a heavy skillet. Prepare a batter by beating the eggs in a small bowl and adding the flour and parsley. Dip the fish steaks in the batter, coating lightly. Fry for about 3 minutes per side, turning once, or until the steaks are cooked. Serve hot, garnished with lemon wedges.

Aunt Sweet's Seafood Gumbo
(New Orleans)

I met Lionel Keyes at a Southern Foodways Alliance conference, where he demonstrated how he prepares filé from sassafras in the traditional manner that he learned from his Uncle Bill. I was intrigued by the method, by his quiet gentleness, and by the massive mortar in which he pounds the leaves. The large mortar of worn wood and the smooth pestle reminded me of ones I'd seen in Africa, and I was thrilled to see this New World variety. Over time, we became e-mail buddies and, when I began to write Beyond Gumbo, *I knew that I'd like to have one of Lionel's recipes. He sent this one: the filé gumbo that his Aunt Sweet, Uncle Bill's wife, used to make. The only way that you can finish off a gumbo of this type is with a pinch of filé, so turn to the glossary and order up a bottle or two of Uncle Bill's filé to go with the gumbo.*

SERVES ABOUT 20

1½ cups of oil
1½ cups flour
2 cups celery, chopped fine
3 cups onions, chopped fine
6 cloves garlic, minced
Salt and freshly ground black pepper, to taste
Red pepper flakes, to taste
2 pounds shrimp, peeled and deveined
2 pounds smoked sausage
2 pounds roasted chicken, cut into serving pieces
2 pounds ham, cut in chunks
2 1-pound cans crabmeat, picked over
2 teaspoons minced flat-leaf parsley

2 bay leaves
Uncle Bill's Creole filé
White rice, for serving
French bread, for serving

Prepare a *roux:* Pour the oil into the bottom of a heavy gumbo pot and heat until oil is hot. Gradually stir in the flour. Lower the heat, stirring constantly. After all the flour has been added, lower the heat, and cook until golden brown, stirring constantly.

Add the celery and onions to the roux. Cook, over low heat, for 5 minutes, or until onions are wilted. Add one gallon water and the garlic. Raise the heat and cook in heavy uncovered pot over medium heat for 20 minutes. Season to taste with salt, black, and red pepper flakes. Add the shrimp, sausage, chicken, ham, crabmeat, and parsley and cook 30 minutes. Add the bay leaves and bring to a boil. Cook for 10 minutes. Remove from heat. Serve in soup bowls with cooked rice, accompanied by French bread. Finish each plate with a dash of Uncle Bill's Creole filé, if desired.

Sopa de Guingambo

Okra Soup

(Puerto Rico)

Okra is emblematic of the cooking of the African Atlantic world. From the gumbos of New Orleans and the pepperpot of Philadelphia all the way to the caruru *of Brazil and beyond, it pokes its green nose in many dishes, indicating Africa's culinary presence in the hemisphere. This recipe, from my buddy Patricia Wilson, is one way with okra from Puerto Rico that is in direct line with gumbo's African ancestry.*

SERVES 6 TO 8

1 quart chicken stock
3 tablespoons *Sofrito* (p. 130)
1 pound (about 2 medium) yautias, peeled and cut into small chunks
1 pound okra, trimmed, washed, dried, and sliced
½ pound calabaza, peeled and cut into small chunks
2 tomatoes, seeded and chopped
Salt and freshly ground black pepper, to taste

Bring the chicken stock to a simmer. Add the sofrito and the yautia and cook for 15 minutes, until almost tender. Add the okra and calabaza and cook for 5 minutes, until tender. Add the tomatoes and cook for 2 minutes more. Taste for seasonings. Serve hot.

San Antonio Gumbo
(United States)

This is a Texas variation on the gumbo theme, notable because the roux is made with bacon fat, which gives it intense flavor. This was probably the original way that many of the heartier gumbos were prepared. It is also different in that it is from San Antonio, which is inland. My friend Patrick Dunne recounts that when he was growing up in Texas in the fifties, his father wouldn't even allow him to eat seafood in San Antonio!

SERVES 6 TO 8

5 tablespoons bacon fat

6 teaspoons flour

2 medium onions, minced

1½ cups minced celery

1 clove garlic, minced

4 large ripe tomatoes, peeled, seeded, and coarsely chopped

2 tablespoons tomato paste

1 teaspoon chile powder

Salt and freshly ground black pepper, to taste

5 cups water

Cayenne pepper, to taste

Hot sauce, to taste

2 cups sliced okra

1½ pounds fresh shrimp, peeled and deveined

1 pound lump crabmeat, picked through

White rice, for serving

continued on next page

San Antonio Gumbo (*cont.*)

Prepare a *roux* by cooking the bacon fat and flour in a heavy gumbo pot or saucepan over low heat, until deep brown, stirring constantly. Add the onions, celery, and garlic and cook until they are slightly brown and translucent. Add the tomatoes, tomato paste, chile powder, salt, pepper, and water. Bring to a boil over medium heat. Lower the heat and simmer for about 1 hour. Add the okra and cook for 30 minutes, or until the desired thickness is reached. Add the seafood and continue to cook for 10 minutes. Serve hot over rice.

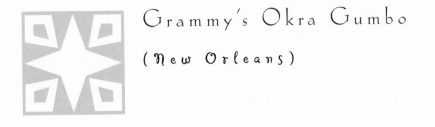

Grammy's Okra Gumbo

(New Orleans)

My friend Lolis Eric Elie is an acknowledged barbecue specialist, and his book, Smoke-stack Lightning, *is a must for any connoisseur of that culinary art. What many folks don't know about him is that he's a fierce hand at the gumbo pot as well. Here's his version of a gumbo that was prepared in his household when his eighty-five-plus-year-old grandma dined. She was allergic to some shellfish, so this gumbo uses only dried shrimp, which she could eat. Grammy passed away in August of 2002, but her recipe and her memory are family treasures.*

SERVES 12

2 pounds (8 cups) of okra, cut into 1" pieces

2 smoked turkey wings

12 ounces dried shrimp

2 pounds smoked sausage, cut into bite-sized pieces

½ cup plus 2 to 3 tablespoons vegetable oil

¾ cup flour

1 tomato, chopped, or 3 tablespoons tomato sauce

2 bell peppers, chopped

3 onions, chopped

4 ribs celery, chopped

1 bunch flat-leaf parsley, chopped

12 cloves garlic, chopped

4 bay leaves

White rice, for serving

continued on next page

Soak the shrimp in 1 quart water. Set aside. In a large stockpot, place the smoked turkey wings in a gallon of water. Cook over medium heat for about 1 hour, or until the wings are tender and have started to separate from the bone. Reserving the turkey stock in the pot, remove the wings. Discard the bones and the skin. Break the meat into 3" or 4" pieces. Return the stock to the heat and simmer over low-to-medium heat.

Place ¼ cup oil in a large skillet over medium heat. When the oil is hot, reduce the heat, and add the okra and tomato. Cook for 45 minutes to 1 hour, or until the okra is fairly dry and much of its gelatinous consistency has been cooked out. Pour the mixture into the simmering stock.

In a large skillet, heat the oil over medium-high heat. Prepare a roux by adding flour to the oil, stirring constantly. The bubbling roux should be the consistency of pancake batter. Once the roux is a color somewhere between caramel and chocolate, add two cups of turkey stock to the skillet. Stir well, being certain that there are no lumps. Pour into the stock pot.

Without washing the skillet, add the chopped onion and 2 or 3 tablespoons of vegetable oil. Cook over medium heat until the onions are soft and have taken on some of the brown color of the roux. Add the onions to the stockpot.

Add the celery, parsley, and garlic to the skillet and fry until they are soft. Add them to the stockpot.

Separate the smoked sausage into 2 or 3 batches. Over medium heat, brown the sausage, rendering as much fat as possible. Discard the excess fat before putting the sausage in the stockpot. Add the bay leaves, shrimp, and the water in which they've been soaking to the stockpot. Add salt, black pepper, cayenne pepper, and hot sauce to taste. Be generous with the seasonings.

Cook the gumbo over low heat for about 2 hours. The consistency should be like that of vegetable soup; add water if needed. Serve in a bowl over steamed rice.

Julie Tronchet Masson's Okra Gumbo

(New Orleans)

Julie Tronchet Masson was the ancestor of my friend Lou Costa, who has the distinction of being a descendant of one of New Orleans's oldest families. This version of gumbo is one of the treasured family recipes that Lou and his family whip up when they entertain in their glorious antique-filled house that used to be a Freedman's Bureau. I've spent many an evening there, sitting on a stool in the kitchen chopping and helping out.

SERVES 6

1½ pounds okra
2 tablespoons vegetable oil
2 medium onions, chopped
4 cloves garlic, minced
¾ pound ham, cut into ½" pieces
2½ pounds medium to large shrimp
1 pound lump crabmeat, picked over
Salt and freshly ground black pepper, to taste
White rice, for serving

Slice the okra and place in a heavy Dutch oven. Fry for 20 minutes, or until all stickiness is gone. Add the onion, garlic, and ham, and cook for 5 minutes, or until the onions are wilted but not browned. Add the shrimp and crabmeat and 2 cups of water. Cook for 15 minutes and add the seasonings. Cook for an additional 10 minutes. Serve hot over white rice.

Gerri Elie's Creole Filé Gumbo
(New Orleans)

As a native New Yorker, I was not born into the gumbo tradition. However, I number among my New Orleans friends and adopted family enough folks who have made gumbo for generations, so that I just need to put the word out. This recipe is one that I received from a friend who makes vats of it. A gumbo is always the first course at her Thanksgiving dinner, for which I have been fortunate enough to snag a seat for the past few years.

SERVES 12 TO 15

2 pounds medium to large shrimp, peeled (reserve and wash shells for
   seafood stock)

1 pound smoked sausage

1 pound andouille sausage

¾ pound Creole hot sausage

½ dozen fresh crabs

½ dozen large boiled (seasoned) crabs

6 cloves garlic, chopped

1 bunch flat-leaf parsley, chopped

5 stalks celery, chopped

1 bunch scallions, including the green parts, chopped

¾ cup vegetable or olive oil

¾ cup all-purpose flour

2 large onions, coarsely chopped

3 quarts seafood stock (2 quarts seafood stock, plus 1 quart chicken stock
   may be substituted)

2 tablespoons margarine

2 bell peppers, chopped

4 bay leaves
1 pound crabmeat, picked over
1 tablespoon seasoned salt, such as Lawry's
Salt and freshly ground black pepper, to taste
4 tablespoons filé powder
White rice, for serving

Clean and devein the shrimp and set aside. Place the washed shrimp shells in 3 quarts boiling water in a stockpot. Cook for about 20 minutes, strain it, and discard the shrimp shells. Reserve the stock. Cut the sausages into bite-sized pieces and cook in an ungreased frying pan over medium heat, turning occasionally until they are slightly browned. Drain the excess fat from sausages, place them into a 12-quart pot; set aside. Wash the fresh crabs in cold water, clean them, and cut them in half, keeping the claws in place. Place in a large bowl and sprinkle with seasoned salt. Reserve cooked crabs in a separate bowl.

Place the vegetable oil in a gumbo pot or heavy saucepan over medium heat. When heated, prepare a roux by slowly adding the flour and stirring constantly, until a paste is formed. Allow flour to brown to desired color (somewhere between caramel and chocolate). Add the onions to the roux, stirring constantly until onions are wilted and slightly browned. Add the uncooked crabs to the roux and brown slightly.

Add two cups shrimp stock to the roux and stir and scrape the roux and crabs into the large gumbo pot and add the rest of the shrimp stock.

Place the margarine in a skillet to heat. Add the chopped garlic, parsley, celery, shallots, and bell pepper and cook for 5 minutes or until the vegetables wilt; do not brown. Add the vegetable mixture and bay leaves to the gumbo pot. Cook over medium heat for about 30 minutes. Add the cooked crabs and peeled shrimp and cook for an additional 15 minutes. Add the crabmeat, lower the heat, and cook for 10 minutes. Adjust seasoning. Remove the gumbo pot from the heat, and add the filé.

Allow the gumbo to sit for about 15 minutes before serving. Serve in soup bowls over white rice.

Four-Generation Filé Gumbo

(New Orleans)

My friend Lou Costa's mother, Myldred Masson Costa, received this recipe from her mother, Julie Tronchet Masson. Today, it's made not only by Lou but also by his daughter Lenora, making it a gumbo recipe that's appealed to the taste of four generations. Try it and you'll see why.

SERVES 6

1 pint oysters, freshly shelled with their liquid
2 pounds poultry (turkey, chicken, or other domestic fowl), cut into pieces
½ pound diced cooked ham
2 bunches green onions, chopped
4 to 6 ribs celery, thinly sliced
4 to 6 cloves garlic, minced
3 tablespoons unsalted butter
Freshly ground white pepper, to taste
Fresh or dried thyme, to taste
Salt, to taste
Fresh filé

Drain the oysters, reserving the liquid. Pick the shell from the oysters, but do not wash them, and set them aside.

Melt the butter in heavy pot. Brown the poultry, turning as needed. Cover and allow the poultry to cook until the meat is tender and falls off the bone. Remove from the heat and allow the meat to cool. Then, remove the skin, pull the meat from the bones, and set it aside.

Add the onions, celery, and garlic to liquid from the poultry and cook until translucent. Add the diced ham and poultry and stir to distribute evenly among the vegetables. Season to taste with white pepper, thyme, and salt.

Add the reserved oyster liquid with enough water to make 1 quart. Bring the pot to a slow simmer. (You may stop at this point and heat the gumbo up again right before serving.)

With the gumbo at a simmer, add oysters and cook gently until they begin to ruffle around the edges. Do not overcook. Adjust the seasoning.

You may add the filé to the gumbo at this point, or each guest can add filé at the table to suit their own taste. If adding the filé at the cooking stage, make sure that once the filé is added the gumbo does not return to a boil.

Note: Be sure that the filé is fresh by testing before use. It will dissolve quickly in liquid.

Asturia's Guingambo with Mofongo

(Puerto Rico)

Several years back, when I appeared as the resident culinary historian on Sara Moulton's
Prime Time Live, *I received a recipe from an interested viewer who was excited to give
me his mother's version of okra stew. Her name was Asturia, and she came from Puerto
Rico. She made a rich stew of okra and root vegetables that went by the Bantu-sounding
name* guingambo. *I have left the recipe as given because I feel that José Millan's culinary
memory of his mother is a fitting way to end this chapter.*

*Thank you for your kind words on television about my Puerto Rican heritage. I am
delighted that you have been to the island and to Loiza Aldea. I spent some wonderful days there eating Alcapurrias de Jueyes, cooked in the large Black Iron Pots used
by the descendants of the Yorubas. Our heritage includes African, Taino and
Boricua, Indians, Spanish and French; it is truly a rainbow coalition and I would
not have it otherwise. My own ancestry as far as I know includes all of the above.
The recipe you asked for on air regrettably died with my Mother and only she knew
the secret ingredients and spices and in what proportions they were used. Neverthe-
less, I will try to give you what I saw her do hundreds of times in her kitchen. My
Mother's name was Asturia and she began practically every dish, or so it seemed to
me, with a Sofrito.*

Sofrito

1 large tablespoon of vegetable or olive oil, or one piece of pork fat. (My mother preferred the pork fat, or "tocino," which is what we call it.)

2 ounces of smoked ham, chopped into small pieces

3 or 4 garlic cloves, minced

¼ tablespoon oregano

Salt and pepper to taste

Cilantro to taste, chopped fine

1 medium-sized onion, chopped

Seeds of 3 small sweet peppers

½ large green pepper, chopped

2 to 3 chorizos (Spanish sausage), sliced into thin pieces (This is optional but terrific.)

1 small can of tomato sauce (Some people prefer to use annatto seeds or achiote, as we call it for coloring and taste. I prefer the tomato sauce because we begin with pork fat and ham and more oil is a bit much for my taste and cholesterol.)

1 cup, black-eyed peas, soaked

1 pound okra, topped and tailed

My Mother would begin by placing the salt pork in a saucepan with a bit of oil and letting this fry for 4 or 5 minutes, then she would add the smoked ham for a minute or two until they both rendered their fat. She would grind the garlic in a mortar and pestle with the oregano, salt and pepper, and cilantro, and then add it to the pork fat together with the onion, sweet peppers, and the green bell pepper. After all this was mixed, she would add the chorizo and a few minutes later the tomato sauce.

The soaked black-eyed peas, which she had kept in cold water that same morning, would then be added.

continued on next page

The okra, which she also kept in salted water, would then be rinsed in cold water and added some 10 to 15 minutes later. Sometimes she added calabaza or potatoes cut into bite-sized pieces; I liked it without the calabaza or potatoes.

This was then left to cook for approximately 45 minutes. While this was cooking, she prepared the Mofongo.

 Mofongo

4 green plantains
4 to 6 cloves of garlic
Salt
1 tablespoon olive oil
Fried pork rinds, to taste
Vegetable oil for frying

Peel and cut the green plantains into 4 to 6 diagonal pieces. Place them in salted water. In a deep-frying pan, heat the vegetable oil to about 300 degrees. Fry for 15 minutes, until they are cooked but not toasted. Remove and dry on paper towels.

In a mortar, crush the garlic cloves with a pinch of salt and the olive oil. Remove and set aside.

Add the cooked plantains to the mortar with pieces of pork rind and mash together. Once the pork rind is incorporated, add the garlic and olive oil mixture.

Continue to incorporate, then using your hands form balls of the Mofongo and serve warm.

After watching your show I began to wonder where the names of our Puerto Rican dishes come from. We have one called "Mondongo," which is a tripe stew, and another called "Gandinga," which is made of innards, hearts, kidneys, and liver, all cut into bite-sized pieces and braised. My name is José Millan, Cheo is a nickname for José.

Banana seller, Martinique.

Starches

Red Rice (Charleston, South Carolina)

Limpin' Susan (Charleston, South Carolina)

Dirty Rice (New Orleans)

Riz aux Gombos — Okra and Rice (Guadeloupe)

Gallo Pinto — Costa Rican Rice and Beans (Costa Rica)

Hoppin' John — South Carolina Black-Eyed Peas and Rice (United States)

Arroz con Gandules — Rice and Pigeon Peas (Puerto Rico)

Red Beans and Rice (New Orleans)

Arroz a la Criolla — Creole Rice (Argentina)

Coconut Rice (Curaçao)

Green Rice (Curaçao)

Sopa Seca con Huevos — Rice with Eggs (Panama)

Moros y Cristianos — Black Beans and White Rice (Cuba)

Yuca Frita — Fried Yuca (Costa Rica)

Mashed Sweet Potatoes with Pineapple (United States)

French-Fried Sweet Potatoes (United States)

Baked Sweet Potatoes (New Orleans)

Tutu — Cornmeal with Black-Eyed Peas (Curaçao)

Tutu a Mineira — Minas Gerais Black Beans (Brazil)

Frijoles Negros — Black Beans (Cuba)

Tacu Tacu — Peruvian Lima Beans and Rice (Peru)

Coo-coo — Turned Cornmeal and Okra (Barbados)

Red-Rice Epiphany
Charleston, South Carolina—1983

IT'S A FAIRLY LONG DRIVE from Columbia to Charleston, but my friends and I had never been to the city that houses Catfish Row, and we were determined to see it during the College Language Association conference. After all, some of us would never have journeyed to South Carolina if we hadn't fallen for the lure of the place that some call the Holy City. We piled into a car and hit the road, forsaking panels on multiculturalism and deconstructing the works of Haitian author Jacques Roumain. We talked and drove and I stared out of the window, mesmerized by the dense landscape and wondering what the Africans enslaved in the Low Country must have thought of the dense palmetto forests and swampy terrain. We passed basket sellers, and I saw at a glance how their baskets were the cousins of the fanner baskets and containers that I'd purchased by the scores in the markets of Dakar, Senegal.

We drove into the center of town and parked near the market where, in the nineteenth century, enslaved Africans hawked wares and carried on lively commerce. We had no idea where to eat, and just headed into the first place we saw. As it turned out, it was probably not one of Charleston's finest places, but we'd made our pilgrimage and weren't leaving without a meal. We ordered, and the waitress asked if we'd like rice or potatoes. "Rice," we all replied, and were delighted when it came to find that it was fluffy, flecked with bits of bell pepper and red with tomato. We dipped our forks in and said, virtually in unison, *"thiebou dienn."* We'd all spent time in Senegal and our mouths told us what I'd later confirm through research: The food of South Carolina's Low Country is closely related to that of the rice-growing regions of western Africa that include southern Senegal. Charleston's red rice, in fact, is but a variant of the red rice that is the national dish of Senegal.

I've returned to Charleston many times and now count it among my favorite places. I've had grand meals there, in fancy restaurants and at kitchen tables, but none has informed me as much as my first meal, when I learned to trust my tastebuds. When sitting down to a meal, be it grand or humble, always be prepared to have a culinary epiphany.

Red Rice

(Charleston, South Carolina)

This rice is one of the links between the food of West Africa and that of African Americans. Indeed, the link becomes clearer when one realizes that the Casamance region of southern Senegal is a rice-growing area, and that slaves were taken from there to work in Carolina's rice fields. This is not a pre-European African dish, for there were no tomatoes in West Africa before the Columbian exchange. Also, in Muslim Senegal, there would be no bacon in the dish. In spite of this, the dish definitely reflects the tastes of West Africa in the New World.

SERVES 4 TO 6

6 strips lean bacon
1 medium onion, chopped
3 scallions, minced, including the green parts
2 cups coarsely chopped, seeded, and peeled ripe tomatoes
1 cup uncooked long-grain rice
¾ cup minced, cooked ham
Salt and freshly ground black pepper, to taste
Hot sauce, to taste

Preheat the oven to 350 degrees. Heat a heavy cast-iron skillet, over medium heat, add the bacon, and cook until crisp. Remove and drain on paper towels. Cook the onion and scallions in the remaining bacon fat until translucent. Crumble the bacon and add it to the skillet with the tomatoes, rice, ham, salt, pepper, and hot sauce. Reduce the heat to low and cook for 10 minutes. Place rice mixture in a greased 1½ quart casserole dish. Adjust the seasonings, cover, and bake for 1 hour, stirring every 15 minutes.

Limpin' Susan

(Charleston, South Carolina)

Ask most folks about the cooking of South Carolina and they will tell you something about rice. If they're a little more knowledgeable, they'll tell you about Hoppin' John. If they're really an expert, they'll tell you about Hoppin' John's little-known cousin, Limpin' Susan. Limpin' Susan is a local Carolina name for one of the region's rice pilaus, or purloos. These composed rice dishes are the jewels of the region's cooking. Many of the dishes have definite links to the cooking of other areas of the African-Atlantic world and to West Africa itself. This dish is prepared with okra and pieces of bacon. Occasionally, tomatoes are added to this pilau, *but the classic dish simply calls for rice, bacon, okra, and seasonings. It requires, as do many South Carolina rice dishes, a rice steamer, which makes an excellent gift. If you don't have a rice steamer, you can approximate one with a colander and a covered saucepan.*

SERVES 4

5 strips lean bacon
3 cups thinly sliced okra
1 small onion, minced
1 cup washed, raw long-grain rice
Salt and freshly ground black pepper, to taste

Cut the bacon into 1" pieces and fry in a heavy skillet until crisp and most of the fat is rendered. Add the okra and onion and sauté in the bacon fat, stirring occasionally, until the onion is translucent and the okra is tender. Add the rice, 1 cup water, and salt and pepper and continue to cook for 5 minutes, mixing well. Transfer the rice and okra mixture to the top section of a steamer, add water to the bottom, cover,

Roadside market women, Jamaica.

and cook until the rice is fluffy and dry. The cooking times will vary depending on the type of rice, but this should take from 45 minutes to 1 hour. Serve hot. Use a rice spoon, if you have one, to serve. In the rest of the world, this is a long-handled stuffing spoon. In rice-eating Charleston, it's called a *rice spoon*.

Dirty Rice

(New Orleans)

Composed rice dishes are one of the hallmarks of African-American cooking in the New World. They range from hoppin' John to the Caribbean's rice and peas, peas and rice, and moros y cristianos, to the red beans and rice that Louis Armstrong loved so much. New Orleans's dirty rice is just another addition to the list. The dish gets its name because chopped chicken innards and savory seasonings give it a "dirty" appearance.

SERVES 6 TO 8

1½ cups raw long-grain rice
3 tablespoons vegetable oil
1 large red onion, chopped
1 clove garlic, minced
½ pound chicken livers, minced
4 ounces chicken gizzards, minced
2 scallions, including green tops, chopped
2 stalks celery, including leaves, minced
¼ cup minced green bell pepper
1 sprig flat-leaf parsley, minced
2 preserved bird pepper chiles, minced, or to taste
Salt and freshly ground black pepper, to taste

Cook the rice according to the directions on page 265 until almost done, about 15 minutes. While the rice is cooking, brown the onion and garlic in the vegetable oil, in a heavy skillet. Add the chicken livers and gizzards and sauté until they are cooked and crumbly, about 4 minutes. Add the scallions, celery, bell pepper, parsley, chiles, salt, pepper, and drained rice and continue to cook over medium heat, until the rice is thoroughly cooked. Stir gently until the ingredients are well mixed, and serve immediately.

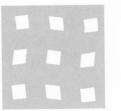

Riz aux Gombos

Okra and Rice

(Guadeloupe)

This mixture of okra and rice would be at home on a South Carolina table, but it is, in fact, from Guadeloupe. Its roots are pure African and it is indeed a close Caribbean country cousin of Limpin' Susan. I learned this version from Carmelita Jeanne, one of Guadeloupe's famous cuisinieres. It is Creole culinary magic.

SERVES 6 TO 8

2 teaspoons olive oil
½ pound fresh okra, topped, tailed, and cut into rounds
3 scallions, minced
1 tablespoon minced flat-leaf parsley
1 teaspoon minced fresh thyme leaves
2 cloves garlic, minced
1 teaspoon minced habanero chile
Salt and freshly ground black pepper, to taste
2⅓ cups raw long-grain rice

Heat the oil in a heavy saucepan over medium heat and lightly brown the okra for 3 minutes. Add 1 quart water, scallions, parsley, thyme, garlic, chile, and salt and pepper. Bring the mixture to a boil over medium-high heat and boil for 5 minutes. Add the rice, lower the heat to medium, and allow the rice to continue to boil gently for 8 to 10 minutes. Drain the mixture and place it in a large sieve or colander or on top of a rice cooker over a pot of boiling water. Cover and steam for 7 minutes, or until the rice is tender. Fluff the rice, adjust the seasonings, transfer to a serving bowl, and serve hot.

Gallo Pinto

Costa Rican Rice and Beans

(Costa Rica)

Unlike the myriad Caribbean versions of this dish that are made from scratch, this version is composed of well-seasoned leftover rice and beans.

SERVES 6 TO 8

3 tablespoons minced onion
1 tablespoon minced green bell pepper
1 tablespoon minced red bell pepper
3 tablespoons vegetable oil
3 cups cooked black beans
4 cups cooked rice
2½ tablespoons minced coriander
2 teaspoons Worcestershire sauce
Hot pepper sauce, to taste
5 strips bacon, cooked, drained, and crumbled
Sour cream, for serving
Minced onion, for garnish

In a skillet, sauté the onion and bell peppers in the oil until the onion is translucent. Add the beans and cook for 2 minutes. Add the rice and cook for 3 minutes more. Add the coriander and the Worcestershire sauce, stir well, taste, and adjust seasonings. Cook for 2 minutes and serve mounded on a platter topped with the crumbled bacon bits, a dollop of sour cream, and onion.

Hoppin' John

South Carolina Black-Eyed Peas and Rice

(United States)

1 pound dried black-eyed peas
½ slab bacon, chopped
Salt and freshly ground black pepper, to taste
1 teaspoon dried fresh thyme
2 teaspoons minced garlic
1 bay leaf
1½ cups long grain rice

Pick over the peas and soak them in water to cover overnight. Drain. Fry bacon in heavy casserole to render the fat. Add the black-eyed peas, 1 quart water, thyme, garlic, and bay leaf. Cover and cook over low heat for 30 minutes, or until tender.

In a separate saucepan, bring 3 cups hot water to boil and add long-grain rice. Cook for 20 minutes, or until rice is tender. Mix ingredients together, adjust seasoning, and serve hot.

Arroz con Gandules

Rice and Pigeon Peas

(Puerto Rico)

The litany of rice dishes spreads from north to south and is one of the indicators of Creole fusion. Rice, indigenous to Africa as well as to Asia, is enhanced with the additions that each culture brings to it. From the relative simplicity of Hoppin' John from the rice-growing regions of South Carolina to rice and peas from Jamaica—so common there that it's called coat of arms—the list seems endless. Here, my Puerto Rican friend Patricia Wilson weighs in again with her version of rice with pigeon peas, called gandules *in Spanish. These peas are also called* gungo pea *in Jamaica and Belize or even* Congo peas *in Barbados, Grenada, Guyana, and other points south. They are tender yellow-greenish peas, related to the more familiar black-eyed peas.*

2 tablespoons Annatto Oil (p. 135)
3 ounces slab bacon or ham, diced
1 onion, chopped
2 tablespoons Green *Sofrito* (p. 131)
1 red pepper, seeded and diced
1½ cups long-grain rice
1 tablespoon capers
1 tablespoon salt
1 cup fresh, frozen, or canned pigeon peas, drained

Heat the annatto oil in a saucepan. Brown the bacon or ham, add the onion, and cook until softened. Add the green sofrito and cook for 1 to 2 minutes over medium heat, mixing well. Add the red pepper and rice and stir well to coat with oil. Add 3 cups water, capers, salt, and pigeon peas. Bring to a boil, then lower the heat, cover tightly, and simmer for 20 minutes. Fluff with a fork. Adjust seasonings. Serve hot.

Red Beans and Rice

(New Orleans)

Red beans and rice are so much a part of the culinary life of New Orleans that master trumpeter Louis Armstrong used to sign his letters "Red beans and ricely yours." Camellia red beans are traditional in New Orleans, as opposed to the more common kidney bean, and they are served slightly creamy. This recipe came from my friend Lionel Keyes, who makes Uncle Bill's filé by hand in Louisiana.

SERVES 4 TO 6

1 pound Camellia red beans
1 large yellow onion, minced
3 tablespoons garlic powder
1 tablespoon freshly ground black pepper
3 cups cooked ham or other meat of your choice
1 tablespoon Uncle Bill's filé
Salt and freshly ground black pepper, to taste
Rice, for serving

In a large saucepan, soak red beans overnight in water to cover, according to package directions. When ready to cook, drain the water and add 2 cups fresh water. Then add the onion, garlic powder, meat, filé, salt, and pepper. Cover and cook over medium heat, stirring occasionally, for 1 hour, then lower the heat and continue to cook, stirring more frequently during the second hour. Add warm water as needed. The beans should be creamy, and served hot over the rice of your choice.

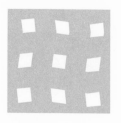

Arroz a la Criolla

Creole Rice

(Argentina)

Cordoba, in Argentina, is one of many New World cities named for Old World places that evoked nostalgia. No doubt, the colonists who founded the city that lies between the Pampas and the Andes thought with longing of the Spanish center of Moorish learning and art that the poet Frederico de Garcia Lorca had called lejana y sola *(far away and lonely). Argentina's second largest city after Buenos Aires, this New World Cordoba is a university town, one with a tradition of learning that goes back to the seventeenth century. The food of Cordoba also reflects its lengthy history and mixed ingredients from several traditions. This Creole rice is a case in point, mixing African rice with the bell peppers of the New World, and a European cooking technique. The trick here is in browning the seasonings and the rice before cooking.*

SERVES 6

1 medium onion, minced
½ teaspoon minced garlic
1½ tablespoons minced green bell pepper
1½ cups long-grain rice
1½ teaspoons olive oil
½ teaspoons salt, or to taste

Cook the onions, garlic, bell pepper, and rice in the oil in the bottom of a heavy saucepan for three minutes or until the onion is lightly browned. Add the salt and 3 cups boiling water, and stir. Cover, lower the heat, and cook for 25 minutes, or until the water has evaporated and the rice is tender. Fluff and serve hot.

Coconut Rice

(Curaçao)

This simple yet flavorful rice dish from Curaçao is an example of the extent to which foods have mixed in this hemisphere. The hint of lemon grass more than the use of coconut milk, which is pervasive in the East and West Indies, speaks to the Southeast Asian origins of this dish. I suspect that the Dutch brought this rice to Curaçao along with rijstaffel *and other dishes that they'd become fond of in Indonesia and in other parts of their colonial empire.*

SERVES 4 TO 6

3 cups coconut milk
1 cup long-grain rice
Salt and freshly ground white pepper, to taste
1 stalk lemongrass, slightly crushed

Bring the coconut milk to a boil in a medium saucepan. Add the rice, salt, pepper, and lemongrass. Cover. Lower the heat and simmer for 25 minutes or until the rice is dry. Remove the lemongrass and serve hot.

Green Rice

(Curaçao)

This rice uses a cilantro paste, instead of the sofrito that is typically used in the cooking of the Hispanic Caribbean. It combines the saffronlike hue of turmeric from Asia with the taste of cilantro from the Americas and the surprise of a good old European beer.

SERVES 8 TO 10

1 medium onion, minced
1⅛ teaspoon minced chile
2 garlic cloves, minced
1 teaspoon turmeric
Salt and freshly ground black pepper, to taste
2 teaspoons Cilantro Paste (p. 134)
2 tablespoons olive oil
2 cups chicken stock
10 ounces beer
3 cups long-grain rice
1 cup frozen green peas
Red and yellow bell pepper julienne, for garnish

Fry the onion, chile, garlic, turmeric, salt, pepper, and cilantro paste in the oil for 3 minutes, or until the onions are lightly browned. Add the chicken stock, 1 cup water, and beer, and bring to a boil. Drizzle in the rice, stirring with a fork. Reduce the heat, cover, and simmer for 20 minutes or until the rice is cooked but not soft. Stir in the peas and cook for an additional 5 minutes. Serve hot, decorated with the pepper strips.

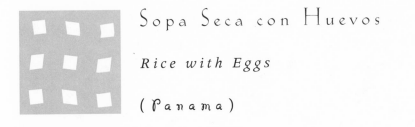

Sopa Seca con Huevos

Rice with Eggs

(Panama)

This so-called dry soup is a typical rice dish in the Hispanic Caribbean and is a good way to use leftover meat. Here, in a meatless version, eggs are cooked in the rice for an interesting combination. You may add minced pieces of cooked leftover chicken or ham for a heartier dish.

SERVES 4 TO 6

1½ cups long-grain rice
1 medium onion, minced
1 clove garlic, minced
2 tablespoons olive oil
¼ teaspoon salt, or to taste
2 cups chicken stock
1 cup boiling water
Pinch saffron
6 eggs
Minced flat-leaf parsley, for garnish

In a heavy saucepan, sauté the rice, onion, and garlic in the olive oil until the onion is lightly browned. In a second small saucepan, bring the chicken stock and water to a boil, add the saffron and pour over the rice mixture, stirring constantly. Lower the heat, cover, and cook for 20 minutes. Make six wells in the rice. Break an egg into each one. Cover and cook for an additional 5 minutes, or until the eggs are firm. Slide the rice carefully onto a platter, trying not to break the eggs. Sprinkle with parsley and serve immediately.

Valdimaide Sao Pedro "Te"
Salvador da Bahia, Brazil

"A tabuleiro da Baiana tem — vatapa, caruru, mugunza, tem umbo . . ." (The Baiana's tray has vatapa, caruru, mugunza, and umbu.)

I HAVE FAMILY IN BRAZIL. As the first American to be initiated into one of the city's oldest houses of Candomble, there are people in the town of Salvador to whom I am not related by blood, but for whom I am sister and mother, daughter and aunt. As a daughter of Casa Branca, I have spent time in the ritual kitchen of the big white house on the hill, watching and cooking, praying and learning, listening and laughing. I have savored the ritual community that was one of the ways in which the enslaved Africans in Brazil were able to keep an astonishing amount of their cultural heritage intact. I have watched as the *iya basse,* or ritual cook, prepared meals for the African gods or *orixas,* harkening back to recipes that were transmitted by word of mouth from their African sources, and begin with instructions to take one hundred okra pods and cut them lengthwise and crosswise into a mass of tiny, sticky chips. They then go on to detail every stroke of the knife blade and turn of the wooden spoon, and how they have been prepared just so for centuries.

I have climbed the hills and entered the holy precincts and served these dishes that are survivors of the Atlantic slave trade as offerings to the African gods who also made the Middle Passage to watch over the enslaved. I have sat at the communal table and eaten with other votaries after the feasts, marveling at how the Candomble religion in Bahia transcends the divisions of race, class, and age so palpable in Brazil, and how the sense of community is similar to that of the churches of my youth.

One of my sisters in religion is Valdimaide— known to all as *Te,* her *Oxum.* When she is possessed by the African *orixa,* or goddess, of love and wealth she is wondrous to behold. I'd watched her as she prepared things with a sure hand and marveled because she and her sister had founded their own *terreiro,* an offshoot of the mother house. One night, as the members of the community were stopping in to pay their respects before heading home from work, Te appeared. She was beautifully clothed in her traditional finery of brightly flowered skirt atop a froth of multiple petticoats; pristine, white, starched lace blouse; turban tied just so; and wearing the glass bead necklaces that signaled her devotion to the *orixas.* Carrying a tray covered with an immaculate lace cloth and topped with sweet treats like *cocadas* and coconut patties, she was heading off to work. Te, I discovered, was a *Baiana de tabuleiro:* one of the tray-carrying vendors who are the repositories of the Afro-Bahian culinary arts. Like many Creole women past and present, she had turned her skill in the kitchen into her livelihood, purveying sweets on a street corner to people who had no idea that with each bite they were not only savoring a delicious coconut morsel, but also enjoying a taste of history.

Moros y Cristianos

Black Beans and White Rice

(Cuba)

This is the Cuban entry into the region's beans and rice sweepstakes. Here, the rice is cooked in the liquid from the beans. Some cooks remove a tablespoon or two of the cooked beans and mash them before returning them to the pot, giving the cooked dish a creamier texture.

SERVES 6 TO 8

2 cups dry black turtle beans
1½ tablespoons olive oil
1 small onion, minced
4 garlic cloves, minced
¼ Scotch bonnet chile, seeded and minced, or to taste
1 tablespoon minced green bell pepper
1 small tomato, peeled, seeded, and minced
1 sprig fresh thyme
⅛ teaspoon dried oregano
Salt and freshly ground black pepper, to taste
2 cups raw long-grain white rice

Soak the beans according to package directions and cook until tender. Drain the beans, reserving the cooking liquid. Add enough water, if necessary, to make six cups. Place the oil in a heavy saucepan, and add the onion, garlic, chile, bell pepper, tomato, thyme, oregano, salt, and pepper. Cook over medium heat for 5 minutes, stirring occasionally. Add the rice and the reserved bean water, continuing to stir. Bring to a boil, stirring constantly, then lower the heat, cover, and cook for about 20 minutes, or until the rice is cooked. Adjust the seasonings and serve hot.

Yuca Frita

Fried Yuca

(Costa Rica)

This dish, also known as boca, *can be found in much of the Spanish-speaking Caribbean as well as Costa Rica. Here, the trick is that the yuca is cooked in bouillon before being fried. Traditionally chicken bouillon is used, but I have switched to vegetable bouillon so that the dish can be served to vegetarians.*

SERVES 4 TO 6

1 pound yuca
2 low-sodium vegetable bouillon cubes
2 tablespoons vegetable oil
1 tablespoon butter

Wash the yuca, peel it, and cut into 3" rounds. Place 4 cups water in a saucepan with the yuca, add the bouillon cubes, and cook for 15 minutes, or until fork tender. Drain and cut the pieces into thick julienne, as you would for French fries. Heat the oil in a heavy skillet and fry the pieces until all sides are golden brown. Drain on absorbent paper and serve immediately.

Mashed Sweet Potatoes with Pineapple

(United States)

The sweet potatoes in this dish are called garnet yams *in the supermarket, thereby underlining the endless confusion about root vegetables that exists in the English-speaking regions of the hemisphere. We, in the northern part, who have only had sweet potatoes until very recently, began to listen to the descendants of the Africans who named the vegetable for the things that were closest to their experience . . . yams. The name stuck, and now, in many parts of the South, certain varieties of sweet potatoes are marketed as yams. This recipe is not really traditional, but does combine the best of north and south using two American natives; the sweet potato from central America and the pineapple (probably a native of Brazil, but it has been cultivated in the Caribbean region since before Columbus). Even if you've never seen a yam, don't be fooled. A yam is an entirely different thing, as you'll discover if you cook any of the recipes using them.*

SERVES 4 TO 6

3 large garnet yams
2 large carrots, grated
1 cup freshly squeezed orange juice
Pinch ginger powder
1½ cups minced fresh pineapple

Wash the yams, peel them, and cut them into 1" pieces. Place the yams and carrots into a saucepan with the orange juice and the ginger. Bring to a boil, lower the heat, and simmer for 10 to 15 minutes, or until the yams are fork tender. Remove the yams and reserve the liquid. Force the mixture through a ricer into a bowl, adding a bit of the cooking liquid, if necessary, to make the yams smooth and creamy. Add the pineapple and stir to mix well. Serve hot.

French-Fried Sweet Potatoes

(United States)

This way with sweet potatoes has become so common in restaurants that it is difficult to believe that the dish is fairly new.

SERVES 4

Vegetable oil, for frying
1 large sweet potato, peeled, and cut into French fry shapes

Preheat 3" of oil in a heavy saucepan to 375 degrees. Place the sweet potatoes in the oil a few at a time and fry for 3 to 5 minutes or until lightly browned and cooked through. Drain on absorbent paper and keep warm while you continue frying. Salt to taste, and serve hot.

Baked Sweet Potatoes

(New Orleans)

Louisiana is one of the places in the United States where the yam–sweet potato confusion runs riot. Although they are marketed as yams, it must be said that Louisiana yams are sweet potatoes. A yam is something completely different. This recipe could be made with yams or with sweet potatoes, but will be much tastier when made with sweet potatoes.

SERVES 6

6 medium sweet potatoes
6 tablespoons butter
Salt, to taste
Powdered cayenne pepper, to taste
Freshly ground nutmeg, to taste

Preheat the oven to 450 degrees. Scrub the potatoes. Coat their skins lightly with vegetable oil and place them on a rack in the oven. Cook for 45 minutes or until they are cooked through. Slit them open and place a tablespoon of butter and salt, a dash of cayenne, and freshly ground nutmeg to taste in each. Mash it together and eat while piping hot.

Tutu

Cornmeal with Black-Eyed Peas

(Curaçao)

It is amazing how close the Sephardic culture of Curaçao is to that of parts of Brazil. A listing of traditional dishes collected by the sisterhood of Mikve Israel contains such typically Brazilian dishes as kala, *Curaçao's version of the black-eyed pea fritter known as* acaraje *in Brazil;* Bolo Pretu, *a dark, rich, fruitcakelike confection, also found in Brazil; and this dish—tutu, which keeps its Brazilian name, but is prepared with black-eyed peas and cornmeal instead of Brazil's traditional black beans and cassava meal. The Curaçaoan version is sweeter, as well. None of this is surprising, when you remember that many Sephardic Jews came to Curaçao from the Pernambuco region in northern Brazil. They brought with them not only the idea of the plantation system of agriculture that subsequently transformed all of the Caribbean region and much of the American South, but also their food, which fused Europe, Africa, and the Americas.*

SERVES 6

1 pound dry black-eyed peas
1½ cups yellow cornmeal
½ cup sugar
2 teaspoons salt, or to taste
4 tablespoons salted butter
1 cup grated Edam cheese

Soak the black-eyed peas according to package directions; cook them in their soaking water for 45 minutes or until tender. Drain and place in a large saucepan. Add 2 cups water, bring to a boil, then mash the peas coarsely with a whisk. When the peas are broken, gradually add the cornmeal, sugar, and salt, and continue to beat into a

Bread seller, Cuba.

smooth mash with no lumps. The cooking time will be approximately 15 minutes. Reduce the heat and continue to mash the mixture until it begins to pull away from the side of the pan. Add the butter and mix well. When finished, invert the *tutu* onto a platter and garnish with butter and grated cheese. Serve hot.

Tutu a Mineira

Minas Gerais Black Beans

(Brazil)

Minas Gerais is a Brazilian state that is known for its jewel and gold mines and its cooking, and for the voice of singer Milton Nascimento. The food of the region is hearty and many of the dishes are baked or grilled. Cheeses are a specialty and, at times, it seems that Mineiros have their own way with all of the Brazilian classics. This is their take on the bean dish called feijoada *in much of the rest of the country. Traditionally, it is eaten with fried pork chops, the greens known as* couve, *and fried pieces of linguiça sausage.*

SERVES 4

¼ pound streaky slab bacon, cut into 1" pieces
1 medium onion, chopped
1 clove garlic, minced
3 cups drained cooked black beans
Salt and freshly ground black pepper, to taste
1 cup cassava meal (p. 27)
½ pound fried linguiça sausage pieces

Fry the bacon bits in a heavy skillet until crisp. Remove and drain on absorbent paper. Cook the onion and garlic in the bacon fat over medium heat until they are golden. Add the beans, stir well, and season to taste. Reduce the heat to low and slowly add the cassava meal, stirring until the mixture thickens. To serve, pour onto a platter and decorate it with the reserved bacon pieces and the linguiça sausage. Serve hot. You may want to have some *Molho Brasileiro* (p. 143) available for those who might want it a bit spicier.

Frijoles Negros

Black Beans

(Cuba)

While black beans are cooked in several parts of the Caribbean, it seems that Cuba has a lock on their preparation. From the black-bean soup that makes exiles head to restaurants like Versailles in Miami and Victor's in New York, to the rich soupy beans that come as an accompaniment to almost every dish, they are emblematic of Cuba's cooking. It is surprising, then, to note that the island is bisected by a line of bean demarcation and that the black beans that have become so connected with Cuba in our minds are only eaten in the western part of the island, which includes Havana. In the eastern regions, including Santiago, red beans or kidney beans are preferred, as they are in Haiti, Jamaica, and New Orleans.

1 pound black beans
4 tablespoons olive oil
1 medium onion, coarsely chopped
1 small green pepper, minced
2 cloves garlic, minced
1 bay leaf
1 teaspoon oregano
1 teaspoon sugar
Salt and freshly ground black pepper, to taste
White rice, for serving

Prepare the beans and soak them overnight according to package directions. Cook the beans in their soaking water for 45 minutes. Place 2 tablespoons olive oil in a heavy skillet and sauté the onion, bell pepper, and garlic for 2 to 3 minutes, or until the onion is lightly browned. Add the onion mixture to the beans along with the bay leaf, oregano, sugar, salt, and pepper. Cook for an additional 15 minutes, or until the beans are creamy. Serve hot with white rice.

Tacu Tacu

Peruvian Lima Beans and Rice

(Peru)

It comes as a surprise to many people who haven't heard the music of Sonia Baca that there are people of African descent in Peru. Africans were enslaved in Peru from the earliest days of the Spanish conquest and worked in the silver mines. Later, during colonial times, they worked in the coastal cotton and sugar plantations. This dish of rice and lima beans is a part of their culinary legacy. Traditionally, tacu tacu *is eaten with a fried egg, fried bananas, a slice of breaded fried beef tenderloin, and a garnish of julienned red onion and hot chile strips for a truly hearty stick-to-your ribs meal. Some folks feel that* tacu tacu *is best the day after preparation, but I think it's pretty darned good anytime.*

SERVES 4 TO 6

1 pound lima beans, soaked overnight
1 pound fatback cut into ¼" dice
3 tablespoons vegetable oil
1 large red onion, chopped
4 cloves garlic, minced
½ cup *aji amarillo* paste (p. 20)
1 tablespoon dried oregano
2½ cups cooked rice
Salt and freshly ground black pepper, to taste
Breaded beef tenderloin, for serving
Fried banana, for serving
Fried egg, for serving
Thinly sliced red onion, for serving

Place the beans in a large saucepan with the fatback and water to cover, and cook for 1½ hours, or until tender. Place them in a mortar and pestle or into the bowl of a food processor and mash or process them into a thick purée.

Heat 2 tablespoons oil in a heavy skillet and sauté the onion and garlic over medium heat until golden. Add the *aji amarillo* paste and oregano and cook for 3 minutes. Add the rice and mashed beans and stir to mix well. Season and remove from the heat.

Prepare the *tacu tacu* by heating a tablespoon of vegetable oil in another skillet and taking ¼ of the bean mixture and forming it into a thick cake using a spatula. Place the cake on a serving plate. Repeat with the remaining mixture.

Top the *tacu tacu* with breaded beef tenderloin cooked to your liking, a fried banana, a fried egg, and a sprinkling of thinly sliced red onion. Serve hot.

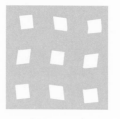

Coo-coo

Turned Cornmeal and Okra

(Barbados)

This dish is found throughout the Caribbean region under a variety of different names. It is known as fungi *or* fungee *in the U.S. Virgin Islands, Dominica, Anguilla, and Antigua; as* coucou *in the British Virgin Islands, Saint Vincent, and Guyana;* coo-coo *in Barbados, Grenada, and other parts of Guyana; as* turn corn *in Saint Kits and Nevis; and as* turn cornmeal *or* turn meal *in Jamaica. Usually served with steamed fish of some sort, it is a part of the Barbadian national dish of flying fish and* coo-coo. *It's usually made from cornmeal, but can also be prepared from breadfruit, calabaza, cassava meal, or potato. The smooth oblong piece of wood called a* coucou *stick is used to stir the* coo-coo *and shape it. (It's also used for disciplining Caribbean children in some households.) Making* coo-coo *is an art that takes practice, so don't be discouraged if it doesn't work exactly right the first time.*

SERVES 4

12 okra pods, topped and tailed
1 teaspoon salt
1 small onion, minced
3 cloves garlic, minced
3 tablespoons butter
2 cups fine cornmeal

Wash the okra and slice it into thin rounds, place in a medium saucepan with 3 cups water, salt, onion, garlic, and 2 tablespoons butter. Bring to a boil, lower the heat, and simmer for 10 minutes. Combine the cornmeal and 3 cups water in a separate bowl, stirring occasionally to saturate the meal. When the okra is cooked, strain the water into a bowl and reserve the okra in another. Pour the cornmeal into the pot over medium heat, whisking constantly to make sure that there are no lumps. Slowly drizzle in the cooking liquid, stirring constantly. When the mixture begins to thicken, reduce the heat to low, add the remaining butter and okra and continue to cook for about 10 minutes, beating the *coo-coo* with a *coucou* stick or wooden spoon. The *coo-coo* is ready when the mixture becomes stiff and breaks away from the sides and bottom of the pan. Pour the *coo-coo* into a well-buttered medium bowl. Allow the *coo-coo* to cool for about 10 minutes, then unmold it. (It will keep its shape when turned out onto a serving dish.) Serve hot.

Fruit market, Havana.

Desserts

Lemon-Pecan Pound Cake (United States)

Home-Made Peach Ice Cream (United States)

Mildred Oliver's Nut Cake (New Orleans)

Creole Fluff (New Orleans)

Flan de Queso — Cheese Flan (Puerto Rico)

Flan Tres Leches — Three-Milk Flan (Costa Rica)

Pralines (New Orleans)

Cajeta de Leche — Milk Fudge (Costa Rica)

Tamarind Balls (Trinidad)

Stuffed Dates (Curaçao)

Stuffed Figs (New Orleans)

Canjica de Erminhia — Brazilian Sweet Hominy (Brazil)

Arroz con Leche — Milk Rice (Costa Rica)

Rice Pudding (United States)

Historic Calas — Rice Fritters (New Orleans)

Calas — Rice Fritters (New Orleans)

Fruit Fritters (United States)

Gateau Sirop — Syrup Cake (New Orleans)

Country Calas — Rice Fritters (Louisiana)

Creole Cream Cheese (New Orleans)

Creole Cream Cheese Ice Cream (New Orleans)

Dewberry Juice Pie (Louisiana)

Three Dessert Sauces

Plantain Crisps (U.S. Virgin Islands)

Conkies (Barbados)

Bajan Bread Pudding (Barbados)

Rum Sauce (Barbados)

DELIA MADURO
Curaçao

Yaft Elohim l'Yefet, v'yishkon b'ahole Shem.
(May God enlarge Jafeth, and let him dwell in
the tents of Shem.) (Gen.9:27) 1730 Inscription
over the doors of Synagogue Mikve Israel-
Emmanuel, Curaçao

THE DUTCH WERE TRADERS, and came from a northern tradition of austerity and frugality. They came from the seafaring Netherlands first to Brazil and, when they were expelled from their homes in northeastern Brazil they moved on to the Caribbean. Many of them were Sephardic Jews who had journeyed to the hemisphere in search of religious freedom. While prosperous centers of trade, none of the Dutch Caribbean possessions ever attained the sugar wealth of the rest of the region. However, they played a major role in the culinary history of the region, for those expelled from Brazil brought their knowledge of the plantation system and sugar cultivation to the southern Caribbean, thereby paving the way for the reign of King Sugar. They also had a hand in developing the beverage we know as rum, for it is said that one of the enslaved Africans the Dutch brought with them from Brazil brought the knowledge of the distillation process that produced some of the first rum to the Caribbean region.

Delia Maduro was a matriarch of the congregation Mikve Israel-Emmanuel in Curaçao, the Jewish community with the longest continuous history in the Americas. White haired and elegant, she sat in the living room of her Willemstad house and spoke lovingly of the festive sweets that are traditionally prepared for the dessert tables that are an integral part of many of the congregation's holiday meals. Years earlier, I had attended a Sukkout service at Mikve Israel and marveled at the history that fairly seeped from the walls of the temple, where the sand on the floor symbolized the Israelites' wanderings in the desert. The sense of tradition was palpable. After the service, members of the congregation sang songs in Ladino that were haunting with the keening sonorities of Andalucia and North Africa. I recalled that night vividly while talking to Mrs. Maduro. My mouth watered as she described *dushi de leite,* a milk fudge; *garosa,* a confection prepared from peanuts, cashews, brown sugar, dried fruit, and kosher wine; that is their version of the Sephardic Passover charoset, and more, much more. She brought out folded, age-stained recipes for the nut cookies, sponge cake, matzo balls, and other delicacies that are a part of the Passover celebration. As I listened to her soft voice, tinged with nostalgia for times past, and heard the vestiges of Brazilian Portuguese in the *Papiamento*-named dishes like *cocadas* and *pan bolo,* I marveled at the perseverance of a people who have given mightily to the Creole world and whose history, like my own, could be read on their plates.

Lemon-Pecan Pound Cake

(United States)

The pound cake is the picnic cake of choice for much of the African-American South. Its consistency or its taste just seem to bear up to the strains of travel better than any other frosted goody or homemade pie. This is one of the many changes that can be rung on the traditional recipe.

SERVES 10

2½ cups flour
¼ teaspoon salt
⅛ teaspoon freshly grated nutmeg
1 cup unsalted butter, softened
1 cup sugar
5 eggs, separated, plus 1 egg white
1 teaspoon vanilla extract
½ teaspoon lemon extract
1 tablespoon freshly grated lemon zest
½ cup finely chopped pecans
Home-Made Peach Ice Cream, for serving (p. 296)

Preheat the oven to 350 degrees. Grease a 9-inch loaf pan. Sift the flour, salt, and nutmeg into a small bowl and set aside. In another bowl, cream the butter, slowly add the sugar, continuing to beat until light and fluffy. Beat the egg yolks until thick and slowly drizzle them into the butter-sugar mixture while continuing to beat. Gradually blend in the flour mixture, add the vanilla, and lemon extract, and zest, and beat until smooth. Stir in the pecans. In a separate bowl, beat the egg whites to

Strawberry pickers, Florida.

soft peaks and fold them into the batter. Pour the batter into the pan and bake for 1 hour, or until the cake pulls slightly from the sides of the pan. (A clean broom straw should remain clean when inserted and removed from the middle of the cake.) Let cool. Serve with Home-Made Peach Ice Cream.

Home-Made Peach Ice Cream

(United States)

Ice cream is the classic summer dessert in the South. Those who have had rural childhoods or childhoods filled with family reunions fondly recall the race to get to the dasher in the ice-cream freezer and the strength it took to make those last turns of the handle before the ice cream was pronounced finished. This version celebrates the peaches that grow in such abundance in Georgia—they are the state symbol—and it has the extra kick of peach schnapps.

MAKES ABOUT ¾ GALLON

½ gallon whole milk
1 can sweetened condensed milk
1 tablespoon vanilla extract
2 tablespoons peach schnapps
2 cups minced fresh peaches (canned peaches may be substituted, but the
  taste will not be the same)

Mix the milk, condensed milk, vanilla, and peach schnapps together in a large bowl. Add the peaches, and freeze according to the instructions for your ice cream maker.

Mildred Oliver's Nut Cake

(New Orleans)

I tasted this cake one Thanksgiving at the home of my friends Louis and Mary Len Costa, where it had been brought by Jan Batty, a friend of ours who is the curator of both the Hermann Grima House and the Gallier House in New Orleans. She sent it along with the following note:

This is a very old recipe that came from Mildred Olivier, a lovely lady who lives in Arlington plantation right outside of Opelousas. She claims this recipe dates back to the early 1800s and all the measurements are given in pounds. Arlington is an 8,000 square ft. plantation home . . . it was built in 1829 by Major Amos Webb. This recipe was rumored to come from its attic.

The cake was delicious, and, for reasons I've forgotten, we decided to serve it with molasses cream—whipped cream flavored with molasses—that I had concocted when I was writing A Kwanzaa Keepsake. *The khaki-colored cream, with its slightly sweetish taste, was fantastic, and harmonized perfectly with the slightly dry cake. Imagine my surprise several years later, when I discovered a recipe for a similar confection called Creole Fluff (p. 299) in a cookbook as I was researching recipes for* Beyond Gumbo.

1 quart pecans
1 pound butter
1 pound sugar
1 pound flour
6 eggs
1 pound white raisins
1 cup bourbon
1 apple, sliced

continued on next page

Chop the pecans. Preheat the oven to 300 degrees. Grease a large bundt or tube pan and line it with wax paper. Cream the sugar and butter, add the eggs, one at a time. Beat until smooth. Add the bourbon and flour, alternating each ingredient, and beat well after each addition. Fold in the raisins and chopped pecans. Place a shallow pan of water at the bottom of the oven for added moisture. Bake at 300 degrees for 1½ hours. Remove cake from oven and leave out overnight. The next day, poke holes in the cake and sprinkle it with the bourbon. Place a sliced apple in center of cake and put it in a cake tin. Allow the cake to sit for a few days, and then serve with Creole fluff.

Note: The cake never gets really brown. The cooking time depends on the oven; sometimes it only takes one hour. Jan always uses dark raisins for contrast.

Creole Fluff
(New Orleans)

The Williams Research Center at the Historic Old New Orleans Collection in New Orleans is a wondrous place to work. Not only is it blessed with some of the most helpful staff around, it has modern facilities complete with ports for computers and the like. And, most important in the dog days of summer in New Orleans, it is air conditioned! I was busily typing away and making note of recipes I wanted to check again and books that I wanted to read in more detail when I happened across a recipe for Creole Fluff. I was so amazed that I forgot to note its origin. Anyhow, it is the recipe that I had invented and called Molasses Cream in A Kwanzaa Keepsake. *The only difference was a dash of cinnamon.*

MAKES ABOUT 2 CUPS

½ pint heavy whipping cream
3 tablespoons dark molasses
Dash cinnamon

Place the whipping cream in a medium bowl, add a dash of cinnamon, and whisk it with a wire whisk, slowly drizzling the molasses into the cream. When the cream is whipped into firm peaks, spoon it onto whatever you're serving it with and eat immediately.

Flan de Queso

Cheese Flan

(Puerto Rico)

My friend Patricia Wilson declared: "This recipe is so simple it's embarrassing." The important thing is that it works and it's delicious.

SERVES 6 TO 8

1 14-ounce can sweetened condensed milk
1 5-ounce can evaporated milk
1 teaspoon vanilla extract or rum
8 ounces cream cheese, softened
4 large eggs, well beaten

Caramelize the bottom of a 1-quart mold with melted sugar. In a large bowl, mix together the milks, vanilla or rum, cheese, and eggs. Pour the mixture into the mold. Bake in a *bain marie* at 350 degrees until a toothpick inserted in the middle comes out clean, about 45 minutes. Serve hot or at room temperature.

Variations: Add 4 ounces melted guava, mango, or orange paste, apricot leather, or 4 ounces black coffee, to the mixture.

Flan Tres Leches

Three-Milk Flan

(Costa Rica)

Recipes have a way of turning up in the strangest places. While I was finishing this book in Martha's Vineyard, my friend K.T., who runs a fantastic boutique called Vital Signs, and takes a month off each year to visit Costa Rica, was telling me about her favorite dessert. She said that it was stupidly simple but impressively delicious. Her version uses three milks—whole, condensed, and evaporated, yet is unlike the traditional tres leches *dessert, which has a more cakelike consistency.*

K.T. likes to freeze the flan and eat it frozen, but that is a whole different dessert.

SERVES 6 TO 8

Granulated sugar, to taste
1 5-ounce can evaporated milk
1 14-ounce can sweetened condensed milk
2 cups milk
2 eggs
1 egg yolk
1 teaspoon vanilla

Caramelize the bottom of a 1-quart mold with melted sugar. Mix all the ingredients well, and pour into the mold. Cook in a *bain marie* at 350 degrees until a toothpick inserted in the middle comes out clean, 35 to 40 minutes. Serve hot or at room temperature.

CANDY SELLERS

IT'S DIFFICULT FOR ME to describe my love affair with the confections of the African-Atlantic world. I don't know why, but the sticky fudges and fondants that cling to my teeth and make my dentist unhappy are one of the delights of the hemisphere's cooking that I cannot indulge in enough. I tingle with anticipation when I see a candy seller seated atop a stool with a basket or wooden tray of goodies; I can't wait to find out what's inside.

It may be a dark molasses-rich *pe de moleque* in Bahia, Brazil; or a knot of pulled sugar peppermint in Montego Bay, Jamaica; or even a praline in New Orleans (but I really only like the sugary kind). In Jamaica, I might find the jaw-breaking treat known as *Bustamante jawbone* in honor of the debating abilities of one of the country's independence leaders. Perhaps it's a peanut patty known as *pinda-cake* in Jamaica or simply as *pinda* in Curaçao. I delight in the passion-fruit pastes of the French Antilles or even the guava pastes and orange jellies that come wrapped in leaves in San Juan's Plaza del Mercado.

These treats are the other end of the culinary spectrum, designed for frivolity alone and prepared for the delight of children and adults. They are one of my passions.

As much as I love the candy, I love the candy sellers even more. Small and wizened with fingers gnarled from pulling on hot sugar or large and jolly from overindulgence in their own wares, these women are the torchbearers of an art that is too often unheralded in the scheme of general matters culinary. Sassy or sullen, these sisters of the stool and the market tray are special to me, and no cookbook would be complete without a small sampling of some of their wares.

Pralines

(New Orleans)

This New Orleans confection is one of the great links in the chain of Creole cookery. The name harks back to the French Duc du Praslin, *but the New World variant of the candy is found in areas that mark the Creole world. Called* pe de moleque *in Bahia, Brazil;* pinda cake *in Jamaica;* pinda *in Curaçao, peanut patties* in the South; and prasle de cacahuatl *in Texas border towns, the brown-sugar-and-nut confection is a constant.*

When I was working on my book, The Welcome Table, *Leah Chase, the doyenne of African-American-Creole cooking, recalled that the pralines of her youth were coconut patties, white or tinted pink with cochineal. It started me thinking of all of the coconut, peanut, and, yes, pecan confections sold by women of African descent in this hemisphere.*

MAKES ABOUT 12 PRALINES

1 cup firmly packed light-brown sugar
1 cup granulated sugar
½ cup light cream
2 tablespoons salted butter
1 cup pecan halves

Place the sugars and cream in a heavy saucepan and bring to a boil over medium heat, stirring constantly. When the temperature reaches 228 degrees on a candy thermometer, stir in the butter and the pecans, and continue to cook, stirring constantly, until the mixture reaches 236 degrees. Remove the pan from the heat and allow the mixture to cool for 5 minutes.

Beat the mixture with a wooden spoon until the candy coats the pecans but does not lose its gloss. Drop the pralines, 1 tablespoon at a time, onto a well-greased sheet of marble or a well-greased cookie tin. Cool and serve. They keep for several weeks in a tin. You can crumble the pralines over vanilla ice cream for a special treat.

Cajeta de Leche

Milk Fudge

(Costa Rica)

In areas of the Creole world where fresh milk was not always available, condensed milk retains its popularity. It is appreciated for its availability and for its taste; there is a whole range of confectionery prepared from condensed milk. This milk fudge is one part of that tradition. Traditionally, the balls are placed on lemon leaves, to absorb some of the lemon flavor. If you live in an area where lemon leaves are available, you may want to try this method.

MAKES ABOUT 18 FUDGE BALLS

1 5-ounce can condensed milk
1 cup powdered milk
½ tablespoon butter
1 whole clove

Combine the condensed milk, powdered milk, and butter in a small bowl and stir with a wooden spoon until they become smooth and fudgelike. Roll the mixture into small balls in your hands, place a clove in the top of each ball, and place the fudge in small paper candy cups. The fudge can be served immediately, or kept in a cool place for eating later.

Tamarind Balls

(Trinidad)

Tamarind is one of the legacies brought to the Caribbean region by the indentured Indian servants who replaced the enslaved Africans. This confection is a typical sweet in many Caribbean nations; they are particularly prized in the southern Caribbean. Tamarind balls are easy to prepare and are a good project for cooking with children, as no fire is required and the children like kneading the tamarind and sugar together and rolling it into balls. When shopping for tamarind balls in the Caribbean, look for the black seed that is a virtual guarantee that the tamarind balls are homemade.

4 ounces tamarind paste with seeds
1 pound plus 1 cup sugar

Place the tamarind paste and the sugar on a wooden board or tray and knead it together until the mixture becomes light in color and the sugar is nearly absorbed. Take a tablespoon of the mixture and roll it into a ball around one or two of the tamarind seeds. Proceed until you have used all of the paste. Spread the additional cup of sugar on the board and roll each ball in it until coated with sugar. The tamarind balls may be eaten immediately or stored in an air-tight container.

Stuffed Dates

(Curaçao)

These stuffed dates are traditionally served during the feast of Simchat Torah, and are re-markably similar to the North African variation that turns up on dessert trays in Morocco and Tunisia. These, though, are not filled with marzipan, but rather with a mince of walnuts and apricots, perhaps in a subtle nod to Curaçao's Sephardic charoset, known as garosa, that's made from dates, prunes, raisins, figs, orange peel, peanuts, cashews, and more.

MAKES 36 DATES

36 pitted medjool dates
¾ cup chopped walnuts
¾ cup minced dried apricots
2 tablespoons sweet kosher wine

Arrange the dates on a cookie sheet lined with waxed paper. Mix the rest of the in-gredients together and gently spoon about 1 teaspoon of the mixture into each date, being careful not to overfill. When ready to serve, arrange the dates on a serving tray and serve at room temperature.

Stuffed Figs

(New Orleans)

Many a New Orleans backyard boasts a fig tree and, when they are in season, fig preserves are made by the gallon, and the fruit is dried for use in the fruitless seasons. Old recipes use figs in everything from fruitcakes and preserves to candies. This recipe uses marshmallows. Marshmallows have a long history and actually date to the late eighteenth century. This recipe is not an old one, as it uses the light, airy marshmallow with which we're familiar rather than the chewier and denser version that predates it.

SERVES 4 TO 6

12 large dried figs
12 large white marshmallows

Reconstitute the figs by placing them in warm water for 1 hour. Pat dry with absorbent paper, split them open, and stuff with the marshmallows. Serve at room temperature.

Canjica de Erminhia

Brazilian Sweet Hominy

(Brazil)

Salvador da Baia de Todos os Santos, *Brazil, is known as being one of the places on the South American continent where Africa is alive and well. From the hymns to Yoruba gods or* orixas *sung to the sound of drumbeats in temples, called* terreiros, *to the dende oil that flavors much of the region's food, the city affectionately known as Bahia, is a living testimonial to African survivals, culinary and otherwise, in the hemisphere. The city is also a monument to the fusion that has gone on over the ages. In this recipe, the corn of the New World meets up with the coconuts of the old and the Moorish sweet tooth of the cloistered nuns of Portugal. In Bahia, though, they don't worry about the history of the dish, they just enjoy it. It's very, very sweet, so a little goes a long way.*

1½ cups coconut milk
¼ cup sugar
3 tablespoons Goya Coconut in Syrup
4 whole cloves, or to taste
15-ounce can large white hominy
Powdered cinnamon

Place the coconut milk, sugar, coconut, and cloves in a heavy saucepan, and bring to a boil over low heat. Add the hominy, bring to a second boil, and cook for 2 minutes. Remove from heat and serve in small bowls. Sprinkle each bowl with powdered cinnamon.

Arroz con Leche

Milk Rice

(Costa Rica)

The predominance of rice desserts in the Creole world is not really amazing. After all, people in the African-Atlantic sections of the Creole world get rice two ways. The Africans from southern Senegal, Sierra Leone, and Liberia had their own system of rice growing and developed their own dishes. Eventually this African rice was brought to the Iberian Peninsula by the Moors where it became a traditional dish. Rice came to the Americas with the descendants of the Moorish-influenced Iberians as well as with the enslaved Africans.

SERVES 8

4 cups cooked rice
1 5-ounce can sweetened condensed milk
1 4-ounce can evaporated milk
½ cup freshly shredded coconut
2 cinnamon sticks
3 whole cloves
Pinch salt
¼ cup guava jelly

Place all the ingredients, except guava jelly, in a small saucepan and stir until well mixed. Lower the heat, and simmer the mixture for 15 minutes. Serve warm, topping each serving with a dollop of guava jelly.

Rice Pudding

(United States)

My father's favorite dessert was rice pudding. I suspect he'd have been thrilled to know that the rice pudding he so loved is one of the classic desserts of the Creole world.

SERVES 6

4 cups milk
¼ cup uncooked rice
½ cup sugar
½ teaspoon salt
1 teaspoon vanilla extract
¼ teaspoon freshly grated nutmeg

Preheat the oven to 300 degrees. Mix the milk, rice, sugar, and salt in a buttered 6-cup casserole or ovenproof baking dish, and bake the mixture uncovered for 2 hours, stirring 30 minutes. After 2 hours, add the vanilla and the nutmeg, stir well, and bake for an additional 30 minutes, or until a crust forms and the rice is tender. Serve warm. You may also allow it to come to room temperature, refrigerate it, and serve cold.

Historic Calas

Rice Fritters

(New Orleans)

Calas are rice fritters that used to be hawked on the streets of New Orleans by Creole women of African descent whose cry, "Calas, calas, bels calas tout chauds" was a fond memory of those who lived and wrote in nineteenth century New Orleans. This recipe, which I received from my friend Lenora Costa, is an old family one. It's all the more interesting because Lenora's family is one of the oldest in the Crescent City. This recipe was dictated by Pouponne D'Antilly (1809–1887) to her mistress Blanche Livaudais and is still prepared today by Madame Livaudais's descendants.

The rice should be cooked so that it is softer than normal.

MAKES ABOUT 16 FRITTERS

1½ cups cooked rice, soft
1½ cups self-rising flour
½ cup sugar
½ teaspoon salt
Nutmeg, to taste
3 eggs, beaten
¼ cup warm milk
1 teaspoon vanilla
Oil, for frying

Place rice in a bowl and add flour, sugar, salt, and nutmeg. Then add the eggs, milk, and vanilla. Beat until smooth. Drop by the tablespoon in deep hot fat and fry until golden brown in the oil that has been heated to 350 degrees. They will flip themselves over and cook on both side in 2 to 3 minutes.

Dry on absorbent paper and serve hot, sprinkled with powdered sugar.

Calas

Rice Fritters

(New Orleans)

Lyle Saxon, Robert Tallant, and Edward Dreyer in Gumbo Ya-Ya: A Collection of Louisiana Folk Tales, *written in 1945, remind us of the importance of street vending in the Crescent City of centuries past. They also tell of* calas, *the most famous of the street foods. At the time that they were writing, the cala sellers were dying out. There was Clementine, who still wore a* tignon *or headtie, and a long gingham skirt who would solicit clients with the cry:*

*Beeeelles calas—Beeelles calas
Madame, mo gaignin calas,
Madame, mo gaignin calas,
Tou cho, tou cho, tou cho.
Beelles calas—Belles calas
A Madame, mo gaignin calas,
Mo guaranti vous ye bons!*

Beautiful calas—beautiful calas
Madame, I have calas
Madame, I have calas
Good and hot, good and hot
Madame, I have beautiful calas
I guarantee you they're good!

One of the last professional calas *vendors in New Orleans was a man named Richard Gabriel. By the mid-twentieth century, one of the few places that they could be found was*

continued on next page

a small restaurant in the Quarter known as the Coffee Pot. Then an enterprising and in-exhaustible lady named Poppy Tooker took over at the helm of the New Orleans chapter of Slow Food. Thanks to Poppy, the rice fritter has now been placed on the Slow Food Ark of Foods—a list of foods that are endangered—and is having a renaissance. If you want to try the authentic cala *cooked over a wood-burning fire, head to the Hermann Grima historic house in the French Quarter.* Calas *are one of the recipes included in the hearth-cooking demonstration given by docents. Otherwise, make your own with Poppy's recipe.*

MAKES APPROXIMATELY 12 CALAS

2 cups cooked rice (cold or, at least, room temperature)
6 tablespoons flour
2 teaspoons baking powder
3 tablespoons sugar
1 teaspoon vanilla
2 whole eggs
Oil, for frying
Powdered sugar

Place the rice into a medium bowl and sprinkle the flour and the baking powder on top, mixing thoroughly to coat the rice. Mix in the sugar. Sprinkle the vanilla over the rice and mix well. Add the eggs, one at a time, mixing well after each addition. Heat the oil to 375 degrees in a heavy skillet, (you will need at least ¼" to ½" of oil). Form the *calas* with two tablespoons, moving the dough from one to the other until you have an oval. Push the oval off the spoon into the oil and fry, turning once, until it is browned on both sides. Drain well on paper towels and sprinkle with powdered sugar. Serve hot.

Fruit Fritters

(United States)

This can be transformed into a savory fritter batter by eliminating the fruit, and used to fry vegetables like eggplant, zucchini, onions, and okra.

Oil for frying
2 eggs
½ cup milk
1 cup sifted flour
½ teaspoon salt
1 teaspoon melted butter
1½ to 2 cups sliced, peeled fruit, such as peaches, apples, or bananas

Pour about two inches of oil into a heavy deep skillet or saucepan. Over medium-high heat, bring the oil to 375 degrees.

In a medium-sized bowl, beat the eggs while drizzling in the milk. Add the flour, baking powder, salt, and melted butter. Drop the fruit, a piece at a time, into the batter. Remove the fruit and allow the excess batter to drip off.

Drop each piece into the hot oil and fry until golden brown, about two to three minutes in all. Do not crowd the pan.

Gateau Sirop

Syrup Cake

(New Orleans)

I first tasted a gateau sirop on Easter Sunday 2001 when I was taken on a magical excursion into Bayou country by my friend, antiquaire Patrick Dunne. A group of friends lunched and then headed off to visit a folly in the style of the French eighteenth century, constructed by a fellow antique dealer at the edge of a bayou. The contrast between the worldly elegance of the folly and the haunting melancholy of the bayou was startling in its perfection. It was as though I'd visited Sleeping Beauty's castle. One of the best parts was drinking champagne from sparkling crystal flutes and sampling a traditional Louisiana gateau sirop, a densely molasses-tasting confection that is a bit like elegant gingerbread. I couldn't wheedle the recipe out of Patrick, but was delighted to learn that my friend Ken Smith remembered just such a cake from his youth and knew how to make it. You may not get the view of the pink egrets roosting in the branches of the trees in the bayou, and you may not be able to sit in a bergère de l'époque, *but you can savor the taste of a* gateau sirop *along with a flute of your favorite bubbly.*

SERVES 9

½ cup vegetable oil
1½ cups cane syrup (*see* Note)
1 egg, beaten
2½ cups sifted flour
1 teaspoon cinnamon
1 teaspoon ground ginger
½ teaspoon powdered cloves
1½ teaspoon baking soda
Powdered sugar

Heat the oven to 350 degrees. Grease and flour a 9" square baking pan. Combine the oil, syrup, and beaten egg in a medium bowl, and stir until well blended. In a separate bowl, mix and sift the flour, cinnamon, ginger, and cloves. In a small bowl, combine the baking soda and ¾ cup hot water. Alternately add the dry ingredients and the baking soda and water to the egg, syrup, and oil mixture and mix well. Pour into the baking pan and bake for 45 minutes, or until a knife comes out clean when inserted in the middle. Let cool. Turn out of the baking pan and top with powdered sugar.

Note: Ken Smith uses Steen's Cane Syrup (see Mail-Order Sources)

Country Calas

Rice Fritters

(Louisiana)

Calas *were also consumed in other parts of Louisiana and the American South. Historian Sylviane A. Diouf, in her work* Servants of Allah, *finds them under the name* saraka *in the Sea Islands of Georgia and suggests that they may be descendants of the traditional rice ball, given as charity by West African women on Fridays. There is also a rice fritter by the name* calas *among the people of Bong county in Liberia that is hawked on the streets by women. This yeast version from my friend Ken Smith, Louisiana native and executive chef at the Upperline Restaurant, makes a lighter* cala.

MAKES ABOUT 12 CALAS

1 teaspoon dry yeast
½ cup warm water
2 cups cooked rice (rice must be lukewarm)
3 eggs, well beaten
1 cup sifted flour
½ cup sugar
½ teaspoon salt
⅛ teaspoon freshly grated nutmeg
Peanut oil, for frying
Powdered sugar

In a medium bowl, dissolve the yeast in the warm water. Stir in the rice, mixing well, then cover and let rise overnight. When ready to cook, add the flour, sugar, salt, and nutmeg, beat well, and let sit in a warm place for 30 minutes. Heat the oil to 375 degrees in a heavy saucepan or Dutch oven. Drop the mixture into the oil by the tablespoon and fry for 2 to 3 minutes, turning once, or until golden brown. Sprinkle with powdered sugar and serve hot.

Creole Cream Cheese

(New Orleans)

Natives of the Crescent City get misty eyed when the subject of Creole Cream Cheese comes up. It used to be readily available and is a breakfast treat fondly remembered by many. When the last manufacturer of the delicacy closed their doors, the public was forced to make their own or go without. Ever-resourceful Poppy Tooker of Slow Food has seen to it that Creole Cream Cheese is being made again, but she's also got a great recipe for preparing it. Creole Cream Cheese is traditionally eaten topped with half and half and sugar to taste for breakfast, or spread on buttered French bread rounds topped with salt and pepper by those who prefer something savory.

MAKES 6 PINT-SIZED CHEESES

1 gallon skim milk
1 cup buttermilk
6–8 drops liquid rennet (*see* **Note**)

Mix all the ingredients in a bowl and cover loosely with plastic wrap. Allow the mixture to sit at room temperature for 18 to 24 hours, after which time a single large curd will be floating in whey. With a slotted spoon, fill pint-sized molds, adding the cream cheese in as large pieces as possible.

Place the molds on a rack to drain, and cover lightly. Place them in a refrigerator and allow them to drain for 6 to 8 hours. Turn the cheeses out of their molds into containers for storage. Creole Cream Cheese can be stored for up to 2 weeks in the refrigerator.

Note: Rennet is available from cheese-making supply shops (see Mail-Order Sources).

Creole Cream Cheese Ice Cream

(New Orleans)

When the weather gets sultry, there's nothing more refreshing than Creole Cream Cheese Ice Cream.

MAKES ABOUT 5 PINTS

4 pints Creole Cream Cheese (p. 319)
1 pint heavy cream
2 tablespoons vanilla extract
½ cup sugar

Mix all the ingredients thoroughly in a food processor or blender. Place in the bowl of an ice-cream mixer and process according to directions, or place the mixture in a stainless steel bowl in the freezer, and stir every 20 to 30 minutes until the mixture has frozen to the desired consistency.

Dewberry Juice Pie
(Louisiana)

My buddy Ken Smith is a self-proclaimed country boy. It matters not that he is a chef at the Upperline Restaurant, one of the hidden treasures of the New Orleans dining scene, nor that he's lived and worked in that city for many years; his culinary roots are in his country home. He's originally from the Cane River section of Louisiana, and many of his childhood memories are infused with the rich tastes of the countryside. This dewberry pie is one that was prepared from dewberries that grew on his grandmother's farm. Dewberries are similar to blackberries. If you cannot find them, you may substitute blackberries or blueberries.

MAKES 1 8-INCH-SQUARE PIE

FOR THE CRUST:
1 cup all-purpose flour
½ teaspoon salt
¾ cups shortening
2 tablespoons ice water

FOR THE FILLING:
4 cups dewberries (or blackberries)
2 tablespoons cornstarch
4 tablespoons butter, cut into small pieces
Freshly ground nutmeg, to taste
1¼ cup sugar

Prepare the crust by combining the flour and salt in a mixing bowl. Cut in the shortening with a pastry blender or fork until the mixture resembles coarse cornmeal.

continued on next page

Sprinkle the water over the surface. Stir with a fork until the dry ingredients are moistened. Shape into a ball, wrap in waxed paper, and chill in the refrigerator for at least 1 hour.

Prepare the filling by combining the berries and 3 cups water in a saucepan. Cook for 15 to 20 minutes over medium heat until a liquid forms. Strain the berry liquid through a sieve into a medium bowl. Add the sugar and nutmeg. Dissolve the corn-starch in 2 tablespoons cold water and add it to the berry liquid.

Remove the dough from the refrigerator, divide it in half, and roll into ⅛" thick-ness on a lightly floured surface. Place the dough into an 8"-square pan. Add the fill-ing and butter. Roll the remaining pastry out in the same manner and cover the top of the pie, fluting the edges with your fingers. Cut ½" slits in the top of the pie to allow steam to escape and bake for 50 minutes at 350 degrees. Serve warm solo or topped with vanilla ice cream.

Three Dessert Sauces

These sauces can be used over the ice cream or cake of your choice.

Passion Fruit—Caramel Sauce (U.S. Virgin Islands)

2 cups brown sugar
1 cup passion-fruit purée (available in the freezer section of Latin markets)
1 cup heavy cream
1 tablespoon butter
1 tablespoon vanilla extract
1 tablespoon dark rum
1 teaspoon powdered ginger

Place all the ingredients in a medium saucepan, stirring well. Bring to a boil over medium heat. Lower the heat and simmer for 2 to 3 minutes. Remove from the heat, cool, and serve over the ice cream of your choice.

Chocolate Rum Fudge Sauce
(U.S. Virgin Islands)

1 cup sugar
½ cup good-quality cocoa powder
2 ounces unsalted butter
1 cup dark rum
1 cup heavy cream
1 tablespoon vanilla extract

Place all the ingredients in a medium saucepan, stirring well and bring to a gentle boil over medium heat. Lower the heat, and simmer for 2 to 3 minutes. Remove from the heat, cool, and serve over the ice cream of your choice.

Peanut patties and coconut sweets, Guadeloupe.

Patricia's Guava Rum Sauce

(Puerto Rico)

Patricia Wilson serves this sauce with roast leg of pork. I think it's just fine on anything, including drizzled over vanilla ice cream.

8 ounces guava paste, cut into cubes
½ cup Puerto Rican Gold Rum

In a saucepan, mix the guava paste with 1 cup water and the rum. Place over low heat, and simmer until the guava paste has melted. Serve with everything, from ice cream to pork.

Plantain Crisps
(U.S. Virgin Islands)

My friend Robert Oliver is a talented cook who hails from Fiji, which he swears gives him a particular affinity for the food of the tropics. I suspect he's right, in that his tropical desserts are always masterpieces that are as astounding to see as they are to taste. When I organized a chef's week at Almond Resorts in Barbados, he created these plantain crisps as a part of his Bajan Banana Split.

SERVES 4 TO 6

Vegetable oil, for frying
3 green plantains
Sugar
Cinnamon

Heat the oil to 375 degrees in a Dutch oven or heavy saucepan. Slice the plantains lengthwise into very thin slices on a mandolin. Drop the plantain slices into the oil and fry until them for 2 to 3 minutes, or until crisp. Remove them with a slotted spoon and dust with a mixture of sugar and cinnamon. Drain on absorbent paper and serve warm as a snack.

Conkies

(Barbados)

This is a sweet version of delicacies found throughout the Creole world under names like pasteles *and* dukanoo.

2 cups very fine corn flour
½ cup all-purpose flour
1 teaspoon powdered allspice
½ teaspoon freshly grated nutmeg
2 teaspoons salt
¾ cup dark-brown sugar
¾ cup grated calabaza
2 large sweet potatoes, grated
¾ cup dark raisins
1 cup milk
1 teaspoon almond extract
Banana leaves
Vegetable oil, for greasing leaves

Place the flours, spices, and sugar in a large bowl; add the calabaza, sweet potatoes, and raisins and mix well. Add the milk and almond extract and stir to make a thick dough. Pass the banana leaves through a flame to soften them and then oil them with vegetable oil and cut them into 6" squares. Place 3 to 4 tablespoons of the dough in the middle of the banana leaf and fold the ends over, making a small package. Tie the package securely with string. Place the packages on a steamer rack and steam over hot water for 45 minutes. Serve warm. To eat, unwrap the packages and savor the contents.

Bajan Bread Pudding

(Barbados)

This is a variation on the bread puddings that are typical throughout the Creole world. This one is soaked overnight, and comes to the table almost as fluffy as a soufflé.

SERVES 6

½ cup raisins
2 tablespoons dark rum
1 large loaf day-old white bread, crusts removed
½ pound butter, plus additional for buttering bread and topping
2 cups light cream
1 cup evaporated milk
6 eggs
½ cup brown sugar
2 teaspoons vanilla extract
½ teaspoon lemon extract
½ teaspoon cinnamon

Plump the raisins by placing them in a bowl with the rum and letting them sit for two hours. Grease a 2½-quart baking pan. Cut the bread into diagonal slices and butter on each side. Place the butter, cream, milk, eggs, brown sugar, vanilla extract, and lemon extract in a large mixing bowl and whisk until a thin batter forms. Arrange the bread on the bottom of the baking dish, overlapping slightly. Top the bread with raisins and batter. Repeat until pan is full. Top with a sprinkling of cinnamon. Cover with plastic wrap and refrigerate overnight.

When ready to cook, preheat the oven to 350 degrees. Uncover the pudding and dot the top with butter. Bake for 45 minutes, or until set and golden brown. Serve warm.

Rum Sauce

(Barbados)

This is Barbados's answer to the bourbon sauce that traditionally tops many bread puddings of New Orleans.

MAKES ABOUT 1¼ CUPS

1 cup sugar
½ cup dark Barbadian rum
Pinch ground cloves
¼ teaspoon ground cinnamon
¼ teaspoon freshly grated lemon zest.

Place the sugar in a heavy saucepan and let melt over medium heat, stirring occasionally. When it is golden, slowly add ¾ cup water, rum, cloves, cinnamon, and lemon zest. Bring to a boil. Cook for 3 minutes, then cool to room temperature. Serve warm over bread pudding.

Goat's milk the hard way, Cuba.

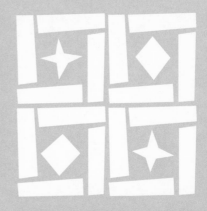

Beverages

Banana Punch (Barbados)

Down the Islands Rum Punch (Trinidad)

Rum and Coconut Water (Dominican Republic)

Coconut Water (Jamaica)

Simple Syrup (All Islands)

Sangaree (Barbados)

Corn and Oil (Barbados)

Ponche — Hot Milk Punch (Costa Rica)

Chaudeau — Milk Punch (Guadeloupe)

Coquito — Rum Eggnog (Puerto Rico)

Ponche Crema — Caribbean Eggnog (Curaçao)

Brandied Milk Punch (New Orleans)

Sorrel and Ginger (Jamaica)

Brown Lemonade (Jamaica)

Lemon Verbena Iced Tea (New Orleans)

Maubi — Mauby (Dominican Republic)

ALEXANDER SMALLS
(South Carolina)

"He's got the whole world in his hands."

I DON'T RECALL EXACTLY how long I've known Alexander Smalls, possibly because I feel that I've known him all my life. We met because he summoned me to Café Beulah, his chic Manhattan eatery that drew crowds of buppies and yuppies, entrepreneurs and entertainers, models, moguls, and just plain old folks to dine on his version of the Low Country foods of his South Carolina youth. He'd selected as his intermediary Bobby Flay, his acquaintance and a friend from my culinary wanderings and someone who has quietly supported chefs of color behind the scenes for years. He'd heard of my books and decided we should meet. We arrived for dinner and Alexander greeted us with beakers of bourbon and a hefty dose of his serious sophistication filtered through "down home, y'all come" warmth.

The first thing that you notice about Alexander is his voice. It's not surprising, as he's a trained musician who still takes vocal classes and has sung professionally in the opera houses of Europe and the

United States. The next is his take-no-prisoners sense of humor. The picture that graced his menu, of elegant African Americans driving near the *Arc de Triomphe* in Paris, hinted that this spot took southern cooking beyond the overworked cliches of so-called soul food. The first taste of the food confirmed my suspicions—the international tastes of his European sojourns, the comfort of the southern food of his birth, and the *je ne sais quoi* that is uniquely Alexander signaled that this was a culinary soulmate to be reckoned with. By the end of dinner, we were gabbing away as though we'd known each other all our lives.

It was several years later, after he'd closed Café Beulah, at which I'd become a virtual regular at the champagne-cork–styled barstools, that I actually got to watch Alexander cook. Seated in the dining room of his apartment, I watched as he whipped around his tiny kitchen assembling dinner as though it were a ballet—a pinch of this, a crumble of that, all the while stirring and accompanying the cooking with a running monologue punctuated with occasional snippets of songs ranging from pop to arias to spirituals. He improvises with food as he would with the *adornos* of an aria: surely, graciously, hitting every note smack on. From the *fortissimo* of his sure hand with the seafood and the swine of his South Carolina home, to the *pianissimo* of his delicate seasonings, to the *brio* of his *tour de force* desserts, cooking is just another part of Alexander's art, an extension of his love of people and his questing mind.

Several years later, as testimonial of our friendship and his generosity, he sang at my mother's memorial service and all who listened said that the angels must have cried. It's fitting that the song was "Kumbaya," 'cause his hospitality at Café Beulah, Sweet Ophelia's, and Shoebox Café, all radiated the same warmth of the phrase, "come by here."

Tortuga

(Haiti)

Named in honor of the pirate haunt that was located off the island's northern coast, this drink is one of my Caribbean favorites.

SERVES 2

½ cup milk
½ cup coconut milk
4 ounces Jane Barbancourt Coconut Rum (*see* Note)
Nutmeg, for topping

Place the milk, coconut milk, and rum in a shaker with ice. Shake until frothy. Pour into chilled highball glasses, top with nutmeg, and serve immediately.

Note: If you cannot get Jane Barbancourt Coconut rum, Malibu brand from Barbados, or any other coconut rum will do.

'Ti Punch

(Guadeloupe)

This is a classic drink of the Creole world. A bit of sugar, a few pieces of limes just cut off the tree and pressed to extract their juice, and enough white rum to give you a buzz. It is, in fact, a French Antillean cousin of Brazil's caipirinha. *In some parts of the French-speaking Caribbean it's known as a C.R.S. for its three ingredients: Citron (lime), Rhum (You know what!), and Sucre (sugar). They're absolutely habit forming, and quite lethal.*

SERVES 1

1 lime, cut into palettes (p. 43)
Unrefined cane sugar, to taste
White rum from the French Antilles, to taste (*see* Note)

Place the lime pieces into a highball glass or a small wide-mouth stemmed glass. Add the sugar and pour in the rum. Stir until well mixed. Some will add an ice cube, but this is considered anathema by many.

Note: You may use any white rum, but the rum of the French Caribbean has a sugar-cane flavor that is not duplicated in the whites of the rest of the region.

Punch au Miel

Punch with Honey

(Guadeloupe)

This is a variation on the popular 'ti punch, but takes its flavoring not only from the rum and the sugar, but from the variety of aromatic honey that is used. Place the bottle of rum and the honey on a tray with the lime pieces and let your guests make the strength of drink that they desire.

SERVES 1

1 lime cut into palettes (p. 43)
Honey, to taste (*see* Note)
White rum from the French Antilles, to taste

Place the lime pieces into a highball glass or a small, wide-mouth stemmed glass. Add the sugar and pour in the rum. Stir until well mixed.

Note: You'll be surprised at the changes in taste that different types of honey will make. You might want to offer a selection of honeys, so that your guests can sample different ones.

Punch au Sirop

Fruit Syrup Punch

(Guadeloupe)

In the French Antilles, many folk have jars of syrup prepared from tropical fruits on hand to use in cooking, and in preparing wonderful punches that have a hint of sunshine. If they don't have time to prepare it themselves, they can usually pick it up at the market or have the number of an older person who can supply them. I never head home without a jar or two of my favorite passion-fruit syrup and perhaps one of surelles *or* surettes. *They're heavy, but a few spoonfuls go a long way and take me right back to* Pointe à Pitre *or* Fort-de-France. *As* Fort-de-France *is a long way off, instead of tropical fruit syrups you may use any tropical fruit jams in this punch.*

SERVES 1

1 teaspoon Goya passion-fruit jam, or to taste
White rum from the French Antilles, to taste

Place the jam in a highball glass. Pour in a teaspoon of the rum. Muddle until well mixed. Top off with rum to taste. Some will add an ice cube, but this is considered anathema by many.

Punch à la Noix de Coco

Coconut Punch

(Martinique)

From piña coladas to rum and coconut water, the fruit of the coconut palm seems a natural pairing with the elixir of the cane reed. Here is a different twist on the rum and coconut theme, one that can be made in a larger quantity and kept on the sideboard or the bar until ready to serve. It only gets better with time.

SERVES 4

1 brown coconut, grated (save the liquid for a different drink)
8 ounces white rum
½ cup sugar, or to taste
2" piece vanilla bean
½ teaspoon lemon zest
½ teaspoon nutmeg

Open the coconut, grate the white meat, and place it in a large bowl. Add the rum and allow it to soak for 1 hour. Place the coconut meat in a square of cheesecloth and squeeze it into a second bowl to remove all the rum. Add whatever rum remains in the first bowl. Add the sugar and the spices, mix well, and serve over ice or plain.

Shrubb

Clementine Liqueur

(Martinique and Guadeloupe)

My friend Maryse says that clementines are traditionally eaten in Guadeloupe at Christmastime. People eat them and keep a few of the seeds in their purses and wallets for good luck throughout the year, in the same way that some African Americans will keep a black-eyed pea in theirs for luck and money. This beverage is a way to use all of the clementines, including the aromatic peel.

MAKES 1 LITER

1 bottle white rum from the French Caribbean
Peels from 8 clementines, pith removed
1 vanilla bean, scraped
3" cinnamon stick
3 or 4 whole cloves

Pour off a bit of rum from the bottle. (You can do this as a holiday libation to the ancestors or just make yourself a 'ti punch.) Add the clementines, vanilla bean, cinnamon stick, and cloves to the bottle, cork lightly, and allow it to macerate in the sun for two weeks. Then store in a cool place until ready to serve. You don't have to wait until Christmas.

Zazerac — Havana Style

(New Orleans)

The use of absinthe shows that this version of this recipe is one of the early forms of the drink that has come to be known as a Sazerac. *Absinthe is currently illegal in the United States, but can be found overseas in Spain and in some parts of Switzerland. A new version, minus the wormwood, is called* Absente *and is becoming more readily available.* La fée verte, *or green fairy, as the drink was called for its enchantment of more than one starving artist in* fin de siècle *France, was very popular in New Orleans, in which there are two competing Old Absinthe House bars. There's even an herbal absinthe substitute called* Herbesainte, *which is also the name of a new restaurant opened by chef Susan Spicer, but that's another story.*

SERVES 1

1 teaspoon sugar
A few drops absinthe
1½ ounces rye whiskey
Dash Angostura bitters
Dash orange bitters

Place all the ingredients in a highball glass with ice. Stir, but do not shake. Serve immediately.

Sazerac

(New Orleans)

Legend has it that the Sazerac is the nation's first cocktail, and was poured in the 1800s by a Monsieur Peychaud, an apothecary in the French Quarter who had invented it as a nostrum for stomach disorders. His tonic was called bitters *and he flavored it with Sazerac-de-forge* cognac *and a dash of absinthe. The creation was served in eggcups called* coquetiers *and the name was soon anglicized into the word cocktail. The drink is revered, and served often at the Sazerac Bar at the Fairmont Hotel, but I prefer to watch my friends sample theirs at Galatoire's, where my friend Kerry Moody never begins dinner without one. Once called the green goblin because of the color they took on from the absinthe, they were considered particularly apropos for Saint Patrick's Day, which is a bigger holiday in New Orleans than you'd expect.*

Today, Sazeracs *are prepared with* Herbesaint, *a local New Orleans liqueur that is an absinthe substitute. Both Herbesaint and M. Peychaud's bitters are available in New Orleans. The latter can be mail ordered (see Mail-Order Sources).*

SERVES 1

1 teaspoon superfine sugar
Dash or two Peychaud's bitters
Dash Herbesaint
1½ ounces rye whiskey
Lemon zest

Muddle the sugar and the bitters together with the whiskey. Pour enough Herbesaint into an old-fashioned glass to rinse it well. Add 2 or 3 ice cubes and the whiskey. Rub the rim of the glass with lemon zest and serve.

Fancy Alcoholic Champola

(Cuba)

This Cuban punch, prepared from fresh soursop juice, is a favorite at bembes, Lucumi re-*ligious ceremonies. There it is served without the rum, and used to salute the* orisha, *Obatala, who is a lover of all things white. Cuban ethnologist Fernando Ortiz suggests that the name may come from the Congolese word* sampula, *which means to shake rapidly. A version of the punch is also prepared in Mexico and keeps its Cuban name. In other places in Latin America this beverage goes by the name of* guanabana *or* guanabada. *With the addition of a tot or two of rum, it's a great summer punch; without, it's a cooling tropical twist anytime.*

SERVES 12

2 cans soursop nectar (*see* Note)
2 packages frozen soursop pulp (*see* Note)
2 bottles coconut soda (*see* Note)
½ cup ginger beer
½ pint vanilla or coconut ice cream
Dark Puerto Rican rum, to taste (Unless you've got a contraband bottle of
    Havana Club hidden away), optional
Freshly grated nutmeg

Chill the liquid ingredients and place in a punch bowl. Add the ice cream and serve immediately, topped with freshly grated nutmeg.

Note: Goya Products makes all of these; they are available at supermarkets and shops that specialize in Hispanic ingredients.

Champola

Chilled Soursop Liquid

(Mexico)

This is the purist's version, as it is prepared in Veracruz, Mexico by Afro-Mexicans.

SERVES 2

2 cups soursop pulp
2 cups whole milk

Place the soursop pulp and the milk in a blender and beat into a froth. Serve over ice in large, chilled glasses.

Mauby vendor, Guadeloupe.

Watermelon Agua Fresca

(Mexico)

Agua frescas, or cool waters, are prepared from all sorts of fruits, and take the place of fizzed-up sugary sodas in traditional Mexican life. This one is a natural and takes advantage of the fruit's high water content. It's a great cooler in the summer. Save the rind—you can use it for Watermelon Rind Pickle (p. 144).

MAKES ABOUT 1½ GALLONS

8 cups puréed watermelon
16 cups water
1 cup sugar
¼ cup freshly squeezed lime juice
Watermelon wedges, for garnish

Place all the ingredients in a large glass crock. Stir well to mix and then refrigerate overnight or for several hours until well chilled. Serve chilled in tall glasses garnished with watermelon wedges.

Banana Punch

(Barbados)

The banana-boat song and the United Fruit Company notwithstanding, bananas are not originally from the Caribbean. Thought to have originated in Malaysia, they belong to the same family as the lily and the orchid. The banana turns up in India in the sixth or fifth century B.C., and an Indian legend says that it was the banana, not the apple, that was offered to Adam—a legend that is the reason behind the Latin name for the plantain—musa paradisiaca. They grow in tropical and subtropical climates and are available in many varieties, from the ones with which we are most familiar to small, delicate ones with reddish skins. Any variety will do for this punch, including good old Chiquitas.

SERVES 1

½ ripe banana
4 ounces fresh coconut milk
1 ounce dark Barbadian rum, or to taste
Sugar, to taste
Freshly grated nutmeg

Place the banana, coconut milk, rum, and sugar in a blender and blend until frothy. Pour into an ice-filled glass, top with a few shavings of nutmeg, and serve.

MOUNTAINTOP MADNESS
Haiti, 1987

MANY OF MY FRIENDS don't understand it, but Haiti is one of my favorite islands in the Caribbean. It manages to combine the sophistication of Europe in Petionville's parlors and drawing rooms, with the deep bedrock of an African soul. It's also one of the most spiritual places in the hemisphere, right along with Bahia and New Orleans. It's certainly a place that will leave no one indifferent. I've been going to Haiti for over twenty years, and have seen the island through many changes.

On one of my last trips to the island, I took my mother, who, ever perspicacious, understood it the minute she got off the plane, and loved it as much as I did. I showed her the Iron Market and the presidential palace and the museum of art that then housed works by Hector Hippolyte and other Haitian masters. We ate a spicy peanut butter called *mamba* for breakfast by the pool at the Villa Creole and dined lavishly at some of Petionville's finest restaurants.

I even managed to take her to the castle built by

the Jane Barbancourt family that was a Baskin-Robbins for rum lovers. One of my favorite spots, I'd been taken by a friend on my first trip to Haiti in 1972 and had returned on each subsequent trip, sampling yet more and more of the flavored rums. The crenellated tasting rooms looked out over a valley and, as you sat and enjoyed the view, waiters would circulate with trays bearing the different types of rum that the house made and sold. There was a super sweet hibiscus, that I now realize must have been made from the pods of the plant known as sorrel in the English-speaking Caribbean, a winey mango, and a seemingly endless array of tropical fruits. I'd always try to hold out for the coconut rum. Not as cloyingly sweet as other coconut rums, this one had a purity and intensity that instantly made it my favorite. It was also served not only plain but in a frothy milk mix known as a Tortuga. The serving of the Tortugas was always my signal that it was time for me to drink up, buy my several bottles of coconut rum, and head home.

My mother died in May 2000, as I was writing this book and, in cleaning out her house, the one in which I'd lived from age six, I discovered, in the back of the drinks cabinet, a bottle of Jane Barbancourt coconut rum. I've kept it, saving it for some special occasion. Then, I'll open it, pour some on the ground for Mom, and try my hand with a Tortuga of my own.

Down the Islands Rum Punch

(Trinidad)

Many years ago, on a trip to Trinidad, I was fortunate enough to find myself heading "down the islands" one weekend. That is the way Trinnies refer to heading down to the islands that are off the coast of South America. We had a leisurely trip and, by the time I returned, I was well lubricated with rum punch, hence the name. I like this punch, as it is not as sweet as fruit-juice based punches often are. There's even a rhyme to help the incipient inebriated remember the recipe: These proportions can make one drink or many.

1 of sour
2 of sweet
3 of strong
4 of weak

The ingredients are respectively freshly squeezed lime juice, sugar or simple syrup, rum, and water. Mix your own, adjust to your taste, and drink away.

Rum and Coconut Water

(Dominican Republic)

Years ago, on an exceptionally memorable trip to the Dominican Republic, I was with a group of folk who had headed to the North coast by small private plane. When it was time to return, the plane wouldn't start. We were left on a small landing strip in a not-yet-developed Samana, while the pilot tinkered and prodded. An obliging youngster climbed a tree and provided us with coconuts, and one of our band had purchased a bottle of rum. We proceeded to make the natural pairing and added the rum to the coconut water. It was wonderful, and we staggered slightly onto the plane after it was repaired. I'm sure the rum had kicked in by the time that we were aloft, because there wasn't the slightest murmur when we found out that the pilot had jump started the engine with a coat hanger!

SERVES 1

4 ounces coconut water
Dark Dominican rum, to taste

Mix the ingredients and pour into a large glass over ice.

Coconut Water

(Jamaica)

My friend Norma Shirley, who runs Norma's on the Terrace at Devon House in Kingston, arguably the best restaurant in Jamaica, has a secret. There is always a pitcher of coconut water in the refrigerator at her restaurant. It is the most cooling beverage one can find. Better than rum, better than red wine, even better than water, it's the taste of the tropics. If you find a coconut vendor along the side of the road, whether in Bahia, or Barbados, if the sign says cocos frescos *or chilled coconuts . . . indulge. Nowadays, coconut water can be found canned in many supermarkets and in Caribbean neighborhoods like my own in New York. Vendors are on the streets throughout the summer with chilled green coconuts, ready to slash them open and allow you to have a swig or transport the liquid home in plastic bottles.*

Cooling coconut water, Guadeloupe.

Simple Syrup

(All Islands)

Many people in the tropical parts of the Creole world feel that sugar doesn't mix properly with their beverages, so they prepare a clear syrup that will dissolve more easily. There are two different ways to prepare it; I've listed both here.

MAKES ABOUT 1 CUP

1 cup water
1 cup superfine sugar

Place the sugar and water in a small saucepan and cook over low heat, stirring constantly, until the sugar is completely blended and you have a thin syrup. Allow the syrup to cool and decant it into a small bottle. It will keep, refrigerated, indefinitely.

Alternately, you may try this method, which is even simpler.

4 ounces superfine sugar
1 pint water

Place the sugar and water in a bottle and shake from time to time, until the sugar is dissolved. Refrigerate it, and use as needed.

Sangaree

(Barbados)

A nineteenth-century traveler to the region reported on the quantity of rum consumed in the Caribbean and wrote this note about one fête:

> A marble basin, built in the middle of the garden especially for the occasion, served as a bowl. Into it were poured 1,200 bottles of rum, 1,200 bottles of Malaga wine, and 400 quarts of boiling water. Then 600 pounds of the best cane sugar and 200 powdered nutmegs were added. The juice of 2,600 lemons were squeezed into the liquor. Onto the surface was launched a handsome mahogany boat piloted by a boy of twelve who rowed about a few moments, then coasted to the side and began to serve the assembled company of six hundred, which gradually drank up the ocean upon which he floated.

Back in the colonial period, Barbadian plantation owners, who were the nouveau riche *of the period, really knew how to throw a party! One of the punches that might have been served was sangaree, a midmorning drink*

SERVES 1

1 ounce Madeira
1 ounce dark Barbadian rum
1 cup water
1 tablespoon freshly squeezed lime juice
A few gratings nutmeg
Sugar, to taste
Angostura Bitters, optional

Place all the ingredients in a cocktail shaker. Shake well and pour into a tall glass over ice. Top with a dash of Angostura Bitters.

Corn and Oil

(Barbados)

Barbados is a small island, yet there seems to be a church on every corner. What is even more astonishing is that there seems to be at least one rum shop for every church. Specialists in the art of hospitality since the seventeenth century, Barbadians know how to be welcoming. George Washington even slept there. While the women go to church, the men adjourn to these small shacks where the members of the bar association convene to fire off a few corn and oils.

2 ounces Barbadian white rum
Falernum, to taste (*see* Note)

Mix together and serve over ice in a highball glass.

Note: Falernum is a Barbadian sweet syrup prepared from lime juice, sugar, rum, and water, flavored with almond essence (see Mail-Order Sources, p. 61).

Coffee sorting, Mexico.

Ponche

Hot Milk Punch

(Costa Rica)

Formerly, in Costa Rica, people kept farmer's hours and dined between 5 and 6 P.M., before retiring around 8:30 P.M. Before they went to bed, they always had a cup of hot ponche. The milk punch is similar to the Ponche Crema *(p. 359), a favorite Christmas beverage of the Hispanic Caribbean, and to the* Brandied Milk Punch *(p. 360) of New Orleans.*

SERVES 4

4 cups whole milk
2 egg yolks
Sugar, to taste
½ teaspoon vanilla
2 teaspoons cornstarch
Rum or brandy, optional, to taste
Cinnamon

Combine the milk, egg yolks, sugar, vanilla, and cornstarch in a small saucepan, and bring to a boil over low heat. Add the liquor and whisk until the ponche becomes frothy. Serve immediately, topped with a pinch of cinnamon.

Chaudeau

Milk Punch

(Guadeloupe)

This drink is the traditional beverage of first communions in Guadeloupe. (In Martinique, they seem to prefer hot chocolate.) It falls right in under the category of milk punches, but without alcohol.

SERVES 4 TO 6

1 pint milk, plus 2 tablespoons for eggs
Zest of 1 lime
1 vanilla bean
4 eggs
3" stick cinnamon
⅓ cup sugar, or to taste
Vanilla extract
Grated nutmeg

Pour the milk into a medium saucepan and add the lime zest and vanilla bean. Cook the mixture over medium heat until just below boiling. Remove it from the heat. Break the eggs into a small bowl and whip them as though for an omelet, pour a little milk over the eggs, then pour the eggs into the milk mixture, being careful not to cook the eggs. Replace the saucepan on low heat and cook the *chaudeau* for 20 minutes, never allowing it to come to a boil. Remove the cinnamon and the lime zest and add one or two drops of vanilla extract and grated nutmeg. Serve warm in small cups.

Coquito

Rum Eggnog

(Puerto Rico)

The word coquito *means "little coconut" and indeed, coconut milk is the basic ingredient in this deceptively potent punch. It is traditionally served at Christmas celebrations and no* Noche Buena *(Christmas Eve) or* Año Nuevo *(New Year's Eve) would be complete without it.*

SERVES 6 TO 8

3 cinnamon sticks
1½ cups coconut milk
1½ cups evaporated milk
1½ cups sweetened condensed milk
1½ cups Puerto Rican white rum, or to taste
4 egg yolks, well beaten
Ground cinnamon, for garnish
Freshly grated nutmeg, for garnish
Slivers of toasted coconut, for garnish

Place 1½ cups water and the cinnamon sticks in a small saucepan and bring to a boil. Remove the cinnamon and allow water to cool to room temperature. Combine all of the milks and the rum in a blender. Add the water and blend until you have a frothy liquid. Decant into sterilized jars with a glass stopper placed loosely over them. Store in the refrigerator until ready to serve. When ready to serve, pour into small glasses and top each one with a sprinkle of cinnamon, a grinding of nutmeg, and a sliver of toasted coconut.

Ponche Crema

Caribbean Eggnog

(Curaçao)

This is a classic holiday drink in much of the Carribean region. It is so popular that it is now bottled and sold all year round.

SERVES 6 TO 8

4 egg yolks, beaten
1 4-ounce can sweetened condensed milk
1 cup dark rum, or to taste
1 teaspoon vanilla

Place all the ingredients in a blender and mix well. Pour into a sterilized jar, cork, and keep in the refrigerator until ready for serving.

Brandied Milk Punch
(New Orleans)

One of my favorite New Orleans memories has to do with a group of women from Natchez, Mississippi, who have an annual luncheon at Galatoire's—the only mandate is that all come dressed in white. The luncheon is lengthy and raucous and full of the kind of wacky camaraderie that only seems to truly exist among Southern women. (Think The YaYa Sisterhood *meets the* Sweet Potato Queens.*) Lunch lasted for hours, then we adjourned to their hotel room to giggle some more, this time with paper cups and bathroom glasses full of brandied milk punch that one of them had thoughtfully brought in a cooler. I made it back to another white lunch in 2002, and will go again next year for the friendship and for the brandied milk punch, which I learned how to make.*

SERVES 1

1 tablespoon superfine sugar
Brandy to taste
8 ounces milk
Crushed ice

Dissolve the sugar in the brandy and pour it into the milk. Add crushed ice and serve.

Sorrel and Ginger

(Jamaica)

Sorrel is what the relative of the hibiscus plant, Hibiscus sabdariffa, *is called in Jamaica. Ironically, is is called* flor de Jamaica *in Mexico. The plant is also known as* karkadeeh *or* carcade *in Egypt, where it is used to brew a ruby-hued beverage. In the Caribbean, sorrel signals Christmas, although it is increasingly consumed year 'round. There are many variations of how to prepare the drink—some are heavier on spices and sugar than others. This one is a simple version, calling only for a bit of cinnamon, allspice, and lots of ginger for zing. It can be served with or without rum. I make my sorrel unsweetened and allow folks to sweeten it themselves with sugar syrup.*

MAKES ABOUT 1 QUART

3 cups dried sorrel
2 2" cinnamon sticks
8 whole cloves
3 2" pieces scraped fresh ginger
1 quart water

Place all the ingredients in a heavy saucepan and bring to a boil over medium heat. Lower the heat to a simmer and cook for 10 minutes. Remove from heat and bring to room temperature. Strain and decant into a sterilized quart bottle. Chill the bottle. The sorrel may be served with rum or by itself. This drink looks lovely in a crystal decanter.

Brown Lemonade
(Jamaica)

On one of my early trips to Jamaica, I was startled to discover the lemonade that my girl-friend Maria was serving me was a light brown. She reminded me that it was prepared with not our stateside white sugar, but with the rich molasses-y brown sugar available in Jamaican grocery stores. Black sugar, as it used to be called, was rich with the taste of cane and molasses. It's hard to find in Jamaica today, but you can get a fair approximation if you use dark brown sugar.

MAKES 1 QUART

Juice of 8 lemons
Dark brown sugar, to taste
1 quart water
1 sprig fresh mint, for garnish

Mix all the ingredients together in a large pitcher. Chill and serve over ice, garnished with a sprig of fresh mint.

Lemon Verbena Iced Tea

(New Orleans)

½ cup dried lemon verbena leaves
Sugar to taste
6 lemon slices, for garnish

Place the lemon verbena leaves in a teapot, cover with 3 cups boiling water, and allow to steep, as for regular tea. Sweeten to taste. Allow the verbena to cool to room temperature. When ready to serve, pour the verbena into a large pitcher, add 6 cups cold water and ice, and serve garnished with a thin slice of lemon.

Back from the river, Guatemala.

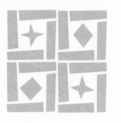

Maubi

Mauby

(Dominican Republic)

Mauby is a cool, refreshing beverage that is prepared from the bark of a small, shrubby tree. The tree, Colubrina elliptica, *grows on several West Indian islands. In bygone days, vendors would carry a container filled with the beverage through the streets on their heads and dispense the beverage with a tilt of the container and a smile. The original drink, reported by earlier colonists, was prepared from sweet potatoes, but that one is no longer found. It is thought that the name of the drink comes from the Carib word* mabi, *meaning edible roots or tubers.*

SERVES 6

6 ounces mauby bark
3" stick cinnamon
1 cup dark brown sugar, or to taste

Place the mauby and the cinnamon in a saucepan with 3 cups water, and bring to a boil. Lower the heat and simmer for 15 to 20 minutes or until golden brown. Let it cool to room temperature, and then add the sugar and 3 more cups water, stirring until the mixture is well mixed and slightly frothy. Pour into a glass bottle, leaving space at the top for fermentation. Close the bottle tightly, and allow it to rest at room temperature for 3 or 4 days. When ready, decant the mauby into a second sterilized bottle through a sieve. Chill, and serve cold.

Menus

Carnival Jump Up
Down the Islands Rum Punch
Crab Backs
Curried Lamb
White Rice
Creole Okra

Late Night Bajan Bash
Corn and Oil
Baxter's Road Fried Chicken
Coconut Rice
Bajan Bread Pudding
Rum Sauce

Puerto Rican Lenten Meal
Caldo Santo

A Get-Together in the French Antilles
Punch Vieux
Oeufs Mayonnaise aux Crabes
Maryse's Salade Mixte

Maryse's Vinaigrette
Giraumonade
Caribbean-style Zucchini
Courtbouillon de Poisson

A CREOLE CHRISTENING
Chaudeau
Lemon-Pecan Pound Cake
Dewberry Juice Pie
Home-Made Peach Ice Cream

CARIBBEAN COCKTAIL PARTY
'Ti punch
Down the Islands Rum Punch

Cigar seller, Cuba.

Pulping cacao, Jamaica.

Tortuga
Fancy Alcoholic Champola
Souskai de Mangues Verts
Oeufs Mayonnaises aux Crabes
Janga

Passion-fruit Party
Punch au Sirop
Maryse's Salade Verte
Passion Fruit Vinaigrette
Pernil
Passion Fruit–Peach Salsa
White Rice

New Orleans Tea
Creole Fluff
Mildred Oliver's Nut Cake
Creole Cream Cheese Ice Cream
Gateau Sirop
Café Brulot
Brandied Milk Punch

Early tourist hotel, Jamaica.

LUNCH IN EL YUNQUE

Green Banana Escabeche

Asopao de Pollo

Arroz con Gandules

Flan de Queso

Some Of My Favorite Cookbooks from the World Beyond Gumbo

In addition to my own *Hot Stuff, Iron Pots and Wooden Spoon, Sky Juice and Flying Fish,* and *Tasting Brazil,* I adore the classics of the cooking of the African-American World such as Lafcadio Hearn's *La Cuisine Creole* and the *Times Picayune Cookbook,* the *Dooky Chase Cookbook* by the redoubtable Leah Chase, and a host of other works. Some of my favorite less well-known and hard to find ones include the following baker's dozen.

Adams, Paul M. D. *La Cocina Cubana Sencilla: Simple Cuban Cooking,* Louisville, KY: Butler, 1998.

Bateman, Michael. *Café Brazil.* Chicago: Contemporary, 1999.

Benghiat, Norma. *Traditional Jamaican Cookery.* London: Penguin, 1985.

Elwin, Hyacinth I. R. *A Taste of Nature Island Cooking: The Cuisine of Dominica.* London: Macmillan Caribbean, 1998.

Gardner, Kenneth. *Creole Caribbean Cookery.* London: Collins, 1986.

Girard, Sylvia. *Antilles.* Paris: Editions de Fanal, 1996.

Gravette, Andy. *Classic Cuban Cuisine.* London: Fusion, 1999.

Jorge Amado, Paloma. *As Frutas de Jorge Amado ou o livro de delicias de Fadul Abdala.* Sao Paulo: Companhia das Letras, 1997.

Land, Mary. *Louisiana Cookery.* Baton Rouge: Louisiana State University Press, 1954.

———. *New Orleans Cuisine.* Cranbury, NJ: A. S. Barnes, 1969.

Mayard, Louise and Adeline Moravia. *Tropical Cooking: Cuisines des Pays Chaud.* Haiti: Henri Deschamps, n.d.

Rojas-Lombardi, Felipe. *The Art of South American Cooking.* New York: HarperCollins, 1991.

Saveurs des Iles: Cuisine des Iles et des pays tropicaux. 2 vols. Paris: Orphie, 1996.

The Saint Rita Guild. *Havana Hospitality Havana.* N.p.: n.d.

Index

Metric Equivalencies

Liquid and Dry Measure Equivalencies

Customary	Metric
¼ teaspoon	1.25 milliliters
½ teaspoon	2.5 milliliters
1 teaspoon	5 milliliters
1 tablespoon	15 milliliters
1 fluid ounce	30 milliliters
¼ cup	60 milliliters
⅓ cup	80 milliliters
½ cup	120 milliliters
1 cup	240 milliliters
1 pint (2 cups)	480 milliliters
1 quart (4 cups)	960 milliliters (.96 liter)
1 gallon (4 quarts)	3.84 liters
1 ounce (by weight)	28 grams
¼ pound (4 ounces)	114 grams
1 pound (16 ounces)	454 grams
2.2 pounds	1 kilogram (1000 grams)

Oven-Temperature Equivalencies

Description	°Fahrenheit	°Celsius
Cool	200	90
Very slow	250	120
Slow	300–325	150–160
Moderately slow	325–350	160–180
Moderate	350–375	180–190
Moderately hot	375–400	190–200
Hot	400–450	200–230
Very hot	450–500	230–260